FAMILY POLICY MATTERS

Responding to family change in Europe

Linda Hantrais

The POLICY
P P
P R E S S

D0242200

First published in Great Britain in April 2004 by

The Policy Press
University of Bristol
Fourth Floor
Beacon House
Queen's Road
Bristol BS8 1QU
UK

Tel +44 (0)117 331 4054
Fax +44 (0)117 331 4093
e-mail tpp-info@bristol.ac.uk
www.policypress.org.uk

British Library Cataloguing in Publication Data
A catalogue record for this book is available from the British Library.

Library of Congress Cataloging-in-Publication Data
A catalog record for this book has been requested.

ISBN 1 86134 471 6 paperback

A hardcover version of this book is also available.

Linda Hantrais is Director of the European Research Centre at Loughborough University, UK.

Cover design by Qube Design Associates, Bristol.
Front cover: photograph supplied by kind permission of Christian Goupi.
Printed and bound in Great Britain by Hobbs the Printers Ltd, Southampton.

Contents

List of tables and figures

Tables

Figures

Acknowledgements

This book draws heavily on three European multinational collaborative research projects, co-ordinated by the author, and carried out between 1994 and 2003. The first project (1994-96), which was based on a series of international seminars and supported by the Economic and Social Research Council (United Kingdom), the European Commission's Directorate General for Employment and Social Affairs, and the Caisse nationale des allocations familiales in Paris, examined concepts and contexts in international comparisons of family policies in Europe. The second project (1998-99), commissioned by the Directorate General for Employment and Social Affairs, drew on secondary literature to study the interaction between socio-demographic change and social and economic policies across the European Union (EU), with particular reference to France, Germany, Ireland, Italy, Spain, Sweden and the UK. The third project, entitled 'Improving Policy Responses and Outcomes to Socio-Economic Challenges (IPROSEC): changing family structures, policy and practice' (HPSE-CT-1999-00031, 2000-03) was funded by the European Commission's Directorate General for Research under Framework Programme 5. The project team carried out secondary analysis of national debates and policy contexts, in combination with new empirical work, involving interviews with policy actors, and surveys and in-depth interviews with men and women belonging to different family types in eight EU member states (France, Germany, Greece, Ireland, Italy, Spain, Sweden, UK) and three candidate countries (Estonia, Hungary, Poland). The 11 countries were chosen to represent consecutive waves of EU membership and different policy regimes. The project was designed to examine policy and practice comparatively, and to look at ways of improving policy responses to the socio-economic challenges associated with changing family structures and policy outcomes.

We are grateful to the funding organisations mentioned above for making the research possible. The contents of this book do not necessarily reflect their opinions or positions. The author is also indebted to participants in the three projects, especially members of the IPROSEC research team, and the anonymous respondents who agreed to answer our questionnaires and to be interviewed. She takes full responsibility for any errors of interpretation in the analysis of the materials they supplied.

IPROSEC Co-ordinating Team at Loughborough University
Peter Ackers, Business School; Louise Appleton, European Research Centre; Paul Byrne, Jeremy Leaman and Monica Threlfall, Department of Politics, International Relations and European Studies; Tess Kay, School of Sport and Exercise Sciences

IPROSEC partners and research assistants

Estonia – Dagmar Kutsar, Tartu University, with Kati Karelson
France – Marie-Thérèse Letablier, Centre d'études de l'emploi, Noisy-le-Grand, and Sophie Pennec, Institut national d'études démographiques, Paris, with Olivier Büttner
Germany – Dieter Eißel, Justus Liebig Universität, Gießen, with Jutta Träger
Greece – Loukia Moussourou and Maria Stratigaki, Panteion University, Athens, with Dimitra Taki and Spyridon Tryfonas
Hungary – Mária Neményi, Institute of Sociology, Hungarian Academy of Science, Budapest, with Ágnes Kende, Judit Takács and Olga Tóth
Ireland – John Garry and Tarjinder Gill, Trinity College, Dublin
Italy – Alisa Del Re, Padua University, with Valentina Longo and Devi Sacchetto
Poland – Wielisława Warzywoda-Kruszyńska, Łódź University, with Małgorzata Potoczna and Lucyna Prorok-Mamińska
Spain – Mònica Badia i Ibáñez and Celia Valiente
Sweden – Ingrid Jönsson, Lund University, with Olga Niméus
United Kingdom – Moira Ackers, Julia Griggs, Elizabeth Monaghan and Elizabeth Such, Loughborough University

The author also wishes to acknowledge the guidance and support provided by the Commission, especially their scientific officer, Virginia Vitorino, and members of the IPROSEC Advisory Committee: Anthony Abela, John Ditch, Anne-Marie McGauran, Keith Pringle, Ceridwen Roberts and Bruce Stafford.

Hannele Sauli and Leena Kartovaara of Statistics Finland supplied comments on Finnish statistics, and Anthony Abela of the University of Malta provided access to Maltese sources. Other information about countries not included in the three European projects was drawn from secondary materials, which are cited in the body of the text.

Finally, the author is grateful for the assistance received from Julia Griggs and David Stirling at the European Research Centre, and from staff at the Pilkington Library, Loughborough University, in locating, processing and checking data for this publication.

ONE

The changing family–policy relationship

Across Europe and beyond, the close of the 20th century was marked by a surge of interest in the well being of families. This core institution was depicted in the media, and in political and academic debate, as a driving force for socio-economic change while also being a victim of it, in both instances presenting new challenges for governments.

Concepts, definitions, measurements and perceptions of family life, family policies and policies that impact on families are not constant over time or space. Historians, demographers, sociologists, political and moral philosophers, lawyers and politicians generally agree that family and household structure underwent far-reaching change in the course of the 20th century in European societies (for example Seccombe, 1993; Kumar, 1995; Fox Harding, 1996; Cheal, 1999; Coleman, 2000; Halsey, 2000). Whether the extent of change was greater than in previous eras, whether conjugal instability and high rates of family dissolution constitute the historical norm, or whether the married couple family headed by a male breadwinner, which peaked in the 1950s, represents a break in the continuity thesis are mote points that will continue to fuel debate for many years to come. Whatever the outcome of such deliberations, the early 21st century seems set to be distinguished by greater family diversity, increasingly endorsed by formal legal codes.

In western Europe, it is widely recognised that what came to be idealised in the middle of the last century as the traditional or conventional family no longer constitutes the only dominant family form or the principal normative environment in which children are born and reared. Few observers would argue that 'the' family has ceased to exist as a viable unit. The tentative answer to the question already being posed in the 1960s and 1970s (for example by Cooper, 1971) about the chances of 'the' family surviving the pressures it is facing may be that the concept is not destined to disappear in the foreseeable future. The prognosis is rather that family forms will continue to evolve, possibly in an ever more reflexive and self-conscious way, as the public at large and its elected representatives react to socio-economic pressures, and as regulatory and analytical frameworks are reconfigured to take account of further socio-demographic change and the associated diversification of family living arrangements.

The relationship between public policy and family life is complex. The policy process is made more complicated by the many ways in which different policy actors shape the strategies adopted by families as they seek to develop a sustainable work–life balance. Despite the widely acknowledged trend towards more individualistic value systems, characteristic of postmodern societies (Lesthaeghe, 1995; Cheal, 1999; McRae, 1999), a basic premise in the present volume is that families, in the plural, do not form and develop in isolation from wider societal contexts. Rather, they are socially, economically, culturally and, it is argued, politically constructed by the environments within which they evolve, and where policies are formulated and implemented. Moreover, families are not simply passive recipients and beneficiaries of policy measures, they are also agents and actors in the policy process. Their behaviour, in terms of family formation, development and dissolution, and their attitudes concerning the legitimacy and acceptability of public policy can influence the decisions of politicians. This book explores the ways in which family life is socially and culturally constructed in the early 21st century in the member states of the European Union (EU), and looks at how families interact with the political, economic and civil society actors contributing to the policy process.

Already during the 1990s, the renewed debate over the implications for society of socio-economic change had spawned a series of academic and think-tank studies, which fed into the policy process. For example, in the United Kingdom, a country renowned for its hands-off approach to government intervention in what are considered as private matters, public concern over the link frequently made by the media between family breakdown, delinquency and other social ills prompted a more proactive stance among politicians towards government regulation of family life. For some observers (for example Morgan, 1995, with reference to American and British society), governments cannot escape their share of responsibility for the breakdown of the traditional married family. As well as reacting to change, policy makers play a proactive role. Whether or not they are explicitly targeting particular family forms, and whether or not individuals wittingly adapt their living arrangements accordingly, it can be argued that the frameworks established in legal provisions regulating marriage, family formation, parenting and unmarried cohabitation, tax and benefits systems, and social support services directly or indirectly set the parameters for family life. These interpretations beg questions about the motives and objectives underlying policy formulation, which are rarely unambiguous and not necessarily explicit. The title of this book, *Family policy matters*, reflects the ambiguity of the relationship between family change and policy responses, and the ways in which policy measures can have both intended and unintended impacts on families.

A second underlying assumption in this volume is that the extent and impact of family change and the policy responses of governments are dependent on spatial and temporal perspectives (de Singly and Commaille, 1997, pp 5-7). The long-distance view would suggest that a particular model of familial standardisation is characteristic of the present-day European scene, compared with other parts of the world and former times. Evidence can be adduced to demonstrate that, under the influence of homogenising supranational and internal regulatory forces, family patterns across European countries, when viewed from a distance and over a period of many years, appear to be converging towards a lowest common denominator (Coleman and Chandola, 1999, pp 39-41). Similar conclusions could be drawn about the objectives and focus of family policies. Closer scrutiny at national and subnational level indicates, however, that the timing, rate, pace and, sometimes, the direction of change differ markedly between and within countries, as do reactions to it, undermining predictions about how different policy actors, not least families themselves, will respond to external pressures in the longer term. Hence the interest in examining the possible impact of the political structures and frames of reference associated with the different waves of EU membership and, more especially, the eight countries in Central and Eastern European (CEE) and two island states that joined the Union in 2004. Such an approach is also useful in identifying regional clustering of countries along north–south and east–west axes within Europe.

This introductory chapter provides a backcloth for such an analysis by exploring the key concepts and cross-cutting themes in the book, and locating them within the wider European context. It sets out the rationale and structure of the chapters, and presents the core questions they are addressing.

Family as a shifting concept

Although disagreement is rife about the extent to which a western or European family model, or ideal type, based on the logic of individualism can be said to exist (de Singly and Commaille, 1997, pp 11-13), few sociologists would deny that the recognised boundaries of families became more fluid and porous during the closing decades of the 20th century, or that the options available for the organisation of household and family life diversified. For some family sociologists, the passing of the standard, universally applicable theoretical family model associated with the modernisation process, and as represented by the traditional, conventional or bourgeois family in postwar Europe, is symptomatic of the 'crisis of modernity' (Cheal, 1999, p 57).

The definitions of the family proffered in the English language literature of the 1940s and 1950s were influential in setting the parameters of family sociology in structural-functionalist terms and in providing a reference point for theorists. George Peter Murdock's (1949) normative definition of the family identified four basic functions: common residence, economic co-operation, reproduction and a socially approved sexual relationship. The unit of observation thus consisted of a married couple with children, and was characterised by a sexual division of labour. For Talcott Parsons (Parsons and Bales, 1956), the family was a social subsystem that contributed to the overall efficiency of society. It was based on co-residence and the marriage bond, fulfilled and consolidated by the raising of legitimate children, a single (presumed male) breadwinner role and the sharing of incomes between adult partners.

The advantage of the Parsonian model was that the norms governing family life were readily definable. A common object of study or unit of analysis could be identified. By contrast, sociologists today are hampered by the variability of possible configurations of family living arrangements and relationships, to the extent that doubts are expressed about the feasibility of conducting scientific investigation of 'the' family as a unit for sociological observation. It can be argued that the term is best avoided, since it represents a value-laden concept based on outmoded assumptions (Fox Harding, 1996, pp xi-xii).

David Cheal (1999, pp 61-6) has analysed how sociological theorists have tried to deal with the growing realisation that the concept of the conventional family is no longer a 'cultural universal'. Some analysts have sought to resolve the dilemma by 'concept specification', considering 'the' family as a specific family form, co-existing with other types of family. A more radical response, 'concept abandonment', is to reject entirely the normative concept and look for new paradigms. At the beginning of the 1990s, the Dutch were, for example, experimenting with terms such as 'primary-life forms' to designate different cohabiting relationships (de Hoog et al, 1993). Advocates of 'concept displacement' have taken account of the plurality of forms and meanings of family life within different social contexts, thereby, according to Cheal (1999, p 65), raising questions about the number of models needed to understand societies. An avenue pursued by sociologists reluctant to abandon the concept completely has been to look at 'concept expansion'. For example, the Swedish family sociologist, Jan Trost (1988), identified fundamental social characteristics that could be used to conceptualise what he called 'hyphen-families', including two-parent families, one-parent families, childless families and families with teenagers. The concept of the biological parent–child unit and the spousal unit could, he claimed, be applied irrespective, in the first case, of whether the individuals concerned are living together and, in the second case, of whether they are married. His proposal had the advantage of encompassing non-custodial parents within a parent–child dyad, which statistical definitions of household units do not usually identify.

Another body of theory that is relevant to an understanding of the extent to which the concept of family has evolved in the sociological literature concerns the individualisation thesis of modernity, and the associated notion of moral individualism. These approaches share with exchange and conflict theory an emphasis on issues of autonomy and personal (rational) choice. Although, taken to the extreme, individualism may call into question the capacity of families to function as corporate units, such theories do not exclude the possibility that, as individuals interact, they also develop collective strategies that may serve to promote the interests of the family group (Cheal, 1999, pp 66-7). The related concept of life-course dynamics has been usefully developed in the analysis of changing family structure. While focusing essentially on individual trajectories, and by looking at the way they interlock within families, this approach has enabled sociologists to identify patterns and models, for example with reference to the timing and consequences of family transitions as recorded in panel surveys.

Within Parsonian and role theory, the parameters of family life were premised on sex-role differentiation and specialisation, whereby the wife performed the expressive role of homemaker and the husband the instrumental role of breadwinner. The strong feminist critiques from the early 1970s of the gender inequalities associated with capitalist and patriarchal relations (Walby, 1986), and the emphasis they placed on individual trajectories in life-course analysis, were influential in shifting attention away from the concept of the conventional family to the competing companionate family model dependent on relational and emotional ties, as already depicted in the 1940s (Burgess and Locke, 1945). The literature on patriarchy led to a reconceptualisation of domestic labour as productive work. Families were portrayed as both reproductive and productive units, affording a theoretical framework for the analysis of the incorporation of women into men's work and, at the same time, of women's subordination.

For some observers, as family life has become more democratic, the dependence of the family unit on relational rather than formal contractual bonds has made it more fragile and vulnerable (Castel, 1995, pp 414-15). Following the same logic, unmarried cohabitation, as compared with patriarchal marriage, can be said to leave women more exposed since they lack its legal safeguards (Fox Harding, 1996, p 95). The extreme view, as expressed by postmodern theorists, holds that the apparent failure of 'the' family to survive as a fundamental social unit is symptomatic of the end of scientific rationality and the break with universal reason and order, creating the need for a radical rethinking of social life, based on pluralism, disorder and fragmentation (Cheal, 1999, p 75).

The changing family–policy interface

The relationship between family and state has also been shifting and evolving over time and space. Critics of functionalist theories have argued that, if left to their own devices, families can be dysfunctional not only for individuals but also for society at large, thereby justifying state intervention (Morgan, 1975). Already in the 18th and 19th centuries, the inability of families to function effectively was used to legitimate state involvement in family life and control over the relationships between parents and children. Socio-legal historians have shown how, from the 18th century, in Britain and France, the state was intervening to ensure that parents discharged their moral duties towards their offspring. In extreme cases, state welfarism became absolute, as parents were deprived of the guardianship of their children (Donzelot, 1980; Eekelaar, 1997).

Over the same period, many of the other functions previously attributed to the family were also progressively brought under the control of the state, whether it be family formation, housing, education, work or welfare, thereby contributing to concept specialisation, leaving families to concentrate increasingly on providing emotional support for their members. By the end of the 20th century, under combined social and economic pressures, state coercion was, however, making way for a reassertion of parental and individual responsibility and a reaffirmation of rights, not only for parents but also for children (Eekelaar, 1997). At the same time, questions were being raised about the boundaries between state intervention and personal autonomy, and the ability of families to compensate for any shortfall in public services (Commaille et al, 2002, pp 98, 103; Strobel, 2002, p 11).

When the conventional family was at its peak in the 1950s in western Europe, the CEE countries under post-Stalinist rule were being subjected to a regime intent on destroying the capitalist family model by weakening family ties, replacing family by social solidarity and imposing an alternative normative system. The result was the subjugation of the family institution and the atomisation of the family unit. The state enlarged its sphere of control, putting in place a form of paternalism and patriarchy that dominated social and family life, and discouraged individual participation in public affairs, offering protection in return for obedience and subservience. The political and economic transition that began in 1989 heralded the withdrawal of the state from social protection, leaving families to fend for themselves (Mezei, 1997; Ferge, 2001b). The speed with which transition took place meant that families were ill prepared for self-reliance. The southern European countries had also experienced totalitarian regimes that sought to use families as an instrument for exercising power, but without undermining dependence on family solidarity. By the late 1990s, the CEE and southern European countries had in common their lack of respect for government and their profound mistrust of the state as a family policy actor.

Rationale and structure of the book

The present volume differs from many other book-length studies of family change and public policy published since the mid-1990s in that it is concerned with the two-way interactive process and is not confined to a single country. Other works have examined at length many of the subthemes treated in this book, including family change (McRae, 1999; Berthoud and Gershuny, 2000) and its implications for relationships between the generations (Arber and Attias-Donfut, 2000; Brannen et al, 2002), for policy formation, implementation and analysis (Ditch et al, 1996a, 1996b, 1998a, 1998b; Fox Harding, 1996; Kaufmann et al, 1997, 2002; Carling et al, 2002), and for professional practice (Bogenschneider, 2002).

However, few accounts are structured to the same extent around the family–policy relationship viewed from a consistently cross-national comparative perspective. In addition to covering all the long-standing EU member states, where comparable data are available, *Family policy matters* encompasses the first wave of new members from CEE countries and the two Mediterranean island states. In previous studies of changing families and family policies in the European context (Hantrais and Letablier, 1996; Hantrais, 2000b), the perspective adopted by the author was 'from the outside' and did not take account of the views and experience of family life seen 'from the inside'. This new book has both a wider and a deeper focus, drawing on empirical work to provide novel insights into the interactive relationship between families and policy across a number of European societies. The chapters are illustrated by examples taken from fieldwork conducted in 2001-02 in eight EU15 member states (France, Germany, Greece, Ireland, Italy, Spain, Sweden and the UK) and three of the CEE candidate countries (Estonia, Hungary and Poland), which were chosen to represent different waves of EU membership and contrasting policy environments.

Using the substantial body of available secondary literature to locate the material within a broader theoretical and analytical framework, the primary aim of *Family policy matters* is to analyse comparatively the interaction between family change and policy responses in EU member states, by combining macro- and micro-level perspectives. The book tracks the major socio-economic changes of the late 20th century and explores their impact on family and working life on the eve of the new millennium. The analysis includes the perceptions families have of public policy and the views they express about its relative importance in their lives, in relation to other factors such as employment and working conditions, the economic climate, socio-cultural traditions and expectations.

In bringing together the findings from these various bodies of material, the chapters in the book set out to address five key questions: How are families changing in European societies? What are the challenges raised for society by changing family structures? How are policy makers and practitioners responding to family change? Does family policy matter? What can policy actors learn from experience in other countries?

Chapters Two to Six explore the concepts, definitions and measurements associated with various dimensions of family life and family policies in different policy environments. They analyse the major socio-economic changes that were taking place at the close of the 20th century, their impact on family life, gender and intergenerational relations, and the policy responses of governments. Chapters Six and Seven examine the legitimacy and social acceptability of state intervention as well as the perceptions that families in different countries have of the role played by public policy in decisions about family life.

By the turn of the century, Europe's population had reached an advanced stage of demographic transition, characterised by declining fertility, greater life expectancy and the slowing down of net migration. Chapter Two examines the combined effect of these trends on population growth and ageing. The analysis shows that their impact has not been felt to the same extent in all EU25 member states: marked differences can be found in the intensity, timing and pace of change. CEE countries are, for example, less prone to population ageing, since their life expectancy is relatively low compared with countries from earlier waves of EU membership. Moreover, the countries where the population is most affected by ageing are not necessarily those where political debate and media interest are most prevalent, or where governments are reacting most strongly to the issues being raised: for example, how to pay for pensions, how to cover the costs of caring for the older dependent population or how to sustain labour markets.

Patterns of family formation and dissolution altered markedly across Europe in the last quarter of the 20th century, with the result that less institutionalised and more diversified family forms became widespread. Everywhere family size was declining, while divorce rates and the number of extramarital births were rising. Lone parenthood, one-person households, unmarried and same-sex cohabitation, and reconstituted families became more common and more socially acceptable living arrangements. Chapter Three shows how these changes have taken place at differing rates and to differing degrees both within and between countries. After reviewing the ways in which families are defined, conceptualised and measured across countries and over time, the chapter explores the policy debates and challenges socio-demographic change has created for society.

The last two decades of the 20th century saw far-reaching developments in the nature of work, patterns of supply and demand for labour, and working hours and conditions, which were closely intertwined with the changes occurring within families. The fourth chapter examines the changing nature of employment in conjunction with the shifting relationship between paid work and family life, associated with the reduction in the length of working life, increasing levels of female economic activity and employment, greater flexibility in working time and conditions, the spread of temporary work and efforts to stem unemployment. The impact of these changes, insofar as they can be reliably assessed, on gender and intergenerational relations is explored across European societies. The chapter closes with an assessment of policy debates in different countries and the challenges presented by the changing family–employment relationship for both governments and employers.

Despite important differences between European welfare systems, preparation for Economic and Monetary Union, and for EU membership in the case of candidate countries, provided a powerful incentive for welfare reform in the 1990s. The process was further stimulated by concern about the longer-term implications of socio-demographic change. The reaction of most governments was welfare retrenchment and the overhaul of benefits systems, often involving cutbacks in provision for families and privatisation of services. In CEE countries, transition brought far-reaching structural change to the economy, requiring costly adaptations to welfare systems. The debates surrounding welfare reform provide a further indication of the relative importance of family matters on the policy agenda. The fifth chapter examines the legal framework for family life before going on to explore changes in the ways in which families are defined and conceptualised in public policy and administration. The analysis shows to what extent public policy takes account of the welfare needs of the family as a unit, or of its members as individual citizens, and examines how responsibilities and obligations towards family members are shared with the state and with economic and civil society actors.

Chapter Six focuses on the legitimacy and social acceptability of government intervention in family life. It looks at how the state–family relationship is defined, conceptualised and institutionalised at EU level and in member states, and then analyses the extent to which intervention by political, economic and civil society actors is considered to be legitimate and acceptable by society. When families in different countries across Europe are questioned about their attitudes towards policy intervention, responses are usually ambivalent. Even though the general consensus is that governments should intervene to help families in difficulty by providing a safety net, views diverge about the form and extent of such intervention. Opinions differ not only between countries but also within them according to factors such as age, sex, region, socio economic status, religion and previous experience of different living arrangements. The chapter scrutinises these variations and identifies clusters of countries that share similar approaches regarding the legitimacy and acceptability of intervention in family matters.

Even when they acknowledge the legitimacy of government intervention in the private lives of individuals and make full use of the benefits and services to which they are entitled, in most countries, family members are unlikely to admit that decisions about family formation and living arrangements are affected by public policy. This stance is in line with the widely held view that governments should not be prohibitive or proactive by seeking to determine family size or structure. The extent to which linkages are made between policy and behaviour is subject to important variations both between and within countries, as illustrated by Chapter Seven. Decisions about whether couples marry or separate, whether mothers with young children go out to work, when young people leave the family home, and whether older people continue to live by themselves, are examined to determine to what extent they may be directly or indirectly affected by public policy, although not necessarily by policy explicitly targeting families.

The combination of approaches adopted in the book, from the broad-brush scrutiny of statistical data and policy contexts at national level to the fine-grain analysis of the experiences and attitudes of families, provides valuable insights into the way the relationship between public policy and family life is constructed. The book contains an overview of the policy process, while also affording a deeper understanding of how providers and customers perceive the impact of policies. A key theme running through the analysis is diversity, whether it concerns changes in living arrangements across socio-economic groups, the development of gender and intergenerational relations, and perceptions of the effects of policies, or the responses to change formulated and implemented by different policy actors. The fine-grain micro-level analysis carried out in the book and the differences it reveals in the rate and pace of change do not, however, obscure the commonality of many of the issues that western societies were facing as they embarked on the 21st century. The final chapter draws together the various strands of the analysis to identify overlapping patterns between and within countries according to the ways in which the family–policy process operates in different policy environments. It concludes with an assessment of the potential contribution that policy learning and diffusion can make to the development of family policy across countries.

TWO

Population decline and ageing

Analysts of the first demographic transition, which took place in western Europe between the late 19th century and mid-20th century, assumed that the gradual decline in mortality and fertility rates would ultimately result in low population growth across European societies (Coleman, 1996; Bégeot and Fernández Cordón, 1997; Coleman and Chandola, 1999). Following the postwar baby boom, demographic trends within the European Union (EU) were characterised by a sharp fall in fertility from the 1960s, together with a slowing down in the extension of life expectancy and the curtailment of inward migration (Eurostat, 2000, 2002a; European Commission, 2003). These combined trends have resulted in negative natural population growth and population ageing, which distinguish western Europe from countries in the less developed world. The Union, and more especially the enlarged Union of 25 countries, is not, however, a homogeneous mass with regard to demographic trends. Although the direction of change was broadly the same in the closing decades of the 20th century, considerable diversity could be observed both across and within regions, not only in the rate and pace of change but also in the reactions of policy actors to the challenges it poses.

Whether slow or negative population growth and population ageing are a cause, precipitating factor or outcome of changing family structures is a much debated question. Whatever the causal relationship, it is argued in this book that these various demographic phenomena are closely interwoven. In tracking and analysing the process of change, this and the next two chapters, which look at changing family forms and the family–employment relationship, follow the same structure. They begin by examining the problems associated with defining, conceptualising and measuring socio-demographic change from a comparative perspective, in the knowledge that published statistics provide no more than an incomplete snapshot at a given point in time and need to be treated with caution. The chapters then track demographic trends across EU member states, including the pre-accession countries in Central and Eastern Europe (CEE) and the two Mediterranean island states. Reference is made, in particular, to the implications of different waves of EU membership for European population size and social structure.

Subsequent sections review the challenges posed by socio-demographic change for political, economic and civil society actors, and situate them within the wider economic and political context. Chapters Five to Seven explore the options available to policy actors and the possible outcomes of policy developments for society at the macro level, and for families at the micro level. The focus here is the components of population growth and ageing, which provide the canvas for an analysis in the next chapter of change within families and in relationships between family members.

Defining and conceptualising population growth and ageing

Population growth, or change, is defined as the rate at which a population is increasing or decreasing over a given period of time due to the surplus or deficit of births over deaths, and adjusted to take account of net migration (Eurostat, 2000, p 7; 2002a, p 163). Population, or demographic, ageing can be defined as the combined impact of declining fertility rates and falling mortality rates on the age structure of a population (European Commission, 2002e, p 63). Comparisons of population growth and ageing over time and across countries are problematic because of discrepancies and changes in definitions for the main indicators used by demographers to measure their different components: namely fertility and mortality rates, and net migration. These difficulties are compounded when CEE countries are included in comparisons, since their datasets for the period before transition were constructed from sources that are rarely compatible with those used by Eurostat (Kutsar and Tiit, 2000).

In its capacity as the official Statistical Office of the European Communities, Eurostat is charged with issuing recommendations on definitions, methodologies, data collection and processing, and ensuring that they are applied consistently across EU member states, to conform with internationally agreed criteria. Eurostat has devised systems for harmonising data, such as Syscodem, which was used to produce a uniform definition of age for demographic statistics, but it cannot improve on the quality of data collected at national level. Nor can it compel countries to change their definitions or modify their data sources. It can only make recommendations and issue guidelines that member states are expected to follow as far as is feasible, taking account of differences in national circumstances (Eurostat, 1992, 1994, 1999). The recommendations issued for the 2000 census round in EU15 member states were drawn up jointly by the United Nations Economic Commission for Europe (UN/ECE, 1998) and the Statistical Office of the European Communities. This section examines how these recommendations are applied in defining the components of population growth, or decline, and ageing for comparative purposes, and indicates how differences in the interpretation of national data by international agencies may result in discrepancies in outputs.

Defining fertility rates

Of the three components of population growth, the most problematic to define and assess are fertility and migration. Fertility, which for many people is the hallmark of family formation, can be measured by crude annual birth rates, total period or completed fertility rates. Demographers consider that completed fertility rates by generation provide the most reliable indicator of trends in reproductive behaviour, since other measures – crude annual birth rates and total fertility – are influenced by the effects of timing of births.

The crude annual birth rate is the most straightforward indicator of fertility, since it measures the frequency of births per 100,000 inhabitants in a given year. However, the measure is affected not only by the timing of births but also by the structure of the population. A country with a young age profile and, therefore, more women of reproductive age will have more births in a year than a country with an older population.

Although the crude birth rate would appear to be relatively easy to measure and record, differences between countries in definitions of live births and changes in definitions over time affect the comparability of data. Since the early 1990s, Eurostat (1994, p 13) has recommended that EU member states should observe the World Health Organisation (WHO) definition of live births, promulgated in the 1950s. It specifies that the child should either breathe or show other evidence of life at birth, such as a heart beat, irrespective of the duration of the pregnancy (WHO, 1992, code 221).

Compared with the crude birth rate, fertility rates by age provide a more detailed account of the situation for a well-defined population group. The indicator for total period fertility estimates the mean number of children that would be produced by a generation of women throughout their childbearing years if they conformed to the observed fertility rates by age of women in the year selected. The indicator refers to synthetic generations at a particular point in time rather than being calculated from the actual generations concerned. It is, therefore, subject to correction if the actual behaviour of a particular generation departs from what has been predicted. It provides a good indication of fertility if reproductive behaviour is stable, but is less reliable if behaviour suddenly changes. The total fertility rate is also used to indicate replacement level fertility, which is generally taken to be 2.1 children per woman in the more developed regions (Eurostat, 2002a, p 164).

Completed fertility measures the actual number of children produced by a given generation of women, once they have come to the end of their childbearing years (Eurostat, 2002a, p 160). If a fall in the total period fertility rate is not compensated for by a rise in the number of births at a later point in time, the overall effect is a lower completed fertility rate, which has been the case across the Union since the 1980s. Indicators for total period and completed fertility rates thus measure different phenomena, but both assume childbearing to begin at age 15 and to be completed at age 49. Even though few births occur among women aged 40 to 49, the values for completed fertility rates estimated in 2000 for post-1950 generations may be inaccurate, since they are based on the assumption that women in this age group will not have any more children. Only data for generations that have actually reached the end of their natural reproductive period can be used to provide a wholly accurate indication of trends.

Demographers are interested in distinguishing between intensity and timing of births. Although women may be postponing the age of childbirth, they may not be compensating by having larger numbers of children at a later age. Comparisons of data for age at childbirth and birth order are also unreliable due to inconsistencies in the collection of information. Most countries publish the birth order covering the entire reproductive life of the mother, but Belgium, Germany, France, Luxembourg and the United Kingdom, for example, provide the birth order only within the current marriage (Eurostat, 2002a, p 155).

Defining mortality rates

For the purposes of collecting data on mortality rates in EU member states, Eurostat observes the WHO definition of death, excluding foetal death, as "the permanent disappearance of all evidence of life at any time after live birth has taken place" (WHO, 1992, code 241). Mortality rates record the frequency of deaths within a population. The WHO (1999, p 132) definition of perinatal death describes the perinatal period as commencing at 22 completed weeks of gestation, when birth weight is normally 500g, and ending seven days after birth. Infant mortality refers to deaths within the first year of life (Eurostat, 2002a, p 161). WHO (1999, pp xxi, 133) specifies that a spontaneous abortion should be defined as occurring before 20 weeks of pregnancy, or with a birth weight of 500g or less, but leaves countries to define the point in pregnancy when a spontaneous abortion or miscarriage becomes a stillbirth for reporting purposes.

Countries differ in the criteria used to define foetal mortality. Denmark, Greece, Ireland, Italy, Luxembourg, Spain and Sweden base their definition on a minimum period of gestation of 28 weeks. Consequently, they appear to have lower stillbirth rates than countries applying shorter periods, namely Belgium and France (26 weeks), the Netherlands and UK (24), Finland and Portugal (22). If countries alter their criteria, as did the Netherlands and the UK when they reduced the minimum period to less than 28 weeks in the early 1990s, the effect may be that the number of foetal deaths appears to change. Germany applies only a weight condition (1,000g), whereas Austria includes weight and size (500g, 35cm). Portugal and Sweden also stipulate a minimum size of 25 and 35cm respectively (Eurostat, 2002a, p 154).

The example of the CEE countries illustrates how adjustments to definitions can affect the comparability of results over time. Before transition, most CEE countries used the Soviet concept of live births, which excluded infants born with no breath but with other signs of life, described as stillbirths, and those born before the end of the 28th week of pregnancy weighing under 1kg or measuring less than 35cm, and who died during the first week of life (UNICEF, 2001, glossary). Data on live births and perinatal deaths collected in the period before transition may not, therefore, be directly comparable with more recent statistics. Estonia and Poland, for example, moved from the Soviet definition to the WHO definition in 1992 and 1994, respectively, which means that some of the births recorded during the 1990s would not have been registered as live births a decade earlier. In its recommendations for the 2000 census round, the United Nations Statistics Division (UNSD, 1998, § 3.88) endorsed the decision to replace the indicator for birth weight by the contraceptive prevalence rate, a measure that may prove just as problematic to standardise.

As with the crude birth rate, the crude death rate is affected by the age structure of the population. A country with an older age profile is likely to record more deaths in a year than one with a younger population. Data on mortality are, however, more representative and more predictable of the current situation than birth rates because they change less and more slowly, barring a cataclysmic event such as war or a natural disaster. In an attempt to remedy the problem created by differences in age structure, the standard death rate for a population of a standard age distribution measures death rates independently of different age structures as, for example, in the case of deaths in road accidents (Eurostat, 2002d, pp 435, 442).

Definitions of causes of death are based on the WHO international classification of diseases, which most countries have adopted. Despite the use of harmonised definitions, comparability of data for this indicator may be affected not only by different notification procedures but also by inconsistencies when the causes of death are multiple or difficult to identify.

Defining geographical mobility and migration

Net migration, the third component of population growth, measures immigration minus emigration. In some instances, Eurostat (2002a, pp 153, 163) assesses 'corrected' net migration by calculating the difference between total population increase and natural increase, that is between the number of live births and the number of deaths (European Commission, 2002e, p 66). Net migration is of interest for demographers and politicians as it may serve to offset, or compensate for, a deficit in natural population growth. A number of indicators are used to measure trends in international migration. Eurostat produces five broad categories of data on migration: resident population by citizenship, international immigration and emigration, acquisition of citizenship, asylum seekers, employment and unemployment by citizenship (Singleton, 1999; Eurostat, 2000).

Migration is no less difficult to define than fertility. By definition, only migrants who are registered as such can be recorded in the statistics. Eurostat (2000, p 7) admits that it is possible to gain only an 'informed estimate' of the number of international migrants in Europe at a particular point in time. The compilation of comparable data for the five indicators across EU member states is problematic due to substantial differences in sources and definitions, and lack of consistency in their application. Few CEE countries systematically collect information on immigration and emigration. Only the Czech Republic, Hungary, Latvia and Slovenia could supply data on the citizenship of non-EU nationals in 2000 (European Commission, 2002e, p 136). Among EU member states, only Ireland and the UK collect data on ethnicity in their censuses, although several countries, including Finland, France, Estonia, Hungary and Poland, ask questions about nationality or place of birth, or hold such information on their population registers.

The data supplied to Eurostat on intra-European mobility, third-country emigration and immigration, asylum seekers and naturalisations by national statistical offices and ministries depend on an inordinate number of different legislative, administrative and data collection systems across the Union (Eurostat, 2000, pp 6, 8). They include population censuses and surveys, work permits, residence and national insurance records, and asylum applications. Belgium, Denmark, Finland, Luxembourg and Sweden use a computerised central population register to record international migration. Austria, Germany, Italy, the Netherlands and Spain rely on entry and exit forms. Germany also maintains a register of foreigners. Ireland inserts specific questions in the labour force survey, and the UK conducts sample international passenger surveys to record emigration. Indirect sources are used for non-nationals in France, Greece and Portugal (Eurostat, 2000, p 10). Inconsistencies in procedures for reporting data mean that, even when two EU member states are using what are ostensibly the same information sources, they may record different volumes of migratory flows for the same group of people (Singleton, 1999).

Eurostat (2000, p 7; 2002a, p 156; 2002d, p 436) defines immigrants as non-nationals arriving from abroad or nationals returning from abroad with the intention of residing in the country for a specified length of time, most often 12 months, but which can vary from one country to another and from one data source to another. Germans are counted as emigrants when they leave the residence they have been occupying to travel to another country. Ireland bases its definition on the actual duration of stay. The UK applies a 12 months threshold after 12 months of residence.

Eurostat and the Council of Europe use population by citizenship to identify the proportion of foreign nationals in a country, and to assess population movements between countries. Citizenship is, however, a concept that is not based on uniform criteria across the Union. The UNSD (1998, § 2.104) defines citizenship as the legal nationality of individuals, and recommends that both the country of citizenship and the country of birth should be recorded in censuses, since they do not necessarily coincide. France, for example, traditionally accorded citizenship to non-French nationals born on French soil, whereas Germany has been much less liberal in attributing citizenship rights. The concept of 'citizenship of the European Union', which was introduced by the Treaty on European Union in 1992 (title II, article 8), established the right for nationals from another member state to vote and stand as candidates at municipal and European Parliamentary elections under the same conditions as nationals.

Within the Union, the regulations for granting national citizenship or the right to reside remain a matter for the state concerned. The number of years of residence required before being able to apply for naturalisation and the time taken to process applications, therefore, vary from one member state to another. In Germany, for example, under a law that came into force in 2000, foreigners can apply for naturalisation after eight years of residence, compared with 15 years previously. In the UK, candidates for naturalisation must have been permanent residents in the country for a year before being entitled to submit an application. They must then fulfil a five-year residence requirement before naturalisation, if granted, can take effect. Differences in nationality law mean that, depending upon the place of birth and the country to which they or their parents migrate, the children of immigrants may, or may not, be able to acquire another nationality and the citizenship rights it confers.

Since freedom of movement was one of the founding principles of the European Economic Community (EEC), a national with the right to reside moving from one member state to another would not be considered as an emigrant or immigrant. A distinction is made in Eurostat data between intra-European mobility and international migration from and to 'third' countries. Naturalisation rates are higher for citizens from third countries than they are for EU citizens (European Commission, 2002e, p 50). As countries become members of the European Community (EC) and Union, individuals and their families who move from another member state cease to have the status of non-EU immigrants. If and when Turkey, for example, joins the Union, Turks, who have for many years been classified as *Gastarbeiter* in Germany, and have hitherto been entitled to only limited citizenship rights, will no longer be considered as non-EU immigrants, as was the case for Portuguese and Spanish immigrants to EC member states prior to the 1980s.

Despite the best efforts of Eurostat, harmonisation of aggregated data at international level is a well nigh impossible task, due to large gaps in data, problems and inconsistencies that are generated at subnational level and the lack of any international sources that can be used to check data (Singleton, 1999). As a result, many migrants go unrecorded in any system or database. National asylum procedures, usually through a ministry of the interior, are expected to record asylum seekers. Like other data from administrative sources, they are subject to important national variations, for example according to the stage in the process at which asylum seekers are reported, the inclusion or exclusion of dependants and the criteria applied for recognition of refugee status. The problem of collecting reliable data is compounded by the fact that illegal migration, like abortion, is hidden from data collection, since international migration statistics can record only migrants who are known to civil administrative and police authorities.

Defining population ageing and dependency

In combination, two of the components of population growth – fertility and mortality rates – are central to an understanding of the age structure of a population and the phenomenon of population ageing, which is in turn one of the factors affecting the structure of households and families. Declining fertility rates lead to smaller numbers of young people in relation to total population. Falling mortality rates contribute to greater life expectancy and an increase in the proportion of older people in the population. Life expectancy is defined as the average number of additional years a person is expected to live if subjected throughout life to current mortality conditions (Eurostat, 2002a, p 161). It is usually calculated on the basis of information about the probability of dying at each age for a given population group according to prevailing death rates. As with total period fertility, life expectancy assumes that behaviour will remain stable over time. The indicator is, therefore, subject to correction if the actual behaviour of a given generation departs from what has been predicted. In the same way that total period fertility rates fail to take account of generation effects, estimates of life expectancy based on current mortality rates do not represent actual life expectancy, which can only be calculated retrospectively.

The combined effect of falling fertility and greater life expectancy, in the absence of any compensatory net migration, is a rise in average age and median age, or the age separating the population into two groups of equal size. Greater life expectancy leads to population ageing, a shift in dependency ratios in favour of older generations and to what can be described as longer, thinner families. The age dependency ratio is defined as the number of persons of an age at which people are economically inactive for every 100 persons of working age, usually taken to be the population aged either 15-64 or 20-59, according to context (see Chapters Four and Five). The total dependency ratio is the sum of the old and young age dependency ratios (Eurostat, 2002a, tables C-7, C-8, p 159).

Actual dependency ratios vary across countries according to the age at which young people enter the labour market and leave the parental home, and at which older people exit from the labour market and become financially, physically and socially dependent on the intermediate generation of working age. Dependency is thus an important concept in understanding the relationship between the generations both in terms of family structure and the family–employment relationship (see Chapters Three and Four).

Tracking population change

When the EEC was established in the late 1950s, together the six founder member states accounted for nearing 190 million inhabitants. Over the next

40 years, while the natural increase in population size was slowing down, the progressive enlargement to 15 member states contributed to a doubling in the number of 'Europeans'. As a result, with 376 million inhabitants by the year 2000, the Union became the third largest demographic power in the world ahead of the United States. Further enlargement to the east in 2004 bolstered the Union's population by over 100 million inhabitants. The size of the Union will continue to expand during the early decades of the 21st century due to further enlargement. Accession is also likely to stimulate internal westward economic migration flows, as was the case following German unification. Despite relatively low life expectancy, the new member states are not, however, expected to reverse the trend towards slow or negative population growth and population ageing. Although total EU population is predicted to peak in 2022, already by the year 2010, several EU member states will have entered a phase of population decline, where the number of deaths will be greater than the number of births (European Commission, 2002e, p 61). In the absence of a compensating effect from migration, the slowdown in natural population growth is explained essentially by falling fertility rates, which are also characteristic of CEE countries.

Closer scrutiny of socio-demographic change since the 1960s, based on indicators for fertility, mortality and migration, highlights differences in the impact of these three components of population growth and ageing across EU25 member states, and provides the demographic context for an analysis in the next chapter of changing family forms.

Measuring population growth

According to demographers, by the end of the 20th century, the population of the Union had reached an advanced stage of demographic transition, characterised since the 1960s by declining fertility, low mortality and the slowing down of net migration (Coleman, 1996, p ix). According to Eurostat data, annual population growth, which had been increasing at a rate of 7.1 per 1,000 (indicated ‰ from here on) population between 1950 and 1970, slowed down to 4.3‰ between 1970 and 1980, and to 3.3‰ between 1985 and 1993, falling to 2.8‰ by 2000 (Bégeot and Fernández Cordón, 1997, p 24; European Commission, 2002e, p 114). The slowing down of growth was due primarily to the decline in fertility. Completed fertility rates are not available for the less developed countries as a whole but, as shown in Table 2.1, by the year 2000, total fertility rates in the Union were among the lowest in the world. Only the Russian Federation and Japan displayed lower rates. By contrast, crude death rates for EU15, although falling, were higher than in Japan, the US and the less developed regions.

Despite the overall similarity in the direction of trends within the Union, the pace and intensity of socio-demographic change vary between and within member states. Since the EU15 figure for fertility rates, as calculated by Eurostat, is a weighted average that takes account of the size of individual

Table 2.1: Total fertility rates and crude death rates for EU15 member states, and selected countries and regions (1970-2000)

	Total fertility rate (children per woman)			Crude death rate (per 1,000 population)		
	1970/74	1980/84	2000	1970/75	1980/85	1995/00
World	4.48	3.58	2.76	11.6	10.3	9.2
EU15	2.23	1.72	1.48	10.6	10.3	9.8
US	2.02	1.82	2.06	9.2	9.0	8.4
Japan	2.07	1.76	1.41	6.5	6.1	7.6
Russian Federation	1.98	1.99	1.25	9.1	11.1	14.3
More developed regions	2.11	1.84	1.57	9.5	9.7	10.1
China	4.86	2.55	1.82	6.3	6.6	7.0
India	5.43	4.47	3.11	15.9	12.8	9.1
Nigeria	6.90	6.90	5.66	20.6	17.5	13.5
Less developed regions	5.43	4.15	3.05	12.3	10.5	8.9

Note: EU15 death rates are calculated from national data.

Sources: For fertility rates, Eurostat (2002a, table A-3); for death rates, UNESA (2002, http://esa.un.org/unpp).

member states, fluctuations in the more populated countries have a greater effect on the EU average than do those in the smaller countries. In 2000, Germany had the largest population size, with over 82 million inhabitants, accounting for almost 22% of the Union's population. Its contribution to EU population size had increased in the early 1990s by nearly 16 million due to unification. However, the total fertility rate in the former Federal Republic of Germany had sunk to a trough in the mid-1980s, whereas the rate in the eastern *Länder* fell to an all-time low of 0.77 children per woman in 1993, further depressing the figure for Germany as a whole. By 2000, the fertility rate in the eastern *Länder* had risen to 1.22, which was still lower than the average for EU15 member states and for the western *Länder* (Council of Europe, 1997, table GDR-3; 2002, table T3.3).

France, Italy and the UK, which each accounted for 15-16% of EU15 population, exhibited very different profiles in 2000. Italy was displaying one of the lowest total fertility rates in EU15, a position it shared with Spain, although both countries had seen an improvement since the mid-1990s. France and the UK, which had displayed very similar rates since the 1960s, diverged in the late 1990s. While France became one of the member states with the highest rates, close to Ireland, which had retained a strong lead until the late 1980s, the UK continued on its downward trend, as did Greece. Several countries – most notably France and the Netherlands – recorded a marked upturn in 2000, compared with previous years. The rise may be explained by a short-lived 'millennium effect', although the upturn appeared to have been sustained in 2001 in France. The three Nordic states, Denmark, Finland and Sweden, had seen their rates fall to low levels in the mid-1980s. Sweden registered a peak in the early 1990s before falling back again close to the EU15 average, while rates in Denmark and Finland remained among the highest in the Union (Council of Europe, 2002, table T3.3; Eurostat, 2002a, table E-4).

Although the gap widened in 1980, the disparity between the highest and lowest fertility rates diminished over the period as a whole. The difference between Ireland and Luxembourg at the two extremes was greater in 1980 than that between Ireland at one extreme and Sweden at the other in 1960. By 2000, the gap between the extremes, represented by France/Ireland and Italy/Spain, had narrowed to less than half the level in 1960, and the rank order of countries had changed. While these results can be interpreted as a sign of convergence, as noted above, total fertility indicators are too unstable to allow any firm conclusions to be drawn. The upturn recorded in some countries and in the EU15 average at the end of the 20th century may constitute no more than a blip in an otherwise long-term downward trend.

In the short term, enlargement is expected to bring greater heterogeneity rather than convergence, due to the diversity of the demographic profiles among the candidate countries. The new member states in 2004 ranged in size from 384,000 and 759,000 inhabitants for Malta and Cyprus respectively to almost 39 million inhabitants for Poland (European Commission, 2002e, p 136). In 2000, the two small island states were displaying the highest total fertility rates. All the CEE countries reported rates well below the EU15 average, with the Czech Republic below Italy and Spain. Estonia and Slovenia recorded what was seemingly a millennium effect (Council of Europe, 2002, table T3.3; Eurostat, 2002a, table J-8).

Data on completed fertility by generation, as shown in Table 2.2, provide a less volatile picture of the contribution from falling fertility to population decline for women born between 1930 and 1960, the latest date for which information is available for all member states, and the generation in which most women had completed their childbearing years at the beginning of the 20th century. Compared with the 1930s generations, women born in 1960 were producing smaller numbers of children, although the actual decline was less pronounced than that suggested by total period fertility rates. Three EU15 member states – Germany, the Netherlands and Portugal – recorded a continuous fall throughout the period, which was reflected in the EU15 average. The decline began later in most other member states. Figures for the 1955 birth cohorts show an upturn for France, Finland and Sweden, which would seem to have been sustained for the 1960 cohorts in the two Nordic states. The disparities between the countries with the largest and smallest numbers of births per woman for the 1930 and 1960 generations are slightly greater than for total fertility. For the 1960 cohort, France, Ireland and Sweden recorded completed fertility rates above 2.0, with Ireland and France above replacement level. Trends in CEE countries appear to be more erratic.

Table 2.2: Completed fertility rates for EU25 member states, 1930-60 birth cohorts, by membership wave

	1930	1935	1940	1945	1950	1955	1960
EU15	*2.42*	*2.39*	*2.23*	*2.08*	*1.97*	*1.90*	*1.81*
1. Belgium	2.29	2.27	2.16	1.93	1.83	1.83	1.84
1. France	2.63	2.57	2.41	2.22	2.11	2.13	2.10
1. Germany	2.18	2.16	1.97	1.80	1.72	1.67	1.65
1. Italy	2.28	2.28	2.14	2.07	1.89	1.80	1.66
1. Luxembourg	*1.97*	*2.00*	*1.92*	1.82	1.72	1.69	1.75
1. Netherlands	2.67	2.49	2.22	2.00	1.89	1.87	1.85
2. Denmark	2.36	2.38	2.24	2.08	1.90	1.84	1.90
2. Ireland	*3.50*	3.52	3.23	3.27	2.99	2.67	2.41
2. UK	*2.35*	*2.41*	*2.36*	*2.17*	*2.03*	2.01	1.97
3. Greece	*2.21*	*2.02*	2.10	2.00	2.02	2.00	1.93
3. Portugal	2.94	2.88	2.66	2.42	2.08	2.04	1.89
3. Spain	*2.59*	*2.67*	*2.59*	2.42	2.16	1.91	1.76
4. Austria	2.32	2.45	2.12	1.96	1.87	1.76	1.69
4. Finland	2.46	2.29	2.04	1.88	1.86	1.90	1.96
4. Sweden	2.12	2.14	2.05	1.98	2.00	2.03	2.04
5. Cyprus	–	–	–	–	2.29	2.31	2.43
5. Czech Rep	2.14	2.12	2.06	2.03	2.10	2.07	2.03
5. Estonia	–	–	–	1.85	1.97	2.00	2.00
5. Hungary	2.07	1.99	1.92	1.90	1.95	1.94	2.02
5. Latvia	–	–	–	–	1.87	1.84	1.94
5. Lithuania	–	–	1.99	1.97	2.01	1.94	1.88
5. Malta	–	–	–	*1.95*	*1.87*	*1.86*	*1.84*
5. Poland	2.78	2.60	2.41	2.27	2.19	2.17	2.18
5. Slovakia	2.87	2.72	2.55	2.38	2.31	2.22	2.18
5. Slovenia	2.10	2.06	2.01	1.83	1.90	1.96	1.87

Notes: The numbers in column 1 indicate waves of membership: 1. 1957, 2. 1973, 3. 1981/86, 4. 1995, 5. 2004.

Most data in the table are taken from the Council of Europe. Figures in italics are from Eurostat. While data from these two sources are generally consistent, significant unexplained discrepancies were found for Slovakia, with Eurostat reporting much higher figures for the 1945 to 1960 birth cohorts.

Sources: Council of Europe (2002, table T3.7); Eurostat (2002a, table E-6).

No country fell below the EU15 average for the 1960 cohort, and Cyprus, Poland and Slovenia were still above replacement level. Unless the decline in total fertility rates during the 1990s was due merely to a postponement of births, completed fertility rates for the 1965 and 1970 birth cohorts might be expected to fall below the EU15 average.

The overall figures for fertility rates at national level conceal important internal variations within countries (Eurostat, 2002a, table D-1). Regional differences are particularly marked in Germany between the eastern and western *Länder*, as already noted. The *Länder* with the smallest number of live births per 1,000 population in 2000 were Mecklenburg-Vorpommern,

Saxony and Saxony-Anhalt. In Italy, the contrast was between the north-west and south. In Spain, the poorer and less industrialised regions (Extremadura, Andalucia and Murcia) showed higher birth rates than the richer autonomous regions in the north-east. Rural areas in central France, such as Auvergne and Limousin, were distinguished from the major cities by their low fertility rates, as was metropolitan France compared with its overseas territories. The urban–rural divide in Greece was characterised by very low fertility rates in central areas. In the UK, the demographic profile of Northern Ireland was distinct from that of mainland Britain and was closer to the pattern in the Republic, where some of the highest fertility rates in the Union were recorded in the southern and eastern parts of the country (Eurostat, 2002a, table D-1). England and Wales have been described as one of the most demographically homogeneous regions in Europe with respect to geographical variations in the birth rate (Coleman, 2000, p 86), although pockets of very high fertility could be found in London, especially inner London, which recorded the highest rate of all in the Union in 2000. Internal diversity was also marked in CEE countries. In Poland, for example, the main disparity was between the urban and rural populations, with city dwellers registering much lower fertility rates than those living in rural areas (Warzywoda-Kruszyńska and Krzyszkowski, 2000).

Within countries, fertility rates may also vary according to ethnicity or nationality, particularly where new migrants from less developed regions have not adjusted their fertility patterns to those of the host community. In the UK, for example, the fertility rates of mothers born in Bangladesh and Pakistan are found to be more than twice the level for mothers born in the UK (Sporton and White, 2002, tables 2, 3). During the 1990s, the total minority ethnic population grew by 15%, compared to an increase of 1% for the White population, but with important variations between ethnic groups, ranging from 37% for Black Africans and 30% for Bangladeshis to 4% for Indians and 5% for the Chinese group (Scott et al, 2001, p 8). Data from the 1989 and 1999 censuses showed much lower fertility rates for mothers of French or other EU nationalities living in France, compared with mothers of non-EU nationality, particularly women from Black Africa (Legros, 2003, figure 1). In Sweden, the fertility rate for non-EU migrants from former Yugoslavia and Turkey has remained well above that for Swedish nationals (SCB, 2001, table 3.17). Similar observations have been made for Germany (Penn and Lambert, 2002, p 51), and for Finland, where women born in Somalia and Yugoslavia register much higher total fertility rates than women born in Finland. The rates for Somali women living in Finland are, however, lower than in their country of origin. The reverse applies for Russian and Estonian women, who account for the largest proportion of non-Finnish citizens and have usually moved to Finland to marry Finnish men (Statistics Finland, 2003, table 22). In Luxembourg, the high birth rate among foreigners means that, in 2000, births to foreigners accounted for almost 50% of all births recorded (MISSOC, 2002, p 54). In CEE countries, when such information is available, important variations can be found in fertility rates according to ethnicity, especially among the Roma population. For example, in Hungary, a fertility rate of 2.7 was recorded for Gypsy women in a survey in 2000, compared with 1.8 for Hungarian mothers (Kende, 2000, p 50). In Slovakia, the rate was more than three times higher for Roma than for Slovak women (Vagac and Haulikova, 2003, p 8).

Differences between EU15 member states and CEE countries are also found with regard to mortality. At the end of the 20th century, the average crude death rate for EU15 had settled at around 9.7 per 1,000 population, reflecting the fairly homogeneous situation in the countries with the largest population size. The dispersion around the mean was relatively small: Denmark recorded the highest rate (10.9‰) and Ireland the lowest (8.2‰). The picture was more diversified in CEE countries, where Latvia (13.6‰) and Estonia (13.5‰) were reporting the highest rates, and Slovenia the lowest (9.3‰) (Eurostat, 2002a, tables G-2, J-3).

The overall effect of differences in fertility and mortality rates is that, by the end of the century, four EU15 member states – Germany, Greece, Italy and Sweden – were showing negative natural population growth, the number of deaths being greater than the number of births, without a sufficient compensatory effect from immigration. The situation in the candidate countries was rather different. Only Cyprus, Malta, Poland and Slovakia were not registering negative natural population growth. Total population was increasing in the EU15 member states due to net migration, but not in the CEE countries, with the exception of Slovenia (Council of Europe, 2002, tables T1.2-1.4).

Measuring geographical mobility and migration

Since the mid-1980s, immigration to EU15 member states has been falling, although positive net migration has increased as smaller numbers of people have left the EU. In 2000, net migration reached around 700,000 migrants, or a rate of 0.2% of total EU15 population, a proportion greater than for natural population growth. As noted above, in four EU member states, net migration was preventing negative population growth. The sparse data available for CEE countries suggest that they were more often characterised by emigration than by immigration, with the result that net migration was very low and, in some cases, negative. Only in Slovenia was migration a compensating factor for negative natural population growth, and Poland recorded an overall fall in population growth due to negative net migration (European Commission, 2002e, pp 23, 114, 136).

Of the 19 million non-nationals registered in the Union in 2000, representing 5.1% of total population, 13 million, or 3.4% of total population, were from third countries. Although annual naturalisation rates for non-EU nationals have remained stable over time at about 2% of the foreign population, they had risen in Germany, Sweden and the Netherlands, reaching over 11% in the third of these three countries. Between 1988 and

1994, Germany absorbed 1.8 million ethnic Germans (*Aussiedler*), returning with full citizenship rights (European Commission, 2002e, pp 23, 48-50).

Intra-European mobility remained relatively stable during the 1990s at about 1.5% of population. Generally, mobility involved relocation to a neighbouring member state, for example Austrians to Germany, or the Dutch to Germany or Belgium. Germany hosted the largest number of EU citizens (1.9 million) followed by France (1.3 million), the UK (0.8 million) and Belgium (under 0.6 million) (European Commission, 2002e, pp 23, 28-9). At the same time, patterns of migration have been changing. Nationals in the southern European countries are much less mobile than those in the north. Greece, Ireland, Italy, Portugal, in particular, and Spain, which were traditionally countries of emigration, have seen immigration take over. By 2000, net migration had fallen to relatively low levels in Finland, Spain (0.5‰) and France (0.9‰). Luxembourg (8.3‰) and Ireland (5.3‰) were recording the highest levels (European Commission, 2002e, pp 28, 114).

Since the mid-19th century, economic emigration has been a major feature of Ireland's demography, often in the direction of England and Scotland, or the US. In the 1990s, the flow was in the opposite direction, as Ireland became an economically attractive location for returning Irish emigrants (FitzGerald, 2000). The high figures for Luxembourg throughout the 1990s were due to intra-European migration. At the end of the decade, almost 35% of its population were non-nationals, essentially from other EU15 member states. The majority of foreigners in Belgium were also from within the Union. Elsewhere, most nationals from other countries were of non-EU origin. Austria (9.3%) and Germany (6.7%) accounted for the largest share of third-country citizens. Turkish nationals, who were the most common group of non-nationals within EU15, with 2.7 million, were concentrated in Germany. In 2000, some 2.3 million North African nationals were registered in EU15 member states. The majority of Algerians and Tunisians were in France. Excluding Turkey, but including Bulgaria and Romania, the 12 candidates accounted for about 850,000 nationals from third countries registered in EU15 (European Commission, 2002e, pp 26, 28, 116).

A characteristic feature of immigration to the Union at the end of the 20th century was that women made up the majority of CEE migrants to Greece, the Netherlands and Finland, and from CEE and South America to Spain and Italy, attracted by the demand for service and domestic workers. The age profile of nationals from third countries was younger than that of EU15 nationals, particularly among Turks, since most migrants are of working age, and a large proportion of older people return to their country of origin on retirement (European Commission, 2002e, pp 26, 28). In the UK in 2001/02, for example, 38% of the Bangladeshi population were aged below 16, compared with 19% of the White group, which recorded the highest proportion of the population aged over 65, at 16%, compared with 9% for Black Caribbeans (ONS, 2002a, online). According to data for 1997-99, 90% of minority ethnic children aged below 15 were born in the UK, while

97% of persons aged over 44 were born outside the UK (Scott et al, 2001, table 4).

Patterns of asylum seeking also changed in the 1990s. Following the fall of the Berlin Wall, applications for asylum rose sharply, more than doubling between 1989 and 1992, to reach a record of 672,400. They dropped off in the mid-1990s and then rose again by the end of the decade. Germany was the main target country for asylum seekers, but applications to the UK increased rapidly during the 1990s to overtake France, which moved into second position. The largest proportions of applications for asylum per 1,000 inhabitants were recorded in Luxembourg (6.8‰), followed by Belgium (3.5‰), Austria and the Netherlands (2.5‰). Denmark, Germany and the UK reported the same level (1.2‰). The proportions were very small in Greece, Spain, Italy, France and Finland (below 1.0‰), falling to zero in Portugal. During the 1990s, applicants from the former Yugoslavia made up the main group of asylum seekers. Most applications from CEE countries were to Austria and Germany (European Commission, 2002e, pp 49, 116).

Much migration goes unrecorded. Estimates suggest that 3 million illegal immigrants were living in EU member states in 1998, with approximately 500,000 new entrants each year. Some countries have attempted to facilitate the integration of illegal immigrants by offering them the opportunity to regularise their situation, thereby enabling an estimated 1.8 million to become legal immigrants since the 1970s (European Commission, 2002e, p 46). Due to problems in defining and recording cross-border mobility and the potentially high fertility rates of some migrant groups, the extent to which inward migration from third countries is sustaining population growth is most probably underestimated.

Measuring population age structure and dependency

The age profile of many EU15 member states during the 20th century was marked by the two world wars, which decimated whole generations of younger men in Europe, followed by an unprecedented baby boom and a prolonged wave of inward labour migration in the postwar reconstruction period. Although population ageing is primarily determined by the combined impact of fertility and mortality rates, migration may also have an effect if the age structure of incoming groups of migrants is substantially different from that of the host population, as indicated above.

Population ageing in the Union is both 'bottom-up', due to falling fertility, and 'top-down', due to falling mortality and greater life expectancy. The decline in fertility has been taking place at the same time as growth in life expectancy due, increasingly, to improvements in survival rates for older age groups. Although women are producing a smaller number of children, relatively few children die in their infancy. Compared with the less developed regions in the world, the survival rate of babies in EU15 member states is very high, resulting in greater life expectancy at birth. In the absence of natural or human-made disasters, the reduction of mortality rates after the first years of life is mainly due to improvements in the standard of health of the population. At the end of the 20th century, with a life expectancy of 78.4 years at birth, EU15 was second only to Japan (80.8); it was ahead of the US (77.1) and far outstripped the Russian Federation (67.4) and less developed regions (62.3) in the world (Eurostat, 2002a, table A-5).

The improvement in life expectancy at birth has been considerable for both men and women throughout the Union since the 1960s, representing a gain of almost 8 years for men and 8.5 years for women between 1960 and 2000. However, the EU15 average conceals important differences between member states and between men and women. Countries that were recording a relatively low life expectancy at the beginning of the period have seen their rates increase markedly, although Portugal has continued to occupy a position at the bottom of the rank order since 1960 for men. At the turn of the century, Denmark and Ireland were displaying the lowest life expectancy for women, whereas it had been relatively high for Danish women in 1960. At the beginning of the period, the Netherlands displayed the longest life expectancy for both men and women, whereas these positions were held by Sweden (77.4 years) for men and, jointly, by France and Spain (82.7 years) for women in 2000. While the disparity between member states was reduced over time for men, it increased for women as they benefited more than men from the relative growth in life expectancy, despite the rise in risk-related behaviour (smoking, alcohol consumption) among women. At the end of the 1990s, the largest gender gap (7.5 years) was found in France and the smallest (4.8 years) in Denmark (Eurostat, 2002a, tables G-4, G-5).

Several of the CEE countries not only suffered heavy losses during the two world wars, but they were also affected during the postwar period by the repression of Soviet rule, which provoked large-scale emigration, mainly among the younger generations. By the end of the 1980s, more Estonian nationals, for example, were living abroad than at home. The upheavals of transition during the 1990s resulted in further demographic disruption, characterised by a combination of low fertility, high mortality, low life expectancy and continued emigration. Throughout the 1990s, life expectancy in CEE countries remained five or more years below the EU15 average. By 2000, particularly low figures were being recorded in Estonia and Latvia, where men could expect to live to the age of 65, compared with the EU15 average of 75 (Eurostat, 2002a, tables J-18, J-19).

By the end of the century, the net outcome of trends in fertility, mortality and migration was not only that natural population growth had slowed down to a much reduced pace, but also that the proportion of older people in the population in EU15 member states had increased more rapidly than in other parts of the more developed regions except Japan. EU15 reported the smallest proportion in the world of population under the age of 15, after Japan, and the largest proportion over the age of 65. The EU15 average age had risen from 32.2 in 1970 to 38 in 2000, compared with 41.3 in Japan and

Table 2.3: Population age structure in EU25 member states, by membership wave (1975, 2000 and 2025)

	1975		2000		2025	
	<15	65>	<15	65>	<15	65>
EU15	24.1	12.6	17.5	15.6	14.8	21.9
1. Belgium	22.2	13.9	17.4	17.0	15.2	23.0
1. France	23.9	13.5	18.8	16.0	16.6	22.0
1. Germany	21.6	14.8	15.7	16.3	13.7	23.8
1. Italy	24.2	12.0	14.3	18.1	11.5	25.5
1. Luxembourg	21.6	13.1	19.0	13.7	16.8	16.5
1. Netherlands	25.3	10.8	18.5	13.6	15.6	21.2
2. Denmark	22.6	13.4	18.3	15.0	15.5	22.0
2. Ireland	31.3	11.0	21.5	11.3	18.6	16.3
2. UK	23.4	14.0	19.0	15.9	16.1	19.6
3. Greece	23.9	12.2	15.1	17.5	12.3	24.0
3. Portugal	27.9	9.9	16.7	15.6	13.9	20.7
3. Spain	27.6	10.0	14.6	16.8	11.9	22.8
4. Austria	23.3	14.9	16.7	15.5	12.6	23.1
4. Finland	22.0	10.6	18.1	14.9	15.7	24.4
4. Sweden	20.7	15.1	18.3	17.4	16.1	23.8
5. Cyprus	25.9	9.8	23.0	11.5	18.3	18.4
5. Czech Republic	22.3	12.9	16.4	13.8	12.6	22.9
5. Estonia	21.7	12.2	18.0	15.1	14.3	21.5
5. Hungary	20.3	12.6	16.9	14.6	13.3	21.2
5. Latvia	21.1	12.7	18.0	15.1	13.4	21.5
5. Lithuania	25.5	11.1	20.1	14.0	16.4	19.2
5. Malta	24.7	9.6	20.0	12.4	16.5	22.3
5. Poland	24.0	9.5	19.2	12.1	14.4	20.3
5. Slovakia	26.2	9.6	19.6	11.3	15.0	18.2
5. Slovenia	23.7	11.0	15.9	13.9	11.8	24.3

Notes: The numbers in column 1 indicate waves of membership: 1. 1957, 2. 1973, 3. 1981/86, 4. 1995, 5. 2004.

United Nations sources provide the most complete dataset for age structure. Some of the data shown in the table, in particular for wave 5 countries, are higher than in Council of Europe and Eurostat sources. EU15 averages are calculated from national data.

Source: UNESA (2002, http://esa.un.org/unpp).

35.2 in the US. By the year 2025, it is expected to reach 45 for EU15, compared with 50.2 in Japan and 37.6 in the US (UNESA, 2002).

Throughout the period, as shown in Table 2.3, Ireland stands out as having a much larger young population than other EU15 member states, due to its relatively high fertility rate. In 1975, almost one third of the Irish population was aged 0-14 and, by 2000, over a fifth, compared with less than 15% of population in Italy and Spain, where fertility rates had been among the lowest in the Union from the early to mid-1980s. Since mortality rates have fluctuated less than those for fertility, the disparity is also marked for the older age group, where Ireland registers the smallest proportion of its population over the age of 65, well below the EU15 average. By the same token, Italy was recording the largest proportion of older people in 2000. By contrast, all but three of the fifth-wave member states were displaying a relatively large young population in 2000, above the EU15 average. None of them was recording an above-average proportion of population over the age of 65. Due to its relatively high figures for life expectancy, Sweden was reporting the largest proportion of population aged over 80 in 2000. In Denmark, Italy and the UK, more than 3.9% of the population was aged over 80. In all CEE countries, the proportion aged over 80 was lower than in EU15 member states (European Commission, 2002e, pp 114, 136).

The intensity and timing of population ageing vary both within and between countries due to internal migration. For example, in France and the UK, older people may migrate to the southern coastal areas in their own countries, resulting in larger concentrations of older people in these regions. North European retirees with generous occupational pensions are often attracted to the warmer climates of the Union's sun belt, with important implications for the provision of care and services in southern Europe.

Changes in the age structure of the population are of interest for the present volume insofar as they affect intergenerational dependency. When total age dependency ratios are calculated as the proportion of the population aged below 15 and over 65 in relation to the population aged 15 to 64, in accordance with the definition used by Eurostat (2002a, p 159, 1st variant), dependency so defined is found to have decreased across EU25 between 1975 and 2000, with the exception of Finland, due to the presence of the baby-boom generations in the active population and the overall decline in fertility rates. The steepest fall was recorded in Ireland, whereas most of the fifth-wave member states registered relatively small changes. In 2000, although falling, the total dependency ratio remained highest in Sweden, the UK and France, in that order (Eurostat, 2002a, table C-7). They were all countries with relatively large young and old age populations above the EU15 average. The low total age dependency ratio reported for Spain was explained by the relatively small proportion of younger people. The picture was different in CEE countries, where the overall dependency ratio was generally lower, and where the balance between young and old age dependency had shifted less towards the older age groups than in the EU15 countries. Since the mid-1970s, the disparity between the countries with the largest and smallest dependent populations and lowest total dependency ratios has been narrowing, mainly due to the decline in the young age dependency ratio in Ireland. The difference at the two extremes, between Ireland and Luxembourg in 1975 and between Sweden and Spain in 2000, was more than halved (Eurostat, 2002a, table C-7).

The combined impact of slow or negative population growth and population ageing is found to vary between EU member states. Figure 2.1

Figure 2.1: Population decline and ageing in EU25 member states (2000)

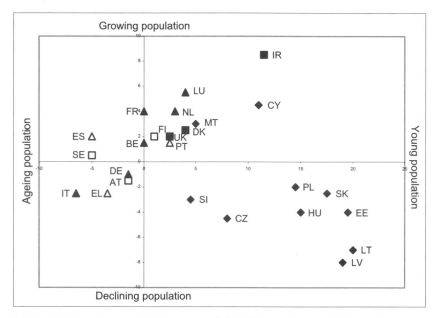

Key: ▲ 1957 members, ■ 1973 members, Δ 1981/86 members, □ 1995 members, ◆ 2004 members.

Notes: For each indicator, the standard deviation has been calculated for the dataset. For each country cell, the deviation of each data point has been calculated from the mean for EU15 (*x*-mean) and has been compared with the value of the standard deviation (SD) for each indicator. Positive or negative values have then been assigned according to the number of SDs (0.5 points for ¼ SD, 1 point for ½ SD, 2 points for 1 SD, 4 points for 2 SDs). The scores for each group of indicators have then been added together and plotted on the *x* and *y* axes.

Sources: Council of Europe (2002, tables T1.2, T1.6, T3.3, T4.6); Eurostat (2002a, tables B-2, B-3, E-4, G-4, G-5, J-8); UNESA (2002, http://esa.un.org/unpp).

locates the 25 EU member states in relation to the EU15 mean in 2000. Indicators for total fertility and population growth rates are plotted on the vertical axis, and for life expectancy at birth, and for population under 15 and over 65 on the horizontal axis. The graph shows that the countries most affected by both population decline and ageing were Italy, followed by Greece, Austria and Germany. Spain and Sweden were exhibiting the effects of ageing, although their population was still growing. France and Belgium matched the EU15 mean for ageing, but both recorded population growth. In relation to the EU15 mean, all the CEE countries were experiencing population decline in 2000. However, they were much less affected by population ageing than almost all EU15 member states, due essentially to the effect of lower life expectancy on the age structure of the population. Lithuania, Latvia, Estonia and Slovakia were displaying the youngest populations in EU25, but the first two were the countries most affected by population decline. By contrast, Cyprus and, especially, Ireland stood out as the member states with relatively young and expanding populations as a result of their high fertility rates and large proportions of young people. Malta clustered with the remaining member states from the different regions in western Europe that were characterised by population growth above the EU15 average but were less affected by population ageing.

Forecasts for the 21st century suggest that the trend towards population ageing within the Union will continue (see Table 2.3). By 2025, more than a fifth of the population will be aged over 65 in most EU25 countries. As the postwar baby boomers reach the age of 65 after 2015, they will temporarily increase the percentage of persons in the older age group, thereby accelerating population ageing. However, the cohorts following the baby boomers into old age will be smaller. Meanwhile, further enlargement to the east will accentuate EU population ageing if fertility remains low, and life expectancy increases. The upturn in fertility at the end of the century in some countries, together with further net migration of around 1 million per year, is not expected to offset pre-programmed population ageing in the 21st century (European Commission, 2002e, p 25).

By 2025, the respective impact of young and old age dependency ratios will be reversed, with the effect that all EU25 member states will experience an increase in total age dependency. According to the figures in Table 2.3, Finland will be most affected between 2000 and 2025 and will become the country with the highest dependency ratio, followed by Sweden. Luxembourg and Slovakia are predicted to be the countries showing the lowest total age dependency ratios. All the CEE countries are expected to remain below the EU15 average.

Policy challenges from population decline and ageing

The information collected about demographic trends by national statistical offices in population surveys, registers and censuses is designed to establish facts that can serve as a basis for policy decisions. The conventions adopted for defining, classifying and analysing data are, therefore, determined by funding bodies in accordance with their requirements and with reference to specific socio-economic contexts (Desrosières, 1996). Consequently, what are held to be facts are social constructs that may only partially capture reality by providing an imperfect or approximate snapshot at a given point in time for a particular purpose. Demographic data are regularly the subject of media scrutiny, often with little regard for their limitations. They constantly fuel public and political debate and are used to underpin policy formulation, as politicians are called upon to respond to the challenges they present. The concluding section to this chapter examines the extent to which the issues raised by statistics showing population decline and ageing are seen as problems at EU level and by national governments. Chapters Six and Seven explore the measures implemented to deal with the implications of demographic change as well as the perceptions that family members have of public policy responses.

Population issues on the EU agenda

Historically, the size of a nation's population has often been portrayed as synonymous with political power and military might in the world arena. During the 20th century, the founding of the EEC in 1957 and its progressive enlargement contributed to a vision of a strong and united Europe capable of being a world player. Documents emanating from EU institutions depict population decline as an issue with which member states should be engaging, together with other more developed countries, if they do not want to lose their pre-eminent world ranking. Since the signing of the Treaty of Maastricht in 1993, article 7 of the Protocol on Social Policy places the European Commission under a treaty obligation to monitor and report on the demographic situation. The first report on the situation in 1994 (European Commission, 1995) highlighted the key role of the Union as a demographic power, but warned that it was in danger of losing its leading position unless population decline was halted. Subsequent Commission reports on the changing social situation in the Union focused on the extent and acceleration of the ageing process and its implications for the economy, social protection, intergenerational solidarity, the dialogue between the social partners and, more especially, the development of a European employment strategy (European Commission, 1996a). The impact of demographic change on the labour market, and the importance of regional variations and of demographic trends in the applicant states were the main themes in the 1997 report (European Commission, 1998). Population ageing, employment, social protection, social cohesion and the linkages between them had become central issues for the Commission by the turn of the century, and were expected to remain high on the social policy agenda. The question of how to sustain the future labour supply in a context of population decline and ageing and against a background of economic stringency reopened the debate about the need for policy measures to tackle immigration, health and social care (European Commission, 2000c, 2001, 2002e, 2003).

In some respects, the Commission has served as the demographic conscience of member states, alerting them to longer-term prospects and drawing attention to the need for pre-emptive action. Few EU member states express concern about population decline per se. Rather, attention focuses on the implications of the slowing down of natural population growth for ageing and migration. The message from demographers (Coleman, 2000, p 80) that any radical disruption to age structure generates problems as the cohorts contributing to the peaks and troughs progress through life has a strong resonance among political historians. European demographic profiles were severely affected by high mortality in the two world wars, followed by high fertility in the postwar period, creating labour shortages together with high demand for schools and housing. In the 1970s and 1980s, the need was to adapt to falling rolls in schools, the bulge in higher education and the demand for jobs at a time when the world economy was suffering from the effects of the oil crises of the early 1970s. Already during the 1990s, in a context of welfare retrenchment, the combination of declining fertility, greater life expectancy and the fall in net migration, characteristic of an advanced stage of demographic transition, was raising questions about the social, economic and political impact of population ageing. The major challenges in the first quarter of the 21st century are how to deal with the needs of the baby boomers as they reach retirement age, how to resolve the labour shortages they leave behind them and how to offset the age imbalance in the population. The demographic fluctuations during the transition period of the 1990s created additional challenges in the case of CEE countries.

As the dependency ratio comes to be weighted more heavily towards older age groups, the demand for social services and healthcare increases, and could reach an unmanageable level in a situation where the generations of working age represent a declining proportion of the population. The shift in dependency towards older generations has, therefore, caused concern about the unduly heavy burden being placed by an older inactive population on the population of working age, and the ensuing need to transfer the financial and practical resources produced by labour to pay for care and pensions. Predictions of further increases in old age dependency raise critical questions about the sustainability of social protection systems and their ability to meet the needs of increasing numbers of older dependants in a situation where the size of the population of working age is stable or declining.

The phenomenon of population ageing may not, however, present insurmountable problems if it is gradual, and if ways can be found to supplement the labour supply, or if the negative aspects of biological ageing can be alleviated by medical advances and improved living conditions. In the late 1990s, disability-free life expectancy at birth was estimated to be 63 years for men and 66 for women (European Commission, 2002e, p 128). The age at which biological deterioration becomes problematic because of the caring needs it entails could be further postponed. It could also be of shorter duration, providing medical advances and a higher level of medical and social care are not used to sustain life artificially for a longer period of time. These issues give rise to a number of ethical questions such as healthcare priorities and euthanasia, which have moved onto the policy agendas of many EU member states.

Population issues on national policy agendas

Not all countries share the same concern about the impending economic and social crises being provoked by low population growth and population ageing. As demonstrated by the statistics, the two phenomena have not occurred at the same rate in all EU member states. Several countries were enjoying a temporary respite in the early years of the 21st century pending the point at which the postwar baby boomers will reach retirement age. For most governments, the major policy issue associated with population ageing is how to pay for the pensions and healthcare of a growing number of older dependants over the coming decades. The extent to which the situation is seen as problematic varies, however, according to the size of the imbalance between the population of working age in employment and the inactive population over retirement age, the way in which welfare is funded and organised and national perceptions of trends. In continental welfare systems, such as those in France, Germany and Italy, where benefits are heavily dependent on earnings-related insurance contributions as well as pay-as-you-go pension schemes, a high dependency ratio may impose an unacceptable burden on the population of working age in employment and also on employers. In countries where social protection has a broader funding base, as in Denmark, Sweden and the UK, the cost of providing pensions, health and social care may be less subject to fluctuations in the dependency ratio, although it can be affected by the wider economic situation and financial markets.

Reactions to socio-demographic change cannot necessarily be predicted from statistical data[1]. The countries that might be expected to be most concerned in the short term about the consequences of population stagnation and decline are those recording the lowest fertility rates at the turn of the century, and where migration does not compensate for low natural population growth. Austria, Germany, Greece, Italy and Sweden were the EU15 member states most affected by low or negative natural population growth in combination with relatively high old age dependency levels in 2000. Sweden was less affected by low completed fertility than by fluctuations in total fertility rates. In the medium term (by 2015), the imbalance in its age structure was predicted to become less problematic, despite high life expectancy. Other EU15 countries were anticipating further deterioration in the age structure of their population. CEE countries had different causes for concern: although the full impact of population decline and ageing had yet to be felt, low fertility, negative natural population growth and low life expectancy were being recorded in a context where, during transition, living standards had fallen to worryingly low levels for large sectors of the population.

The extent to which these potential concerns were reflected in scientific, media and political debate was not necessarily as might have been predicted from the statistics. Public opinion and policy actors in Italy and Sweden were very much aware of the threat posed by the demographic time bomb for

---

[1] Information about national media, academic and political debates is taken mainly from a study of eight EU15 member states and three CEE countries within a Framework Programme 5 project, funded by the European Commission in 2000-03 (see Acknowledgements). Additional information about the remaining candidate countries is derived from a series of unpublished social protection reports prepared for the European Commission in 2003.

the sustainability of pensions and were responding with policies designed to ensure the long-term viability of pensions and care provision. In Sweden, attention was being paid to the burden that would be placed on the shrinking labour force and the possible deterioration in the quality of provision for older people. In Italy, debate was focusing on how to pay and care for an ageing population rather than how to redress the age imbalance. The consequences of population decline were being debated in Germany, in association with the question of immigration, which had staved off the fall in population size during the 1990s. Less concern was expressed in Greece due to the fact that the postwar baby boom had been much less intense than elsewhere in the Union, with the result that the impact of the generations of older people reaching the age of retirement after the year 2010 will be more gradual. Other issues were, however, coming to the fore. Politicians were expressing concern about falling rolls in schools and their implications for local communities. The problems associated with the generation gap resulting from rapid socio-economic change reflected the general debate elsewhere in southern European countries. At the other extreme of the ageing spectrum, Ireland, with a relatively small older population, found itself in the enviable position of being able to plan ahead and take pre-emptive action to avoid some of the problems facing its European neighbours.

Irrespective of their relative situation with regard to population ageing, several countries were debating demographic issues, often in line with traditional national attitudes towards such matters. For example, despite its relatively high completed fertility rate and more favourable age balance, both public opinion and decision makers in France were voicing fears about the threat of population decline. By contrast, in the UK population growth and renewal were not major issues on the policy agenda, except in relation to skill shortages, for which a potential solution under consideration was to adapt policy to accommodate skilled migrant labour. Of greater public interest were the arguments for and against a new wave of immigration. The rights of asylum seekers had become a contentious topic at EU and national level. In Italy and the UK, attention was focusing on asylum not as a demographic concern but as a humanitarian and economic issue. The risk of overpopulation if governments adopt an open door policy was being discussed in several countries in a context where attempts were being made to seal borders against illegal migrants and resolve problems of ethnic identity and racial tension.

The CEE countries were at a different stage of socio-demographic development from most EU15 member states with regard to the ageing process. The later onset of the decline in fertility, in combination with low life expectancy meant that, theoretically, population ageing was not such an immediate problem. Policy makers in Estonia and Latvia, in particular, might have been expected to be concerned to find ways of raising life expectancy among prime-age men by reducing their high premature death rates due to unnatural causes such as alcoholism, suicide, road accidents and violence.

Prompted by the need to adapt to membership of the Union, the issue of how to ensure the longer-term sustainability of pension and healthcare systems had, nonetheless, moved up the social agenda in most CEE countries.

Population decline was of greater concern than ageing in several of the CEE countries. In Estonia, for example, even though completed fertility was above the EU15 average, the falling birth rate was seen as a major threat to the survival of the nation. In Hungary, it was interpreted as a sign of low morale, requiring government action. For several of the candidate countries, a potential danger associated with EU membership was that it would stimulate outward migration of younger people in search of better living and working conditions, endangering both the age balance and the skills base.

Across the Union, the focus of much of the debate was the impact the changing dependency balance was having on 'generational solidarity' (Attias-Donfut and Arber, 2000, p 19). The impending pension crisis was being presented in terms of the growing burden resting on the 'sandwich' generation, after a period when the standard of living of many older people had been improving due to greater income security in old age. The debate surrounding pension reform revealed deep-rooted ideological conflicts within societies. Since the early 1980s, left-wing governments in France, for example, had pursued policies designed to reduce working time and the length of working life in a system highly dependent on redistributing social security contributions from the active to the inactive population. Ways were, therefore, being sought at the turn of the 21st century to make provision for the growing population in retirement without imposing a still heavier burden on the population of working age. The strain on generational solidarity was being felt in several countries, in particular in southern Europe, where families are under a strong moral and legal obligation to care for their relatives. After many years of dependence on the state for welfare, in the CEE countries, the reforms under discussion were premised on greater self-reliance, which was creating further challenges for governments and families alike in a context of fundamental economic restructuring.

THREE

Family diversification

The 'first demographic transition', which lasted from the late 19th and throughout most of the 20th century in the western world, was characterised by low fertility, low mortality and greater life expectancy, resulting in low population growth and ageing. The 'second demographic transition', which began in the 1960s and was still continuing at the turn of the century, entailed a marked rise in divorce, unmarried cohabitation, births outside marriage and lone parenthood. This de-institutionalisation of family life is associated with major shifts in value systems away from collective responsibility and duties towards a post-material conception of individual rights and personal autonomy (Lesthaeghe, 1995; Coleman and Chandola, 1999). Although the sequence of these two demographic transitions places the slowing down of population growth and population ageing before family de-institutionalisation, the processes involved are closely interlocked and mutually reinforcing. The decline in fertility and, more especially, the reduction in the time devoted to childbearing and childrearing made women less dependent on the bonds of formal marriage for their livelihood. In turn, lower levels of commitment to marriage and its instability were conducive to a fall in fertility rates and family size. Greater life expectancy and population ageing called into question relationships between the generations, leading to a rethinking of the 'generational contract' (Attias-Donfut and Arber, 2000, p 1). Changing family forms and structures have raised important policy dilemmas for governments concerned about the threat posed by family breakdown for social order but often reluctant to intervene in what can be considered as strictly private matters.

This chapter analyses the process of family change and its consequences. Like Chapter Two, it begins by examining the problems of defining and conceptualising change from a comparative perspective. It then charts changes in family life, tracking them over time, during the late 20th century, and space, within the European Union (EU), including the countries that became members in 2004. As with population decline and ageing, the impact of different waves of membership, and particularly of enlargement to the east, is relevant to an understanding of the development, or otherwise, of a

European family model. The final section examines the challenges posed by changing family forms for policy actors, with reference to wider social, economic and political contexts.

Defining and conceptualising family change

Family is a shifting concept. What it means to be a member of a family and what is expected of family relationships, as well as the language used to describe them (Allan, 1999, p 4), vary over time and place, at both individual and societal levels. Although the term 'the family' continues to be widely used to refer to an enduring core, or fundamental social unit, it is difficult, if not impossible, to find a universally agreed definition that can be applied across or within societies. Families and households, a more meaningful and tractable umbrella term for demographers, were initially defined for national census purposes in the 19th century. Definitions have subsequently been refined, adapted and extended to achieve international standardisation and to take account of the changing socio-demographic scene. This section briefly reviews attempts to define and conceptualise families from a demographic and international perspective in EU25 member states.

Defining families and households

The United Nations (UN) first established definitions of families and households in 1974 for use in population and housing censuses. These definitions have been widely adopted as international standards. The United Nations Economic Commission for Europe (UN/ECE, 1987, 1998) revises the definitions to be used for each census round in the ECE region. The 1997 revision was carried out in co-operation with Eurostat in preparation for the 2000 censuses. Originally, the UN/ECE definition of the family unit was based on the 'conjugal family concept'. Subsequent revisions can be seen as a response to the growing importance of alternative living arrangements, particularly unmarried cohabitation, and extramarital births. Already in the 1980 censuses within the European Community (EC), unmarried cohabiting couples were recorded as family nuclei in Denmark, France, Ireland, Luxembourg, Portugal and Spain. Ten years later, Italy and the United Kingdom adapted their definitions, while Belgium, Germany, Greece and the Netherlands still did not recognise consensual unions for statistical purposes.

In 1997, all references to marriage as a defining characteristic of the family nucleus were removed from UN/ECE recommendations. The lead paragraph of the 1987 recommendations had read:

> 131. For census purposes, the family should be defined in the narrow sense of a family nucleus, that is, the persons within a private or institutional household who are related as husband and wife or as parent and never-married child by blood or adoption. Thus, a family nucleus comprises a married couple without children or a married

couple with one or more never-married children of any age or one
parent with one or more never-married children of any age.
(UN/ECE, 1987)

In the 1997 version of the UN recommendations, the wording of the
lead definition was changed, by eliminating the term 'married' and
introducing a reference to 'cohabiting partners':

> 191. A family nucleus is defined in the narrow sense as two or more
> persons within a private or institutional household who are related as
> husband and wife, as cohabiting partners, or as parent and child. Thus
> a family comprises a couple without children, or a couple with one or
> more children, or a lone parent with one or more children.
> (UN/ECE, 1998, original emphasis)

From the demographer's standpoint, the family nucleus is a subcategory of a
household. Data collected in national censuses generally refer to private
households rather than families as the unit of measurement. This approach
has the advantage of including one-person households, who are excluded
from counts of family nuclei. In countries where the number of one-person
households is very small, and most households are made up of a single
nuclear two-generation family unit, the distinction between families and
households is minimal, and the terms may be used interchangeably.

The 1997 UN/ECE recommendations provided a definition very close to
that used in 1987 for private, as distinct from 'institutional', households:

> 182. A private household is either:
>> (a) a one-person household, i.e. a person who lives alone in a separate
>> housing unit or who occupies, as a lodger, a separate room (or rooms)
>> of a housing unit but does not join with any of the other occupants of
>> the housing unit to form part of a multi-person household as defined
>> below; or
>> (b) a multi-person household, i.e. a group of two or more persons who
>> combine to occupy the whole or part of a housing unit and to provide
>> themselves with food and possibly other essentials for living.
>> Members of the group may pool their incomes to a greater or lesser
>> extent.
> (UN/ECE, 1998, original emphasis)

National statistical offices in the Nordic states equate private households
with housing units to define the household as a common dwelling unit.
UN/ECE's preferred definition is, however, based on the concept of the
housekeeping unit. It recommends that countries using the household-
dwelling concept should also provide an estimate of the number of
housekeeping units. Statistics Finland (personal communication, 2003) has,
for example, identified 85% of dwelling units as housekeeping units.

Despite the standard definitions laid down at international level for the conduct of censuses, for a number of reasons reliable comparable data are not readily available across Europe to track many of the variables associated with family and household change. Moreover, national censuses are generally held once every 10 years, during which time many changes may occur in individual and family living arrangements, necessitating policy responses. Between censuses, most countries, therefore, carry out their own national sample surveys, and maintain registers and other forms of records.

Progressively, census counts are being replaced or supplemented by population registers and other more frequent surveys, not only to support strategic planning but also to avoid issues of confidentiality, intrusion of privacy or unconstitutionality associated with censuses, in line with the legal frameworks governing data protection. The Nordic states already rely heavily on population registers to compile the information required by Eurostat for its international comparative tables. In the Netherlands, administrative registers are combined with sample household surveys, and Belgium has moved in the same direction. In the 1990 and 2000 census rounds, Germany replaced the national population census, which was deemed to be unconstitutional, by data collected in the annual 1% sample micro census. France introduced an annual sample census in 2004. Statistical services have undergone comprehensive restructuring in the former Soviet states. By 2000, Estonia, Latvia, Lithuania and Slovenia had fairly reliable administrative registers for gathering data on a continuing basis. Although such alternatives are less costly, the data collected are often in a format designed to meet national needs. They are not always harmonised cross nationally and may, consequently, be unsuitable for comparative purposes.

Even countries that conduct conventional censuses do not routinely observe international recommendations or apply them consistently. For example, in the 1990 census round, according to Eurostat (1995b, table 1), single persons were regarded as family units in the Nordic states, and grandchildren living with their grandparents were considered as family nuclei in Germany, Luxembourg, Portugal and the UK.

Discrepancies also result from the way homeless or temporarily mobile individuals are treated, such as those occupying more than one dwelling for professional reasons or absent on the night of the census. UN/ECE (1998, § 30) recommends recording the usual residence (*de jure*), defined as the place where the enumerated person "spends most of his/her daily night-rest", rather than where the person is on the night of the census (*de facto*). The concept of family togetherness is brought into play: "for persons with a spouse/partner and/or children, the usual residence should be that at which they spend the majority of the time with their family" (UN/ECE, 1998, § 36).

A problem of comparability of family units between countries can arise according to whether or not an age limit is used to define the relationship between parents and dependent children. For the purposes of the 2000 censuses, the 1997 UN/ECE (1998, § 192) recommendations did not set an age limit for children to be considered as belonging to a family nucleus. A child was defined "as any person with no partner and no child who has usual residence in the household of at least one of the parents".

According to this definition, a person in their seventies living with an elderly parent in their nineties would be classified as a parent–child dyad. To yield more useful information for policy analysts, UN/ECE (1998, § 202-3) recommends classifying children by age, using 25 as a cut-off point to define children as distinct from sons and daughters within nuclear family households. However, article 1 of the 1989 United Nations Convention on the Rights of the Child defines a child as a person below 18 years of age, unless the age of majority is earlier under national law. In the 1990 round of censuses, Denmark, Finland and Sweden counted children up to the age of 18 as a constituent part of the family unit. In Finland, the practice in presenting statistics is to specify 'underaged children' if the age criterion is relevant for the purpose of the analysis (Statistics Finland, personal communication, 2003). The importance of consistently using an agreed age category can be illustrated by the Danish case: the age change from 26 to 18 in Denmark between the 1980 and 1990 censuses to identify children resulted in a fall of 13.6% in the proportion of married couples without children (Simões Casimiro and Calado Lopes, 1995, p 70).

Age in years is not, in any case, a good indicator of young age family dependency. Eurostat generally considers children to be 'dependent' if they are aged below 15 or are aged 15-24, economically inactive and living with at least one parent (European Commission, 2002e, p 116). Even these boundaries may prove unreliable in a context where young people become financially independent and are leaving the family home at a later age.

A concept that almost disappeared from the statisticians' vocabulary during the 1990s, at least in EU15 member states, was 'head of household'. It has been replaced by the gender-neutral term 'reference person'. While underlining the value of the concept for identifying the structure of households, UN/ECE leaves countries to decide on the criteria to be used to determine who the reference person is, suggesting that:

200. ... the following criteria for selection of the reference person will yield the most fruitful range of explicit kin relationships:
- either the husband or the wife of a married couple living in the household (preferably from the middle generation in a multi-generational household);
- either partner of a consensual union couple living in the household where there is no married couple present;
- the parent, where one parent lives with his or her sons or daughters of any age;
- where none of the above conditions apply, any adult member of the household may be selected.
(UN/ECE, 1998)

Irrespective of the terminology used, the structure of households as recorded in censuses and surveys may be affected by differences in the way the reference person is designated. For example, in Italy and Spain, the members of a household identify the reference person. A child over the age of 16 can be the reference person in Italy. In the UK, the respondent entered on the first line of the survey form as the 'householder' is designated as the reference person, which also leaves the choice to the household. In France, according to the instructions issued to interviewers for labour force surveys, the reference person is determined by using a set of rules that give precedence to sex (male), occupational status (working) and age (oldest), in that order. In Finland, the status is accorded to the person contributing most to household income (Statistics Finland, personal communication, 2003). In Estonia, it is either the owner or tenant of the dwelling, or, if not applicable, an adult household member, who is a permanent resident and present at the time of the census (Statistical Office of Estonia, 1999, § 39.8).

From a comparative perspective, an anomaly may arise if, for example, an economically inactive widow aged over 50 is living in a dwelling she owns with her 25-year-old unmarried son, who is earning a reasonable income. In the UK, she could be identified as the reference person; in Finland or France, this status would be assigned to the son. In cases where no age limit is observed for children, she would be considered as a lone mother. If her elderly father was living with them and was in receipt of a large contributory pension, the way in which the structure of the family and household is described would again differ from one country to another.

Defining marriage and divorce

For its demographic reports, Eurostat collects data from EU member states on marital status (single, married, widowed or divorced and not remarried), gross (or crude) marriage rates, age-specific first marriage rates, frequencies of cumulated first marriages, mean age at first marriage and at all marriages, proportions of first-married men and women by generation, divorce rates by duration of marriage and median duration of marriage at divorce.

According to UN/ECE (1998, § 68), marital status is "the (legal) conjugal status of each individual in relation to the marriage laws (or customs) of the country". It recommends that information should be collected for all persons aged 15 or more, except where the minimum legal age of marriage is lower. The total first marriage rate is defined as the probability of contracting a first marriage if the person concerned conforms to the age-specific first marriage rate in a given year (Eurostat, 2002a, p 164). As with total period fertility rates, the figure represents an estimate for a hypothetical generation based on the sum of the rates observed in a particular year. If the number of marriages fluctuates from year to year, the rate may not accurately reflect the actual situation for completed marriages at the end of the period. The number of marriages recorded may also vary in some countries depending on whether or not religious marriages are recognised by civil authorities, which is a situation that also changes over time (see Chapter Five).

Another problem complicating measurements of marriage rates is that information collected from civil registers may differ from that derived from other sources. Enumerators in Estonia were, for example, instructed to leave the relevant space on the census form blank if the legal spouse was not living in the same household at the time of the census, which meant that the status of being married could apply only to cohabiting married couples.

In addition to data on crude rates, information about divorce covers the number of divorces in relation to the number of marriages and duration of marriage up to the time of divorce. The total divorce rate assumes the size of different marriage cohorts to be the same and is not the divorce rate for a specific marriage cohort. Like total fertility and marriage rates, it is the divorce rate of a hypothetical generation, subjected to current marriage conditions. Eurostat also records duration of marriage. Divorce rates per 100 marriages are calculated by relating the number of divorces at the end of a given number of years of marriage to the number of marriages over the period ending in divorce (Eurostat, 2002a, pp 160, 164).

Comparative data on divorce and separation are often unreliable; in the case of divorce because rates fluctuate with changes in the law. The introduction of more permissive or restrictive regulations may cause sudden variations that are masked by longer-term trends. Even if procedures exist to legalise the situation, as in Ireland in the absence of divorce legislation until 1996, many informal separations may never be officially recorded.

Defining unmarried cohabitation and extramarital births

Consensual unions are generally defined according to two criteria: a shared dwelling and the recognition that two people are living together as man and wife. UN/ECE (1998, § 74) ambiguously defines *de facto* marital status as "the marital status of each individual in terms of his or her actual living arrangements", recommending that:

> 193. The term 'couple' should include married couples and couples who report that they are living in consensual unions, and where feasible, a separate count of consensual unions and of legally married couples should be given. Two persons are understood as partners in a consensual union when they have usual residence in the same household, are not married to each other, and report to have [*sic*] a marriage-like relationship to each other.
>
> (UN/ECE, 1998, original emphasis and punctuation)

In revising the definition of family units to incorporate unmarried cohabiting partners, UN/ECE (1998, § 71) recommends, nevertheless, that "all persons living in consensual unions should be classified as single, married, widowed or divorced in accordance with their *de jure* (legal) status".

Across EU15, the criteria of co-residence, a sexual or emotional and relatively stable relationship, euphemistically described as living together as a couple, and the absence of formal marriage are widely used as defining characteristics of consensual unions. Definitions may not, however, be applied consistently from one country to another. They may change over time, and they may vary between sources. In Finland, for example, the age difference within couples has to be less than 16 years for them to count as consensual unions (Statistics Finland, personal communication, 2003).

As with marriage rates, but to a much greater extent, discrepancies arise between information derived from censuses, official registers and household surveys, and as a result of changes over time in the questions asked. Censuses, like registers, tend to focus on the sharing of the place of residence, whereas surveys often pay more attention to the nature of the relationship within couples. For example, in the UK before 1996, unrelated adults of the opposite sex were classified in the General Household Survey (GHS) as cohabiting if they considered themselves to be living together as a couple. In 1979, questions were introduced on marital history and on pre-marital cohabitation for women aged 16-49. They were extended to all men and women aged 16-59 in 1986. In 1998, a question was added about the number of past cohabitations that did not end in marriage. It was subsequently extended to capture the length of cohabitation. Since 1996, cohabitation has included same-sex couples (ONS, 2001b, p 173).

Census forms often ask separately for information about the relationship to the householder or reference person and about marital status, making it technically possible, by cross-tabulation, to identify individuals living with a partner but who are married to someone other than the person with whom they are living. The Hungarian 2000 census form gave respondents clear instructions to report the number of marriages but not the number of cohabitations. In answer to a separate question about whether the respondent was living 'in cohabitation', the instructions specified that it was not necessary for the partners to live in a common dwelling to be considered as an unmarried cohabiting couple, which contrasts with the practice in Estonia for reporting married couples living apart, as noted above.

Unmarried cohabitation is difficult to define and measure, and interpretation of the available statistics is problematic, not only because of inconsistencies in reporting, but also because the arrangement may be temporary and relatively unstable. At the individual level, the situation can fluctuate over time depending upon how people perceive their relationships, and it may be difficult to obtain honest responses to survey questions. Where marital status affects liability for taxation and eligibility for social security benefits, it may, for example, be in the interest of couples to conceal a *de facto* situation. They may have many personal reasons for not wanting to admit they are living together without being married. Official statistics at international level are usually confined to crude rates by age and sex, with very little information about duration or separation. No EU-wide data are available on same-sex cohabiting couples or couples living together for only part of the time, described as living apart together (LATs).

By definition, extramarital births are the proportion of live births outside formal marriage per 100 live births. They are registered as extramarital in the absence of a declaration that the parents are married at the time of the birth. Across EU member states, information is routinely collected about the date of the parents' present marriage when registering births, which means that the identification of births outside marriage should be straightforward. Not all countries, however, record the individual marital status of each of the parents. Data used in comparisons only take account of the formal marital status of the mother at the time of the birth and disregard whether she has ever been married, making it difficult to distinguish extramarital births to never-married women from those to divorced, separated or widowed women. In practice, therefore, extramarital births represent a variety of situations, including stable unmarried cohabiting relationships that may be formalised contractually at a later date, and where both parents jointly and legally recognise the child.

Defining family formation and non-formation

The blurring of the definition of family formation in the absence of legal marital bonds is removed if family formation is defined by the arrival of children. Although childless couples do qualify as family nuclei according to UN/ECE definitions, for many people 'real' families are expected to contain children. Statistical offices are interested in the number and timing of births. The extent to which these phenomena are determined voluntarily or involuntarily depends to a large extent on access to effective means of birth control. When couples are able to control childbirth, they may decide to postpone family formation through parenting, sometimes indefinitely. Information is not routinely and consistently collected on contraceptive use, abortion and childlessness. Systematic comparisons of trends over time within countries are, therefore, problematic, even more so when they are being compared cross nationally.

Countries that collect data on contraception do not, for example, always include unmarried women. Abortion rates are difficult to compare for a number of reasons. Statistics record only legal abortions and, as noted in the previous chapter, not all countries apply the same criteria to differentiate between foetal death and abortion. In countries such as Poland and Ireland with a ban or restrictions on abortion, the numbers recorded are very small, while 'abortion tourism' to neighbouring countries (the UK for Ireland and the Czech Republic for Poland) inflates the number of abortions recorded in the host countries. Data on childlessness are also unreliable for EU member states. Given the trend towards the postponement of first childbirth, such data can, in any case, only be applied to women who have completed their childbearing period. Furthermore, where time series data are collected for this indicator, they are not usually disaggregated to show the extent to which childlessness is voluntary or due to infertility.

Defining lone parenthood

Statistical comparisons at EU level of the number of lone-parent families are even more unreliable than for extramarital births, because the phenomenon is often conceptualised and measured differently from one society to another and because, like unmarried cohabiting couples, lone-parent families form a particularly unstable and heterogeneous category. Although UN/ECE definitions of the family nucleus and children take account of changes in family structure and recommend that countries should collect data on lone parenthood, good-quality comparable data are difficult to obtain for this indicator. Censuses are too infrequent to capture the dynamics of lone-parenthood, and lone parents tend to be under-represented in surveys such as the European Community Household Panel (ECHP)[1]. Yet, progressively, statisticians have been instructed to provide information about lone parenthood, because lone-parent families are recognised as being particularly likely to suffer from poverty and social exclusion and are, therefore, an important focus of attention for policy makers.

The problems identified in determining and implementing age boundaries for family relationships are compounded in the case of lone parenthood. If no age limit or different age limits are set to define childhood, comparisons of data on lone parenthood become impossible. The UN/ECE (1998, § 192) definition of a child as a person with no partner and no child of his/her own, living in the household of at least one of the parents, is far too broad to be meaningful in policy terms. The European Commission (2002e, p 117) refers to the EU labour force survey rather than its demographic tables or ECHP data to identify the proportion of all children aged under 15 living in families with only one adult who is aged at least 15. This solution arbitrarily reduces the number of lone-parent families, compared with statistics that observe the UN/ECE recommendation on age of majority at 18, or that are designed to capture relationships in families with children aged below 25. For example, France applied an age limit of 25 until 1982, but it was abolished for the 1991 census. The effect was to inflate the proportion of lone-parent families by almost 37% between the two dates (Simões Casimiro and Calado Lopes,

---

[1] The six waves of the ECHP from 1994 provided comparable longitudinal survey data on changing household structure and living arrangements across the Union. Although the usefulness of the ECHP was undermined due to incomplete datasets, varied response rates and limited coverage, it did enable comparative analysis of trends in household formation, transitions between different family living arrangements and intergenerational relations within and between households, such as had not previously been possible. It was replaced in 2001 by a new survey of Statistics on Income and Living Conditions (EU-SILC), indicating the growing interest being shown in household income rather than family structure and dynamics, which panel studies can so successfully capture (Berthoud, 2000).

1995, p 71). For these reasons, disparities between countries and over time in statistics showing the relative importance of lone parenthood may be explained, at least partly, by variations in recording techniques and reporting conventions.

In addition, lone-parent families may originate from a variety of situations, which statistics may fail to capture and differentiate adequately for the purposes of comparisons and policy formulation, including: the death of a spouse; never having lived with a partner or spouse; and the breakdown of consensual and marital unions among couples with children.

Defining reconstituted families

Reliable and comparable data are even more difficult to find for reconstituted families. Statistical definitions have yet to be agreed and accepted to represent the complex family structures that arise when households are composed of one biological parent (although both biological parents may still be alive) and a stepparent living with children from more than one marriage or non-marital relationship.

In line with the growing interest in the phenomenon, for the first time in 1997, UN/ECE recommendations included a definition of a reconstituted family to be used in the 2000 census round:

> 195. A reconstituted family is a family consisting of a married or cohabiting couple with one or more children, where at least one child is a non-common child i.e. either the natural or adopted child of only one member of the couple. If the child (natural or adopted) of one partner is adopted by the other partner, the resulting family is still a reconstituted family.
>
> (UN/ECE, 1998, original emphasis)

This general definition covers a wide variety of situations related to the former and current marital status of the partners involved, dependent on whether one or both parents bring children from a previous union, and whether common children are present. Not all countries observe the UN/ECE definition. Finland, for example, requires at least one child to be aged under 18 and does not consider the family to be reconstituted if the children are adopted (Statistics Finland, personal communication, 2003).

The UN/ECE definition of the child takes account of situations where children spend equal time with each parent:

> 192. ... 'Children' also includes stepchildren and adopted children, but not foster children. A child that alternates between two households (for instance after the parents' divorce) is counted at only one of these households, for instance on the basis of the *de jure* place of usual residence or the number of nights spent at either of the households.
>
> (UN/ECE, 1998)

The ability to identify reconstituted families and their specific forms depends on the availability and quality of information on marital and union history, on children (of parents) in unions, and the ability to attach children correctly to their parent(s). In some cases, this process cannot be recorded unless the new couple marries. In Hungary, for example, because of the way census and micro-census data are collected, the term 'reconstituted family' can refer only to remarried partners. As unmarried cohabitants with children cannot register officially, they cannot be considered as a reconstituted family. Information about unmarried, reconstituted family units can only be drawn from special cross-sectional surveys (Vukovich, 2002).

Defining one-person households

Census returns are required to yield information about one-person households. Data on households containing only one person may be unreliable for comparative purposes due to differences in the practices adopted to record place of residence at the census date. Although UN/ECE provides quite detailed recommendations about how to record persons temporarily absent at the time of a census, it may not be possible to avoid double counting for those who live away from home during the week. As a result, the number of one-person households may be artificially inflated. Anecdotal evidence can be found of older people in Italy reportedly living alone when they are actually living with their children, and of grandchildren taking up residence in the homes of their grandparents, who are counted as living alone for fiscal reasons.

In most countries, people with more than one address are included at the place where they live for the majority of their time, but different practices are adopted to deal with students. In the UK, for example, students who are away from home during term time are registered at their parents' address. The proportion of one-person households or households without children is not, therefore, comparable with that in countries where students are registered at their place of study, as in Estonia, unless they are living in collective dwellings. In France, information is requested on census forms about individuals, including students or non-custodial children, who belong to the household but are temporarily absent.

Defining multigenerational households and extended families

The term 'multigenerational household' is used to describe situations where several generations of family members live together under the same roof and/or have common housekeeping arrangements. The UN/ECE 1997 recommendations provide definitions for households with three generations, while recognising that they will not be relevant units in all countries:

> 194. A three-generation household consists of two or more separate family nuclei or one family nucleus and (an)other family member(s).

> A woman who is living in a household with her own child(ren) should be regarded as being in the same family nucleus as the child(ren) even if she is never-married and even if she is living in the same household as her parents; the same applies in the case of a man who is living in a household with his own child(ren). Thus, the youngest two generations constitute one family nucleus.
>
> (UN/ECE, 1998)

Most national statistical offices in EU member states, and also the ECHP survey, identify the number of multigenerational households by counting the family units within the household and the relationship between each individual and the reference person. Information collected in different types of survey does not, however, produce consistent results for this indicator due to discrepancies in the criteria used to define the reference person. Disparities may also arise between census and household panel data. The relationship between household members is difficult to identify in the census data collected by the Statistical Office of Estonia, to take one example, since generations are defined by age rather than by the relationship between members of the household. Adults of working age, over retirement age and children are distinguished as three separate categories. When representatives of all three categories are found within a single household (a 14-year-old child, a mother of working age and a father who has reached retirement age), they will automatically appear as a multigenerational household, when they are in fact all members of the same family unit. By contrast, the Household Income and Expenditure Survey, which has been the main source of information concerning household composition since 1993, identifies the number of families within a household and the relationship between each individual and the reference person.

The 1997 UN/ECE recommendations also define extended families:

> 198. ... It is suggested that an extended family be defined for census purposes as a group of two or more persons who live together in the same household and who do not constitute a family nucleus but are related to each other (to a specified degree) through blood, marriage (including consensual union) or adoption. Data derived on this basis can have certain advantages for studying the economic relationships of families or kin as spending units, but they also have certain disadvantages for studying and classifying families from a demographic point of view. ...
>
> (UN/ECE, 1998, original emphasis)

According to this definition, relatives such as siblings, uncles and aunts, who are not part of the family nucleus but are living under the same roof, would be considered as belonging to the extended family. They would be counted as members of the household according to the household dwelling definition, but may not necessarily be recorded within the housekeeping unit.

Despite the best efforts at international level to take account of alternative family forms and living arrangements in data collection, incompatibility of sources and data collection methods across countries and over time means that reliable cross-national comparisons of trends in family life are difficult to achieve. The examples given above of consensual unions, lone-parent and reconstituted families, one-person and multigenerational households illustrate the problems that arise when trying to collect and analyse statistical data on families and households across countries, confirming the need to scrutinise national statistical practices and to exercise extreme caution in interpreting information derived from different sources.

Measuring family change

The second demographic transition is said to have involved different phases, determined by the speed at which change has occurred (Lesthaeghe, 1995). The first phase can be located in the 1960s and 1970s. It was characterised by the acceleration of the divorce rate at the same time as the baby boom was coming to an end, and fertility rates were falling sharply, resulting in smaller family size. In some cases, the reduction in fertility was facilitated by the availability of effective methods of artificial contraception, especially the contraceptive pill. The second phase was marked, in the pioneering countries in the 1970s and early 1980s, by an increase in pre-marital cohabitation and the number of children born outside marriage. During the third phase from the 1980s in the same countries, divorce stabilised, while unmarried cohabitation increased. One of the outcomes of these combined trends was the growth in the number of lone-parent families and one-person households.

Despite differences in timing, proponents of the convergence thesis would argue that family forms have been converging towards a shared European family model, reflecting similar living standards and lifestyles (de Singly and Commaille, 1997, pp 11-15). Although this proposition seems justified when the comparison is with the less developed regions in the world, as in the case of population decline and ageing, closer scrutiny reveals a much more differentiated picture across the Union, which has become further diversified with each wave of enlargement. This section analyses and compares the data available on changing family forms, before reviewing the challenges that such change poses for governments in contemporary European societies.

Measuring marriage, divorce and unmarried cohabitation

According to 'traditional' conceptions that were prevalent in the mid-20th century before the second demographic transition gained momentum, families were formed by marriage and consolidated by the arrival of children. While the presence of children was still widely upheld as an important defining criterion of family life at the end of the century, attachment to the institution of marriage as the trigger for family formation had gradually been eroded.

Table 3.1: Marriage and divorce rates, EU15 averages (1960-2000)

	1960	1970	1980	1990	1999/2000
Marriages per 1,000 population	7.7	7.7	6.3	6.0	5.1
Age at first marriage for men	26.7[e]	25.9[e]	26.0[e]	27.7	30.3
Age at first marriage for women	24.1[e]	23.2[e]	23.3[e]	25.3	28.1
Divorces per 1,000 population	0.5	0.8	1.4	1.7	1.9[e]
% of marriages dissolved by divorce by marriage cohort	15.0	22.0	28.0	n.a	n.a

[e] Eurostat estimates

Sources: Eurostat (2002a, tables F-3, F-8, F-9, F-15, F-18).

Table 3.1 summarises trends for the main indicators of marriage and divorce in EU15 member states for the period from the 1960s to the close of the century. According to Eurostat data, the average number of marriages per 1,000 population in EU15 fell by nearly 34% between 1960 and 2000. The rate dipped most sharply in the late 1970s and early 1990s. The average age at first marriage increased by 4.4 years for men, between 1970 and the end of the century, and by almost five years for women. After growing steadily from the early 1980s, the average age at which women were marrying was climbing more steeply at the end of the period. The crude divorce rate per 1,000 population rose by nearly 74% between 1960 and 2000, showing the most marked increase in the early 1970s. As a proportion of the marriages contracted by the 1960 and 1980 marriage cohorts, the number of divorces recorded almost doubled.

Marriage and divorce indicators over the period vary markedly between and within countries. Crude marriage rates are a volatile measure of marital behaviour, subject to short term fluctuations that may be associated with legislative change. Eurostat statistics indicate that the decline of the marriage institution has not followed a uniform pattern across Europe, and in none of the EU15 member states has the fall been consistent over time. Several countries show sudden peaks and troughs. For example, in 1987 Austria saw a steep rise in the number of marriages, accompanying the introduction of a marriage grant, only to be followed by a fall in the following year when the grant was abolished. In Sweden, the figure rose sharply in 1989 to 12.9‰ when the law on pensions payable to widows was changed, but then fell to its lowest level in 1995 at 3.8‰. The millennium effect noted in Chapter Two for fertility rates may help to explain a marked rise in marriage rates in 2000 in Denmark, Finland, France, Ireland and Sweden, which did not appear to be sustained in 2001. Despite these fluctuations, the dispersion around the EU15 mean has been reduced. In 1960, crude marriage rates ranged from 9.5‰ in Germany to 5.5‰ in Ireland. By 2000, the lower overall rate for EU15 was accompanied by less dispersion. The rate ranged from 7.2‰ in Denmark, where it had been rising since the early 1980s, to 4.3‰ in Greece, which had seen a sudden fall at the end of the century. Data for 2001 suggest that, after the 2000 blip, the disparity between countries was further reduced (Eurostat, 1995a, p X, table F-3; 2002a, table F-3).

As with indicators for population decline and ageing, the countries that joined the Union in 2004, taken as a group, display greater heterogeneity than EU15, with marriage rates ranging from 5.9‰ for Malta to 11.0‰ for Latvia in 1960, and from 3.6‰ for Slovenia to 12.9‰ for Cyprus in 2000. Over the period, rates fell steeply in the Baltic states, Slovakia and Slovenia, whereas they rose in Cyprus. By the turn of the century, only Cyprus, the Czech Republic and Malta were displaying rates above the EU15 average (Eurostat, 2002a, table J-13).

The gap has narrowed between the countries with the highest and lowest ages at first marriage for men but increased slightly for women. Different countries were displaying the highest and lowest ages at the beginning and end of the period. In 1960, Ireland recorded the oldest age at first marriage for men, at 30.8, while Belgium reported the youngest age, at 25.1 years. In 2000, these positions were held by Sweden (32.4) and Portugal (27.3). For women, Ireland (27.6) also showed the oldest age in 1960, and Belgium was joined by Denmark (22.8) as the country recording the youngest age. By the end of the century, women in Sweden (30.1) and Portugal (25.2) held the same ranks as for men at the two extremes. Although full datasets are not available for the CEE countries for age at first marriage during the earlier period, the available information suggests that, in the east German *Länder* and the other CEE countries, women were contracting their first marriage at a younger age than in EU15. The lowest age in 2000 was reported for women in Lithuania at 23.5 years (Council of Europe, 2002, table T2.3; Eurostat, 2002a, tables F-8, F-9, J-15).

Large variations are found in divorce rates between countries within EU15. The take off in divorce can be situated in the early 1970s for most of northern Europe. In southern Europe and Ireland, divorce was still not a widespread phenomenon at the end of the 1990s, by which time it had reached a plateau in the north. Divorce rates, like those for marriage, are subject to fluctuations, triggered by changes in the law. For example, an unusually high figure of 3.5 per 1,000 population, compared with 2.0‰ in 1994, was recorded for Belgium in 1995 following a change in divorce legislation. The rate fell back to 2.8‰ in 1996 and had dropped to 2.6‰ by the end of the decade. The Nordic states, Germany, the Netherlands and the UK have consistently displayed divorce rates above the EU15 average since 1970, while Greece, Italy and Spain have maintained relatively low levels. Rates in the east German *Länder* were much higher than in the west until unification. Ireland was the last EU15 member state to legalise divorce in 1996. The crude rate recorded in Ireland in 2000, at 0.7‰, was the lowest, with Italy, in EU15, suggesting that the change in the law had not resulted in a catching-up effect. Far from showing convergence, for this measure, the disparity between the countries with the highest and lowest divorce rates increased over the period by 30% (Eurostat, 2002a, table F-15).

Indicators for the proportion of marriages ending in divorce produce a similar picture to that for the crude divorce rate in terms of clusters of countries. The trend has been consistently upwards, but again with important disparities between countries: the southern European member states display the lowest rates, with Italy recording the lowest rate of all at 3% in 1960 and 8% in 1980, in the absence of data for Ireland. Sweden, Denmark, Finland and the UK reached the highest rates, with over 40%, once more widening the gap between the two ends of the scale (Eurostat, 2002a, table F-18).

The limited data available for CEE countries suggest that their situation is equally varied. In 1960, some countries were already recording higher crude divorce rates than EU15 member states: 2.4 per 1,000 population in Latvia and 2.1‰ in Estonia. Peaks were reached in 1990 in Latvia (4.0‰) and Lithuania (3.4‰). In Estonia, the rate peaked in 1995 at 5.0‰ before falling back to 3.1‰ in 2000, which was the highest figure recorded across EU25 at that date. Poland, the largest CEE country in terms of population, maintained one of the lowest levels throughout the period, together with Slovenia, but again above the lowest level in EU15 (Eurostat, 2002a, table J-16).

As the proportion of marriages ending in divorce has risen, the average duration of marriage at divorce has been declining. For the 1960 cohort, the longest duration for marriages ending in divorce was found in Spain with 28.6 years, which may be attributable to the fact that divorce was not legal during the Franco era. The shortest duration was for Austria, with only 11.3 years. However, for the 1980 cohort, the duration in Austria was slightly greater than for 1960, after peaking for the 1970 cohort. Meanwhile, in Spain the duration of marriage at divorce fell sharply over the period to 16.6, a decline of 12.0 years, and it was continuing to fall. The shortest average duration for marriages contracted in 1980 was found in Denmark and the UK, with 11.8 and 11.9 years respectively. The disparity between the longest and the shortest duration of marriages ending in divorce was substantially reduced over the period from 17.3 years for the 1960 cohort to only 4.8 years for the 1980 cohort (Eurostat, 2002a, table F-19).

The fall in marriage rates and the average duration of marriage has been accompanied by an increase in the number of consensual unions as an alternative form of partnership. Official data are available on unmarried cohabitation in countries where the status is recorded in population registers and surveys, and where it is formally recognised in cohabitation contracts. In France, for example, 16 months after the law introducing cohabitation contracts came into force in November 1999, some 37,000 couples had registered their partnerships. By comparison, and in relation to population size, in 2001 France recorded about 60% more registrations than the Netherlands, where formal registration came into operation in 1998. The number of male same-sex couples registering partnerships when legislation first came into force was much higher in the Netherlands (107 per 1 million inhabitants) than in Denmark (62 per million) or Sweden (28). In the Netherlands, some 6.5% of same-sex couples were registered, or 0.5% of the male population aged 20-69. Overall, men were found to be more likely to register their partnerships than women (Festy, 2001, pp 1-3).

For the reasons outlined earlier in this chapter, data on unmarried cohabitation collected in national censuses, population registers and surveys provide a picture that is far from being complete or consistent. ECHP survey data for 1998 gave an EU15 average figure of 9% for the proportion of couples living in consensual unions, ranging from 1% in Greece and 2% in Italy to 21% in Finland and 23% in Sweden. For the age group 16-29 years, the range was much larger: from 8% in Greece and 11% in Italy to 61% in Finland and 70% in Sweden. Denmark, the Netherlands and the UK also recorded levels over 50% for this age group, clearly distinguishing them from the southern European countries. France, Belgium and Germany displayed rates above the EU15 average for the younger age group (European Commission, 2002e, p 118). Unmarried cohabitation has proved to be more fragile and of shorter duration than marriage. Data from the British Household Panel in the 1990s indicated that, in about 35% of cases, unmarried cohabiting relationships dissolved and, in 60% of cases, they turned into marriage within 10 years (Ermisch and Francesconi, 2000, p 39).

Measuring family formation and non-formation

If family formation is determined by the arrival of children, indicators for the timing of births in EU member states since the 1960s suggest that couples are increasingly delaying the moment when they embark on family life, sometimes indefinitely. The postponement of family formation is a factor contributing to smaller family size, and may also help to explain growing rates of voluntary and, more especially, involuntary childlessness.

Despite inconsistencies between data sources, the available information on individual member states suggests that women born in the 1960s in the Nordic states and the Netherlands were having their first child two or more years later than the 1940s birth cohorts. The shift in timing was much less marked in the southern European countries and Ireland. By contrast, in the Czech Republic, Slovakia and Slovenia, women born in 1960 were having their first child at an earlier age than those born in 1940. Data for more recent cohorts indicate that women everywhere are tending to postpone their first birth (Council of Europe, 2002, table T3.4; Eurostat, 2002a, table E-11; Sardon, 2002, table 6).

Data on mean age at childbearing point to a similar pattern. The Eurostat average for EU15 indicates that mean age at childbearing by generation increased from 26.5 for the 1940 birth cohort to 27.5 for the 1960 cohort. Again, the rise was more marked in northern Europe, whereas CEE countries recorded a fall. Annual snapshots of mean age at childbearing, calculated from fertility rates by age, show that it was rising steadily across EU15 in the late 1990s. Ireland, Italy, the Netherlands and Spain displayed the highest mean age (30 or above) for women at childbearing. The picture in CEE countries was more varied: in 2000, mean age at childbearing was lower in Latvia, Poland and Slovenia than in the early 1960s, although it was higher than in the 1980s and 1990s (Council of Europe, 2002, table T3.5; Eurostat, 2002a, tables E-5, E-7; Sardon, 2002, table 5).

One of the reasons for the rise in mean age at childbirth is that fewer pregnancies are occurring among women under the age of 20, and more women are postponing childbirth until their thirties. Analysis of fertility rates for different age groups shows that, in 1970, the fertility rate was over 30 for 1,000 teenage women in Austria, Denmark, Finland, Germany, Greece, Sweden and the UK, whereas it was 17‰ or less in Ireland, the Netherlands and Spain. By the year 2000, the rate had fallen to single figures in more than half the EU15 member states. Only Portugal and the UK continued to display rates of over 20‰ (Council of Europe, 1997, 2002, country tables - 3). The rate in the UK remained the highest in EU15 despite the fact that 53% of conceptions among girls aged below 16, and nearly 40% among girls aged 16-19, were terminated by an abortion in 1999 (ONS, 2002b, table 2.13). In Sweden, where the rate was much lower, around two thirds of teenage pregnancies were terminated by an abortion in the mid-1990s (Landgren-Möller, 1997, p 274). National studies of the relationship between socio-economic status and teenage pregnancies during the 1990s suggest that, in the UK, teenage girls from disadvantaged backgrounds were most likely to have children at an early age (Kiernan, 1997; Hobcraft and Kiernan, 1999, p 5). By contrast, young Swedish girls on low incomes and with low levels of educational attainment were found to make every effort to avoid early motherhood (Landgren-Möller, 1997, p 271).

Data for CEE countries indicate that teenage pregnancy rates are relatively high compared with EU15 countries. In 1970, six of the eight countries were recording rates over 30‰, and only in Slovenia had the rate fallen to single figures by 2000. In Estonia, Hungary, Latvia, Lithuania and Slovakia, it was over 25‰. Rates in Estonia and Lithuania peaked at over 54‰ and 48‰ respectively in the early 1990s before falling sharply during the rest of the decade (Council of Europe, 1997, 2002, country tables -3).

The extent to which effective methods of contraception and legal abortion are used to limit the number of children and to enable women to exercise control over the timing of births varies between and within countries. The available information suggests that, within EU15, legal abortion may be more widely practised in Denmark, Sweden, France, the east German *Länder*, the UK and Italy than in the other southern European countries, the west German *Länder* or the Netherlands. Sweden was, for example, recording 34 legal abortions for 100 live births in 2000. In Ireland, abortion was still illegal at the end of the century. With the notable exception of Poland, where it was strictly controlled, rates in many of the CEE countries appear to be much higher than in western Europe, reaching nearly 95 per 100 live births in Estonia, 60.9 in Hungary, 46.4 in Slovenia, 38.1 in the Czech Republic and 33.5 in Slovakia in 2000 (Sardon, 2002, table 11B). The need to treat this indicator with caution is demonstrated by the Estonian case. While the absolute number of abortions was decreasing during the 1990s, because the fertility rate was falling more rapidly, the measurement derived from relating abortions to live births gives the impression that the number of abortions was rising (Kutsar and Tiit, 2000, p 31).

Although a direct causal relationship has not been proven, high legal abortion rates and postponement of childbirth may also be contributing factors to the increasing number of women remaining childless. Data for the early 1960s generations indicate that as many as one woman in five was likely to remain childless in Austria, the west German *Länder*, Ireland, England and Wales, compared with nearer one in 10 in Denmark, France, Greece and Spain. In the east German *Länder* and CEE countries, the rates were much lower, with only Poland reaching double figures (Eurostat, 2002a, table E-12; Sardon, 2002, table 7).

The available data imply that the relationship between childlessness and fertility rates is not unidirectional. Austria and West Germany combine relatively high levels of childlessness with low completed fertility rates, whereas France combines low childlessness with high fertility. Spain reports relatively low childlessness and low completed fertility. According to indicators that show low fertility and childlessness in CEE countries, the two phenomena appeared to be mutually reinforcing during the transition period, but they are too unstable to allow predictions about future trends for EU25.

Measuring extramarital births

While marriage and fertility rates have been following a downward trend in most EU member states, the proportion of births outside marriage has been increasing steeply. As can be seen from Table 3.2, the EU15 average rose by 66% between 1960 and 2000, with most of the increase occurring between 1980 and 2000. The EU15 average again conceals marked disparities between member states. Over the period, the gap between the countries with the highest and lowest rates increased by 77%. Greece consistently displayed the lowest rate. From the mid-1960s, Sweden overtook Austria, which had recorded the highest rate in 1960, to register more than 50% of births outside marriage in 2000. The take off in extramarital births was essentially in the 1980s for the countries that were displaying the highest rates by the turn of the century. Ireland moved from being one of the countries with the lowest rates until the mid-1980s to join those with the highest rates above the EU15 average by 2000. Extramarital birth rates have also been increasing steadily over time in the candidate countries, but again with wide disparities between them. At the beginning of the period, rates were lower in the two island states than in all EU15 member states. They were highest in Estonia and Latvia, and at a level above that in Sweden.

By 2000, Cyprus was still recording the lowest rate of all. The east German *Länder* reported rates well above those in the western *Länder*

Table 3.2: Extramarital birth rates, as a percentage of live births, for EU25 member states, by membership wave (1960-2000)

	1960	1970	1980	1990	2000
EU15	*5.1*	*5.6*	*9.6*	*19.6*	*28.4*[e]
1. Belgium	2.1	2.8	4.1	11.6	*22.0*[e]
1. France	6.1	6.8	11.4	30.1	42.6
1. Germany	7.6	7.2	11.9	15.3	23.4
1. Italy	2.4	2.2	4.3	6.5	9.7
1. Luxembourg	3.2	4.0	6.0	12.8	21.1
1. Netherlands	1.4	2.1	4.1	11.4	24.9
2. Denmark	7.8	11.0	33.2	46.4	44.6
2. Ireland	1.6	2.7	5.0	14.6	31.8
2. UK	*5.2*	8.0	11.5	27.9	39.5
3. Greece	*1.2*	1.1	1.5	2.2	*4.1*[e]
3. Portugal	9.5	*6.9*	9.2	14.7	22.2
3. Spain	2.3	*1.3*	3.9	9.0	17.7
4. Austria	13.3	12.8	17.8	23.6	31.3
4. Finland	4.0	5.8	13.1	25.2	39.2
4. Sweden	11.3	18.6	39.7	47.0	55.3
5. Cyprus	*0.2*	0.2	0.6	0.7	2.3
5. Czech Republic	4.9	5.4	5.6	8.6	21.8
5. Estonia	13.7	14.1	18.3	27.1	54.5
5. Hungary	5.5	5.4	7.1	13.1	29.0
5. Latvia	11.9	11.4	12.5	16.9	40.3
5. Lithuania	7.3	6.4	6.3	7.0	22.6
5. Malta	0.7	1.5	1.1	1.8	10.9
6. Poland	4.5	5.0	4.7	6.2	12.1
5. Slovakia	4.7	6.2	5.7	7.6	18.3
5. Slovenia	9.1	8.5	13.1	24.5	37.1

[e] Eurostat estimates

Notes: The numbers in column 1 indicate waves of membership: 1. 1957, 2. 1973, 3. 1981/86, 4. 1995, 5. 2004.

Most of the data in the table are taken from Council of Europe sources. Figures in italics are from Eurostat.

Sources: Council of Europe (2002, table T3.2); Eurostat (2002a, tables E-9, J-12).

throughout the period. Predictably, the countries with the highest unmarried cohabitation rates among younger people were recording the highest proportions of extramarital births, namely Sweden, Denmark, Finland, France and the UK. Sweden showed the highest rates for both indicators. Analysis of patterns of cohabitation among couples with children suggests extramarital birth rates do not necessarily always closely match extramarital conceptions. The extramarital birth rate in France was, for example, almost twice the rate in the Netherlands in 2000, but the proportion of unmarried cohabiting couples that marry when they are expecting a child was less than 10% in France, compared with almost 25% in the Netherlands (Festy, 2001, p 4). The pattern in the UK was closer to that in France (Ermisch and Francesconi, 2000, p 33).

Extramarital births may be jointly registered by both parents: in England and Wales, this was the case for three quarters of extramarital births in 2001, and three in four of these births were to parents living at the same address in the late 1990s (ONS, 2003c, p 50). In France in the mid-1990s, paternity was registered for one in three children even before birth, compared with less than 1% in the 1960s (Munoz-Pérez and Prioux, 1999, p 486). Analysis carried out in the UK suggests, however, that, even if the mother and father jointly register the birth, only 36% of children born outside marriage will spend the whole of their childhood with both parents, compared with 70% of those born within marriage (Ermisch and Francesconi, 2000, p 40). Swedish data for the late 1990s indicated that children of cohabiting couples were twice as likely as children of married couples to experience the separation of their parents (SCB, 2000, p 99).

From the available data, extramarital birth rates would seem to vary according to the mother's ethnic origin. In the UK, 54.6% of births in 2000 to mothers born in the Caribbean were extramarital, compared with 43.5% for UK-born mothers and 1.5% for Pakistani-born mothers (ONS, 2001a, table 9.5). In France, extramarital births were less frequent among foreign mothers (23%) than among those with French nationality (44%) in 1999. The highest rates among foreign mothers were for Black African (39%) and south-east Asian women (37%). The rates were lowest among women with Turkish (5%) or Tunisian (8%) nationality (Legros, 2003, table 1).

Measuring lone parenthood and reconstituted families

Notwithstanding UN/ECE recommendations, datasets on lone parenthood are incomplete and vary between sources. Eurostat labour force survey data for children aged 0-14 living in families with only one adult, as a proportion of all children of that age in families, excluding Denmark, Finland and Sweden, show a progression over time as well as differences between clusters of EU15 countries. In 2000, the highest rates were recorded for the UK, with 19.8%, compared with 11.9% in 1990. The southern European countries reported the lowest rates, with 2.8% for Spain in 2000 (European Commission, 2002e, p 117). Alternative sources, such as the ECHP, indicate that the Nordic states are most probably among the countries with the highest rates. The available data for the CEE countries also provide a partial picture of the situation, with Estonia recording the highest rate in 2000, at 9.4%, and the Slovakia the lowest, at 2.5% (European Commission, 2002e, p 137).

Again, differences can be found within countries according to ethnicity: in the UK, for example, over 50% of families with dependent children from the Black groups were recorded in national statistics as lone-parent families in

2002, compared with 9% from the Indian group and 23% for the White group (ONS, 2003c, table 2.5).

As indicated in the discussion of definitions, the concept of the lone-parent family covers a wide range of situations. Most of the measures produced at EU level for family forms do not break down data according to whether lone parenthood is due to mothers never marrying or cohabiting, the outcome of divorce, the breakdown of a consensual union or widowhood, even though these statuses may represent very different experiences. In some cases, 'lone' mothers may be living in a cohabiting relationship that is not picked up by surveys. Analysis of national data on the marital status of lone mothers collected in the 1996 ECHP survey suggests that, in most EU15 member states, separation and divorce had become the primary reason for lone parenthood, accounting for 57% of lone-parent families. Widowhood, which was the major reason for lone parenthood across the Union in the past, continued to account for over 20% of lone parents in EU15 and for 38% or more in Greece, Italy, Portugal and Spain. In Denmark, more than a third of lone parents had never been married. Never-married parents also accounted for 25% or more of lone parents in Austria, Finland, France, Germany, Ireland and the UK. The great majority of recipients of lone-parent benefit in France are never-married mothers (Algava and Avenel, 2001, table T.01). In more than one case in 10, lone parents were living together with other parents or relatives, generally in a three- or four-generation family. In southern Europe and Ireland, more than 20% of lone parents were living within another household and, thereby, benefiting from family solidarity. The figure rose to 43% in Spain (Chambaz, 2000, tables T.01, T.02).

Lone parenthood is not a stable state. Each year in the UK, for example, about 15% of lone mothers cease to be lone parents, usually as a result of forming a new partnership, which means that, in about 50% of cases, lone parenthood may have a duration of four years or less (ONS, 1998, p 45). When account is taken of marital status, children born within marriage are estimated to spend, on average, 1.7 years living with one of their parents, compared with 4.3 years for children from unmarried cohabiting unions and 6.6 years for lone-parent households (Ermisch and Francesconi, 2000, p 40). Studies in France show that children spend longer in a lone parenthood household if their parents divorce than if one parent dies, a consensual union breaks down or married parents separate (Algava, 2002, table 13).

Growing rates of marital breakdown, unmarried cohabitation, extramarital births and lone parenthood are associated with the development of reconstituted families, as couples repartner and bring with them children from previous relationships. An added complication in collecting data about reconstituted families arises from national differences in the legal status of stepparents. Although the picture they provide about family transitions is limited, data on marriage and remarriage and the number of children in families with other than two biological parents can be informative about the situation at a given point in time.

Statistics collected at national level in some EU15 member states suggest that the phenomenon of family reconstitution is becoming more widespread. For example, in Sweden in 1999, 8% of all children aged 0-17 were recorded as living in reconstituted families (SCB, 2000, p 17). In France, a figure of 10% of families with children was reported in 1999, an increase of 10% since 1990. In two thirds of cases, reconstituted families contained children from a previous partnership together with children from the current relationship. Over 4% of all children lived with stepbrothers and sisters. Mothers in reconstituted families tended to be younger than other mothers and were most often in manual or office work (Barre, 2003). The 2001 British census showed that 10% of dependent children (aged 0-15 or 16-17 if still in education) were living in stepfamilies: 88% of such families contained children from the woman's previous partnership and 9% from that of the man; in 8%, children were from previous marriages or the cohabiting relationships of both partners (ONS, 2001b, table 3.10; 2003a, online). In Italy, 4.3% of families were described as reconstituted in 2000/01, of which 61% contained married and 39% unmarried couples (Istat, 2003, p 9).

Despite the development of alternative family forms, the majority of children still grow up in two-parents families. In Sweden, relatively few children are born into families without two parents but, by the age of 17, only 66% of children are living with both their biological parents (SCB, 2000, p 108). In France, in 1999, 86% of children under the age of 15 were reported to be living with two parents, though not necessarily their two natural parents (Cristofari and Labarthe, 2001, p 2). In the UK, 65% of dependent children were recorded by the 2000 census as living with both natural parents (ONS, 2003a, online). This was the case for 73% of White children aged 0-14 in 1997-99, but for only 35% in the Black Caribbean and 31% in the Black-other (non Caribbean or African) groups. Over 56% of the children in the combined Black groups were living with only their natural mother (Scott et al, 2001, table 5).

Measuring change in family and household size and structure

The modern family can be described as long and thin, in the sense that lower fertility rates and the decline in multigenerational living are resulting in smaller family units and households. Information is not available on average family size, but Eurostat data show that, between 1980 and 2000, average household size decreased in all EU member states, and the EU15 average fell from 2.8 to 2.4, albeit with variations in pace and intensity between countries. In the early 1980s, Ireland and Spain were recording the largest household size and Sweden the smallest. By the end of the century, the rank order had remained almost unchanged, with the Nordic states and Germany showing smaller family size than southern European countries and Ireland. The dispersion around the mean had been reduced, as the proportion of larger households declined (European Commission, 2002e, p 116).

Although data on birth orders are not comparable across countries, they allow trends to be observed over time within member states and provide an indication of changes in the number of children per family. The most striking feature of the data is the extent of the decrease in the number of third and higher order births over time. The fall was most marked in Portugal and Spain between the mid-1980s and the end of the century (Council of Europe, 2002, country tables -5).

The general decline in the number of higher order births means that, in many countries, fewer children are growing up in large families. National trend data for the proportion of dependent children living in different family types in the UK, for example, show that the proportion of couple households with three or more children fell by 50% between 1961 and 2000 (ONS, 2001c, table 2.2). Changes in marriage and divorce patterns also affect family size. British data indicate that, on average, married couples have more children than unmarried cohabiting couples, but that lone parents have more children than cohabiting couples (ONS, 2001b, table 3.8). In France, reconstituted families are twice as likely as other family types to contain four or more children (Barre, 2003, figure 3). Household size also differs according to ethnicity. British labour force survey data for 2002 show that Bangladeshi and Pakistani households are larger than those in other ethnic groups (ONS, 2002a, p 8).

Due to greater life expectancy, today more families are composed of four generations, but it is difficult to establish with any precision the extent to which different generations are living together under the same roof and are dependent on one another financially, physically and psychologically. The available data suggest that, in countries where family de-institutionalisation has been taken furthest and where life expectancy, particularly for women, is greatest, younger and older people are less likely to be living with the intermediate generation. The proportion of extended (three-generation) families appears to be much larger in the southern European countries and Ireland than in the Nordic states (European Commission, 2002e, p 116). Analysis of multigenerational households by ethnicity in the UK indicates that Bangladeshi and Pakistani households are more likely to contain three generations, compared with other ethnic groups (ONS, 2002a, p 8). In Hungary, Roma families are three times more likely to be multigenerational than Hungarian families (Kende, 2000, p 50).

Although the percentage of younger people in the population has fallen as a result of the decline in fertility rates, the age of emancipation (when young people leave their parents' homes) has risen in most member states, but with marked differences between them. Information about the age when at least 50% of young people of the same age group were no longer living with their parents in 1992 and 2000 shows, firstly, that, in most EU15 member states, during the 1990s, young people were postponing the age at which they left the family home and, secondly, that young people in southern European countries and Ireland tended to move out of the parental home at a later age than in northern Europe. Thirdly, men were found to be more likely than women to stay longer in the parental home. Among the countries for which data were available, Finland and the UK were showing the earliest age of emancipation in 2000, with 50% of women leaving home at 19 in Finland and at 20 in the UK. Greece and Italy recorded the latest age, at 31 for men. Greek men were remaining four years longer in the family home than their female counterparts (European Commission, 2002e, p 117; Statistics Finland, personal communication, 2003). No information is available for Denmark and Sweden. The scant data for the candidate countries situate Slovakia and Slovenia close to southern Europe, whereas Cyprus, the Czech Republic, Estonia and Hungary were in the medium range at the turn of the century. Estonia was the only country in EU25 to report the same age of emancipation for men and women (European Commission, 2002e, p 137).

An important contributing factor to the reduction in average household size is the growing proportion of one-person households. In the mid-1980s, the Nordic states and Germany were reporting the largest proportion of one-person households, whereas the southern European countries and Belgium were at the other end of the scale. By 2000, one-person households had become increasingly common across the Union, reaching 30% or more of all private households in most northern European countries, but less than 15% in Portugal and Spain, further reinforcing the north–south divide (Eurostat, 2001, table 9). The limited data available for the countries that joined the Union in 2004 indicate that more people were living alone in Estonia and Hungary than in Slovakia, Cyprus or Malta.

Eurostat predicts that 45% of the population aged over 85 will be living alone by 2010, reaching 62% in Denmark and Sweden, but 30% in Spain and 32% in Portugal. The countries with the largest proportion of one-person households are also those with the smallest average household size. Conversely, those with the smallest proportion of one-person households display the largest household size (European Commission, 2000a, p 21; 2003, pp 180, 199).

Household size and composition are of interest for the present analysis, since they have a bearing on living standards. Data on the risk of poverty by age, sex and household type suggest that one-person and lone-parent households in EU15 countries are more likely to suffer from poverty, when measured as 60% of median equivalised income, than couple households. In the late 1990s, the risk was greater for women living alone than for men, and for younger people under 30 than for older people over 65. It was greatest of all for lone-parent families. The categories most exposed to the risk of poverty were one-person households in Ireland and Portugal composed of older women. Lone-parent families were most vulnerable in Germany and least at risk in Denmark and Finland. Couple families with three or more dependent children were also least at risk in the same two countries, but most at risk in Portugal. One-person households under the age of 30 were most at risk in the Netherlands, whereas they displayed a low risk in Ireland and

Portugal. Older people living alone were least vulnerable to poverty in the Netherlands, Spain and Sweden (European Commission, 2002b, table 3c). In most CEE countries, lone-parent families and families with three or more children have been especially prone to poverty since transition, the more so if they have only one wage earner or if they belong to a minority ethnic group.

The changes in family formation, dissolution and structure examined in this chapter correspond, in broad terms, to those encapsulated in the second demographic transition. In sum, non-institutionalised family forms have become more widespread. Marriage rates have been falling, age at marriage and childbearing is being postponed, and family and household size has been declining. Divorce rates have been rising, and unmarried cohabitation has become a widespread living arrangement in some parts of the Union. The proportion of extramarital births has risen to unprecedented levels in several countries. Lone parenthood, most often as a result of divorce or separation, has become a more common experience. The proportion of one-person households has increased, but the number of multigenerational households has decreased, despite the fact that young people are remaining longer in the parental home.

Although the direction of change in family structure across Europe during the latter part of the 20th century is similar, distinct clusters of countries can be identified that share characteristics with regard to the pace, timing and extent of change in patterns of family formation, family structure and the development of alternative living arrangements, as illustrated by Figure 3.1. When indicators of delayed family formation (late mean age for women at first marriage, and at first child and all childbirths) are plotted against measures of family de-institutionalisation (extramarital births and crude divorce rates), in relation to the EU15 mean in 2000, Denmark and Sweden, followed by France, stand out as the member states where postponement of family formation and the development of alternative family forms seem to have been taken furthest. By contrast, Poland and Slovakia combine the most traditional family forms with the most conventional patterns for the timing of family formation. They share the quadrant with Greece, Portugal, Slovenia and the two Mediterranean island states. Ireland, Italy and Spain all combine delayed family formation with traditional institutionalised family living arrangements. The three Baltic states, Hungary and the Czech Republic cluster together in the quadrant for countries that have gone furthest in de-institutionalising family forms, while retaining more conventional timing of marriage and childbirth. The UK and Finland fall close to the EU15 mean for the timing of family formation but are more advanced in the process of de-institutionalisation. For this composite indicator, the Netherlands and Luxembourg are located on the EU15 mean, while Belgium, Germany and, more especially, Austria combine conventional patterns of family formation with de-institutionalised family forms, but to a lesser degree than CEE countries.

Figure 3.1: Family formation and de-institutionalisation in EU25 member states (2000)

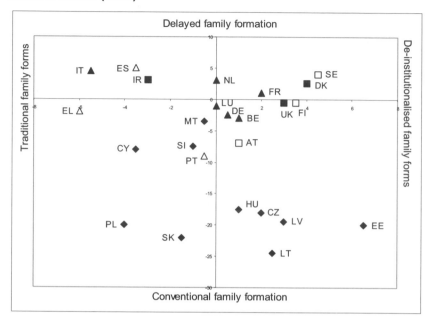

Key: ▲ 1957 members, ■ 1973 members, Δ 1981/86 members, □ 1995 members, ◆ 2004 members.

Notes: For each indicator, the standard deviation (SD) has been calculated for the dataset. For each country cell, the deviation of each data point has been calculated from the mean for EU15 (*x*-mean) and has been compared with the value of the SD for each indicator. Positive or negative values have then been assigned according to the number of SDs (0.5 points for ¼ SD, 1 point for ½ SD, 2 points for 1 SD, 4 points for 2 SDs). The scores for each group of indicators have then been added together and plotted on the *x* and *y* axes.

Sources: Council of Europe (2002, tables T2.3, T2.4, T3.2, T3.4, T3.5); Eurostat (2002a, tables E-5, E-9, F-9, F-15).

Measuring changing value systems

Reports on the findings from population censuses and surveys involve processing and interpreting data collected from a heterogeneous range of sources of varying reliability. Despite the safeguards applied, international statistical agencies can rarely provide an accurate and unbiased record of the situation at a given point in time, the more so over space, as demonstrated by the examples already presented in this chapter. Opinion surveys are even less reliable and more difficult to interpret. As with demographic data, however, they serve as an important source of information for policy actors and feed into media debates. The extent to which popular conceptions of the family precede or follow statistical recognition of change, and are shaped or influenced by political rhetoric, are questions that are addressed in subsequent chapters. Interest in this section is in assessing changing public opinion about family values.

European-wide surveys, such as those conducted at regular intervals by Eurobarometer or the European Values Study (EVS), on what are, as far as possible, comparable population samples, provide insights into public perceptions of value systems concerning family life and shifts in value orientations. The European Value Systems Study Group was formally established in 1978, with the aim of designing and conducting an empirical study of moral and social values in west European countries in relation to both institutions and individual behaviour (Harding et al, 1986). The survey asks questions about attitudes towards the institution of marriage, the rules governing sexual behaviour and factors contributing to successful marriage, relations between parents and children, and also about satisfaction with home and family life.

Comparative findings from a survey carried out in the early 1980s indicated a decline in support for rigid rules. The great majority of respondents in the early survey did not believe marriage to be an outdated institution. Although a small minority were practising unmarried cohabitation, it was seen as a socially acceptable alternative only in the Netherlands and Scandinavia. In Britain, it was still considered as a preliminary to marriage. The survey identified a number of anomalies regarding ideology and practice. For example, a larger proportion of French respondents expressed the view that marriage was an outdated institution, but the percentage that had actually never married was below the European average. Within country variations were found in perceptions of personal morality according to age, level of education, religious belief and political affinity. Young, more highly-educated, more left-wing political supporters and non-religious or atheist respondents showed greatest tolerance in moral outlook (Harding et al, 1986, pp 113-47).

Within families, closeness, sharing of attitudes and transmission of values to children were still of primary importance. Mutual obligations between parents and children were strongly emphasised, but were accompanied by a greater awareness of the need to strike a balance. The overwhelming majority of those interviewed considered that both a mother and a father were necessary to create a family environment in which children could grow up happily. However, approval, or at least tolerance, of lone motherhood as an acceptable family form was increasing and was already widespread in Denmark and France. Acceptance of divorce and abortion for personal and social reasons was also on the increase. Greater permissiveness with regard to the rules for sexual behaviour (extramarital and under-age sex, homosexuality and prostitution) was more readily conceded when applied by respondents to their own lives than to those of other people.

Overall, the findings suggested that a common but changing framework of beliefs and practices with regard to marriage and family life did exist across western Europe, with important variations according to education, religion, political affiliation, age and national culture (Harding et al, 1986, p 116).

Findings from the 1990 and 1999 waves of the EVS showed that, compared with other central life interests, family still had top priority, and had even increased in importance during the 1990s in most EU15 member states (Bréchon and Tchernia, 2002, table 1). Support for marriage as an institution defining the parameters of family life remained very strong, particularly in countries where religion continued to be an influential force shaping attitudes. A successful interpersonal bond based on shared values and mutual interests was seen as a defining characteristic of marriage (Abela, 2003, pp 19-20). The great majority of Europeans considered that two parents are necessary if children are to grow up happily, stating that they were prepared to do their utmost to ensure the well being of their offspring. However, the survey findings indicated that, by the end of the 20th century, the concept of the traditional family composed of two parents in a long-term stable relationship with children had lost its salience as a source of fulfilment in the Nordic states, Ireland and the UK. It was more likely to be upheld in the southern European countries and in continental Europe. Symmetrical or egalitarian views of family life were also more strongly supported in the Nordic states than in southern Europe (Abela, 2003, p 18).

A similarly variegated pattern was found in the candidate countries for the 1999/2000 EVS[2]. In the Baltic states, the importance of family in people's lives was lower than in all other EU25 member states; in Malta and Poland, it was higher than elsewhere. Malta was the EU25 member state where the view that marriage is an outdated institution was most strongly rejected. The marriage institution also commanded strong support in Poland and Slovakia, as did the need for children to grown up with both parents. Respondents in Estonia, Hungary and Latvia attributed a relatively high value to the two-parent home environment and to the need for women to have children to be fulfilled. Lithuanian and Slovenian respondents were more likely to consider marriage to be an outdated institution, and to attach less importance to the two-parent family and the presence of children for women's fulfilment. The Czech Republic was also among the countries where the centrality of children was relatively low.

Analysis of changing value orientations in the EVS has been used to characterise countries as traditional compared with post-traditional, and as materialist compared with post-materialist (Herpin, 2002; Abela, 2003). Whereas traditionalists are more likely to look for companionship, socio-economic security in marriage and close family ties, and to see children as a necessary condition for a fulfilling relationship, post-traditionalists tend to consider marriage as an outdated institution and to prefer a partnership based on mutual respect and understanding, where children are not an essential

---

[2] The full 1999/2000 EVS dataset was supplied by the Zentralarchiv für Empirische Sozialforschung at Cologne University in 2003.

---

ingredient for its success. Using these criteria, some of the southern European and candidate countries, particularly Malta and Poland, are situated at the one end of the traditional–post-traditional continuum, and the Nordic states, especially Sweden, at the other.

Commentators may overestimate the extent to which change in value systems reflects behaviour. Comparisons of the findings from surveys of value systems and the trends recorded in demographic statistics suggest that attitudes in the population as a whole tend to change more slowly than behaviour, although the countries in northern Europe that have undergone the greatest changes in family living arrangements are generally those where attitudes appear to have shifted furthest in the direction of post-materialism. The stimulus for change is most likely to come from the younger generations. The situation in southern Europe is more ambivalent. Some of the evidence indicates that attitudes may be changing more rapidly than behaviour, leading to questioning of traditional assumptions and practices (Badia i Ibañez, 2003; Longo and Sacchetto, 2003; Taki and Tryfonas, 2003). In the CEE countries, by contrast, the experience of transition would seem to have encouraged a return to more traditional attitudes, while patterns of family formation have become more de-institutionalised (Karelson and Pall, 2003; Neményi and Tóth, 2003; Potoczna and Prorok-Mamińska, 2003).

Policy challenges from changing family forms

Just as indications of the slowing down of population growth and ageing collected by statistical offices raise questions about the sustainability of national resources and feed into the policy process, the dissemination of the results of censuses and surveys showing trends in family formation and dissolution provokes lively debate in the media and among policy actors about the future health of society, and calls for policy responses. Disagreement between social historians, sociologists and moral philosophers about the consequences for society of the changes undergone by families during the 20th century is nothing new, as noted in Chapter One. Consensus is no less easy to achieve among policy actors within or between countries about the challenges such change presents. The extent to which legitimacy is accorded to government involvement in formulating policies designed to influence socio-demographic trends, or to which policy can actually impact on the decisions taken by family members about family life, is considered later in the present volume. This concluding section examines the challenges posed by changing patterns of family formation and structure, and reviews the ways in which different societies are reacting to them, as reported in national literature, academic, political and popular debate[3].

[3] Unless otherwise indicated, the information about national debates was supplied by the partners and their research assistants in a Framework Programme 5 project, funded by the European Commission, as noted in the Acknowledgements.

The main question raised by changes in patterns of family formation and dissolution concerns their impact on the future of the family as a basic social institution, and the role the state can and should play in shaping family structure through its economic and social policies. The issue of how society might deal with the consequences of non-institutionalised and de-institutionalised family forms is all the more salient in a context where the realities of social and, more especially, family life for a growing number of Europeans correspond less and less to the normative assumptions that underpinned policy during much of the postwar period. Policy actors, including families, are divided within and between countries over the question of whether public policy should address the consequences of the spread of de-institutionalised family forms. For some governments, the subject is taboo. The challenge governments face is whether to seek to prevent, accompany, encourage or simply ignore change. In addition, as with the relationship between socio-demographic trends, popular attitudes and value systems, a time lag may occur between changes in behaviour and recognition of the need for political action.

The EU25 member states that might have been expected to show most concern about the implications of changing family forms at the turn of the century were Estonia, Sweden, Denmark, Finland, the UK and Latvia, in that order, where family de-institutionalisation had been taken furthest (see Figure 3.1). These were not, however, the countries where the media, social scientists or policy actors were most preoccupied with the risks to family stability. Sweden, in particular, provides an example of a country where alternatives to the married couple and male breadwinner family have resulted in relatively stable living arrangements supported by the state. At the turn of the century, media attention was focusing on more specific questions such as the situation of children living in same-sex couples. In France, where de-institutionalisation had not been taken so far, the long tradition of support for families as a fundamental social institution was not being called into question by the development of alternative living arrangements. However, public opinion and governments were interested in modernising family law to bring it into line with changing behaviour.

Concern was being expressed on religious and moral grounds in Germany (among conservative politicians), Greece, Ireland, Italy (among politicians), and Poland, countries where traditional family forms had been upheld, about the extent to which family de-institutionalisation poses a threat to a social order founded on the commitment to the marital bond within heterosexual couples and the married two-parent family. For example, Irish governments, concerned about the high rate of extramarital births, were seeking to promote the two-parent family and marriage as the ideal. Poland was another country where the traditional married-couple family was strongly supported in policy, to the extent that governments were resorting to restrictive legislation, for example on divorce and abortion, to curb the de-institutionalisation of family life. In Spain, where alternative family forms were relatively uncommon in the 1990s and were considered as having little relevance for social and economic policies, national governments were reluctant to move towards formal recognition of changing practices. In Greece, policy makers were preparing reforms to family law to take account of changing relationships within marriage rather than as alternatives to it.

In countries where it has been recognised that the spread of unmarried cohabitation and divorce, and the growing number of extramarital births cannot be prevented by public policy, attention has turned to questions regarding the rights, duties, responsibilities and obligations of family members towards one another in de-institutionalised families. The specific issues being addressed in policy in the 1990s were whether to legislate to extend the rights and duties enjoyed by married couples to alternative family relationships, for instance in tax and social security law (Ditch et al, 1996a, pp 19-35), following the example already set by Denmark, Sweden and the Netherlands in the 1970s.

In several countries, debate had moved on to consider the formalisation of contracts between same-sex couples. For example, French government proposals to give formal recognition to heterosexual and same-sex cohabiting couples, which had long been on the table, continued to provoke a lively and acrimonious parliamentary and public debate throughout the 1990s (Théry, 1997). The issue revealed the deep-seated divisions in public opinion over the legitimacy and social acceptability of government intervention to introduce permissive legislation, as was already the case in Denmark and Sweden. In Germany, where the Constitution proclaimed the duty of the state to protect marriage and the family, government action to recognise unmarried cohabitation was constrained. The conjugal family was upheld as the symbol of social stability, but debate was ongoing at the turn of the century over the legal rights and status of unmarried cohabiting couples, particularly of the same sex. A proposal from the coalition of Social Democrats and Greens in 1998 to introduce a legally binding cohabitation contract was perceived, and promoted, essentially as a measure applying to same-sex partners.

In the UK, the issue had moved onto the agenda, but governments were showing more interest in supporting the institution of marriage and the relationship between parents and children, irrespective of whether or not parents are married. A contractual commitment between parents and children had been proposed as a 'third way' alternative that would have the advantage of not interfering with the marriage contract while reinforcing the notion of co-parenting (Giddens, 1998, pp 96-8). A more contentious issue, which had already been dealt with in the UK – whether same-sex couples should be allowed to adopt children – was being raised in other countries where same-sex partnerships were formally recognised.

Although it was not new, a topic attracting growing attention in the media was how to deal with another aspect of the breakdown in family relationships, namely abuse within the home environment. The issue was gaining legitimacy as an area for government intervention across the Union, in part due to the fact that the media had been active in raising awareness of the high incidence of 'domestic violence', particularly by men against women and children (Pringle and Hearn, 2003). The problem was also being highlighted as a threat to family life in CEE countries (Pascall and Manning, 2000, p 250). In some cases, growing media coverage resulted in questions being raised about the extent to which couples require assistance in preparing for life together both as partners and as parents. Domestic violence was not the only reason for policy interest in supporting married life and ensuring that spouses fulfil their obligations and duties to one another, or that the weakening of family relationships does not result in abuse. Family harmony was accepted across the political spectrum as an essential component in social cohesion and generational solidarity (Attias-Donfut and Arber, 2000, p 19).

In some countries, the combination of falling marriage rates and the postponement of marriage and childbirth raised a number of questions for governments concerned about the effects of the timing of births on family structure and, ultimately, on the future demographic viability of the nation. A few governments were also showing awareness of the health risks associated with delayed childbirth, while others were worried about the high number of teenage pregnancies and abortions. The failure to reduce the level of teenage pregnancies to that achieved in most other EU15 member states was of continuing policy interest in the UK, where the question is often confused with the debate over lone motherhood. In Spain, although the teenage pregnancy rate was much lower in relative terms, the issue was also attracting attention in public policy and administration. The high rate of teenage pregnancies in Hungary was seen as a problem, insofar as it was frequently associated with social and economic exclusion. By contrast, in Estonia, where the teenage pregnancy rate was also relatively high, but population decline was a major concern, the issue was not how to avoid teenage pregnancies. Policy focused rather on encouraging women to have children irrespective of age, and it was the large number of abortions among teenagers that was seen as a problem.

Across the Union, much of the debate over alternative family forms focused on the consequences of divorce, in particular the risk of poverty, low educational achievement, underemployment and other forms of social exclusion. As noted above, in countries where divorce and extramarital birth rates are relatively high, children living in lone-parent families are found to run a greater risk of falling into poverty than children in two-parent families. During the 1990s, in CEE countries, the increase in the number of children in need of care because their parents had abandoned them was seen as a direct consequence of family breakdown. Such findings heightened the debate about whether governments should intervene to try to reduce the incidence of family breakdown and promote particular family forms that are considered to be more socially secure. The question was also raised about the extent to which the state should play a role in relieving hardship during life transitions and should assist families in managing changing situations.

For so long as lone parenthood was primarily a consequence of widowhood rather than divorce, 'choice' or 'accident', government intervention and support were relatively easy to legitimate. The rapid growth in the incidence of divorce and, in some cases, in the number of never-married lone mothers moved the issue onto the political agenda. The extent to which lone parenthood is seen as a problem for society varies considerably from one country to another, as do the ways in which governments have tried to tackle associated questions of poverty and social exclusion. In the Nordic states and the countries in the geographical centre of EU15, lone parenthood, like unmarried cohabitation and same-sex relationships, was often treated initially as an aberrant family form, until it became sufficiently widespread and socially acceptable to justify being integrated into the institutional framework. In the UK, discussion focused on the causes and consequences of lone parenthood and, in particular, on the cost of providing benefits and services, as well as the effect on government expenditure in areas such as healthcare and personal social services. Evidence from international studies highlighting the relatively high levels of lone parenthood in the UK and the heavy reliance of lone mothers on benefits served to justify the search for policies designed to move lone mothers off benefits and into work. By contrast, in Greece, where the number of lone mothers is relatively small and extramarital births are not socially accepted, the topic had not reached the political agenda by the turn of the century.

Public attitudes towards lone mothers became more tolerant in some of the CEE countries during the 1990s, for example in Estonia, due to the increasing openness of society, the growing number of unmarried cohabiting couples and more pluralistic views of family life. By contrast, in Hungary, where the preference continued to be for the 'classic nuclear family' as established by marriage, and where widowhood still accounted for about 30% of lone parents, no public debate had been initiated on issues relating to lone parenthood. In Poland, where divorce was relatively rare, alternative family forms were not an agenda issue. The government's strong preference was for families to be based on marriage.

Although no consistent data are available for all EU member states to enable tracking of the growth in the number of reconstituted families, issues were already being raised in the 1990s about the rights of children in the first family in relation to those of subsequent families, and also the economic consequences for children of living in reconstituted families. Policy makers in Belgium, France, the Netherlands and the UK were reviewing the legal and material responsibilities of stepparents, as compared with biological parents.

The time lag with which change takes place in family structure, together with differences in the degree and intensity of change, implies that, rather than trends converging across Europe, the latecomers may never catch up, or that, by the time they appear to be doing so, the frontrunners will have moved off in another direction. It also means that, at least in principle, governments might be able to look to other countries and learn from their experience. The extent to which policy learning occurs in the area of family change is examined further in the final chapter. Suffice it here to note, as suggested by the examples above, that governments in democratic societies may find that it is easier to react by working with the grain of change in their own country than to try to resist or counter its momentum.

FOUR

The changing family–employment balance

The slowing down of population growth in combination with population ageing, and changing family forms and structure, characteristic of the first and second demographic transitions, cannot be fully understood without also examining the changing relationship between family life and paid work. One of the main problems associated with low population growth in the developed world is its impact on the size of the population of working age in relation to the inactive dependent population. Changing family forms raise issues about the ability of parents, especially lone parents, to rear children and provide care for relatives, while also securing family income. Much has been written about the relationship between paid work and family life, particularly with reference to the possible causal effects of women's employment on family building, marital harmony and the welfare of children (for example Brannen et al, 1994; García-Ramon and Monk, 1996; Drew et al, 1998; Rubery et al, 1999; Hakim, 2000). Whether fertility levels fell because more women were entering employment outside the home from the late 1960s, and/or whether the ability to control fertility made women available for more continuous employment careers are moot questions.

The issue of how to reconcile employment and family life had been on the policy agenda of governments in northern Europe since the 1970s and acquired visibility in European legislation in the 1990s (European Commission, 1999c; Hantrais, 2000b). A growing concern for policy actors at the beginning of the 21st century in some countries, notably the United Kingdom, was how to enable parents to achieve an equitable work–life balance in the interests of both business and family members (Humphreys et al, 2000; Department of Trade and Industry, 2001). The question became more salient in a context where female labour offered a possible solution to the problems created by a dwindling workforce as a result of low population growth and population ageing (Rubery and Smith, 1999). Not all member states in the European Union (EU) support state involvement in matters encroaching on the private lives of individuals and, even less so, on the relationships between family members. Broader consensus is found, at least at the rhetorical level, that governments should intervene to ensure greater equality of opportunity between women and men at the workplace and in public life, and to reduce the burden created for the working population by the increasingly high old age dependency ratio.

The closing decades of the 20th century saw far-reaching changes in the nature of work, patterns of supply and demand for labour, and working hours and conditions, which were closely intertwined with the changes occurring within families. A major shift had taken place away from employment in industry to the service sector. The demand for skilled labour created by the technological revolution had grown at the same time as the length of working life, the working year and week was being reduced, and as female economic activity and employment rates were expanding more rapidly than those for men. While temporary and casual working arrangements were also spreading, flexibility in working time and conditions was an important issue in negotiations between trade unions and employers. For governments, employability became the keyword. Concerted efforts were made to promote employment through the European employment strategy (COM(2003) 6 final, 14.01.2003), using the open method of co-ordination (OMC), involving benchmarking, exchange of information and peer group review, rather than binding legislation. The candidate countries of Central and Eastern Europe (CEE) were undergoing political, economic and social restructuring, as they strove to meet the criteria for EU membership.

This chapter focuses on the changing relationship between employment, unpaid work and family life in EU25. As in the two previous chapters, the first section is devoted to defining and conceptualising the terms used in discussion and debate. An overview is then provided of trends in working patterns in relation to family responsibilities and the sharing of household tasks. The chapter closes with an assessment of the challenges raised by these changes for political, economic and civil society policy actors.

Defining and conceptualising working life

Chapters Two and Three analysed the problems demographers and statisticians face in reaching agreement over the most appropriate age categories to use, both within and between countries, and in applying them consistently in definitions of intrafamilial relationships and dependency. Similar problems arise in defining the population of working age, the working population, employment and economic activity. Working arrangements, particularly in terms of working hours, are widely seen as important factors contributing to work–life balance, especially when family events and responsibilities are an integral part of the equation. This section reviews the definitions and concepts used by national and international statistical agencies charged with collecting and collating data on various aspects of working life as a basis for policy development and on cross-national comparative analysis of the family–employment relationship.

Defining the working population

Definitions of population ageing and dependency based on fixed age parameters are problematic, as argued in Chapter Two. Disparities in the standard duration of education and training, the legal and actual age of retirement, and movement in and out of the labour market complicate comparisons of the working-age population over time and space. The lower age boundary set for measuring the number of young people entering employment has, for example, been changed over time to reflect the extension of compulsory schooling. The recommendations drawn up jointly by the United Nations Economic Commission for Europe (UN/ECE) and Eurostat, based on definitions that can be applied worldwide, recognise that children below school-leaving age may be in paid work and that children over school-leaving age may still be in education. UN/ECE (1998, § 94) suggests that statistical agencies should distinguish between children under and over the age of 15 to achieve comparability. The 1989 Community Charter of the Fundamental Social Rights of Workers (§ 20) recommended that the minimum employment age should not be lower than 15 within the European Community (EC). By the turn of the century, everywhere the minimum school-leaving age had been raised to 15. Compulsory schooling continued at least to the age of 16 in most EU25 member states, and to 18 in Belgium, Germany, Hungary and Poland, often with the possibility of the last year or two being part time (European Commission, 2000a, p 30; Eurostat, 2002c, p XVIII, figure B1). The Polish Constitution goes so far as to stipulate that young people should continue in education until the age of 18. They are not, therefore, permitted to be in employment before that age.

As the European Commission has pressed for harmonisation of school-leaving age, and member states have raised it above the recommended level, employment rates for the 15-19 age group have lost their statistical relevance. The European Commission (2000a, p 30; 2002e, p 120) now presents data on participation rates of young people aged 16-18 in education and training, rather than employment, and on the average age of students in tertiary education. The interpretation of data on education and training, which also affect labour market entry, is problematic because the definition of training is subject to considerable variation between countries. Initial vocational training may be entirely school based, or it may involve placements in firms. More than half of vocational training in the Union in the late 1990s was being delivered, at least partially, at the workplace. In Austria, training was concentrated at the workplace and, in Denmark, Germany and the Netherlands, it was primarily 'on-and-off the job'. In France and Sweden, it was delivered essentially in educational or training institutions. In the UK, vocational training was carried out in either educational or training institutions as well as being on-and-off the job, whereas the two were rarely associated in Belgium, France and southern European countries (Eurostat, 1998, figure 7; OECD, 2001, p 280).

United Nations recommendations do not specify an upper limit for the population of working age on the grounds that older people beyond retirement age may still be working. Most of the statistical tables drawn up from Eurostat data use 64 as the cut-off point for working-age population, but unemployed persons are defined as being aged 15-74 (Eurostat, 2001, p 9). The actual age at which workers exit from the labour market is, in effect, subject to considerable variation over time both within and between countries. From the 1980s, older people were leaving the labour market at an earlier age, either because they were reaching legal retirement age, which had not previously existed or had been set at a later age, or because they were taking early retirement in a context of economic restructuring or for health reasons. Most countries operate an official retirement age, which opens entitlements to a state pension, but does not necessarily correspond to actual retirement age. Even the official age of retirement may vary between occupations and between men and women, although occupational and gender differences are progressively being eliminated, in the latter case as part of equal opportunities policies, usually by aligning the retirement age of women with that for men (European Commission, 2002d, p 36).

In 2002, the official retirement age opening access to the standard state pension for men and women ranged from 60 in France to 67 in Denmark, although the age of eligibility for a full pension was being lowered to 65 from 2004 (European Commission, 2002d, p 37). In Sweden, workers can formally retire between the ages of 61 and 67, or even later with their employer's agreement. At the turn of the century, in most EU15 member states, legal retirement age was set at 65 for both men and women, but it was still at 60 for women in Austria, Italy and the UK. In Belgium, women could retire at 63 and in Greece at 60, if they were insured before 1992 (MISSOC, 2003, table VI 3.1). Occupations such as mining or the armed forces have traditionally applied a lower age, but it is not uncommon, particularly in the professions, for people in senior positions in the public sector and in private sector management to continue working after the standard age of retirement, or to take partial or phased retirement. National aggregated figures are, therefore, difficult to compare and interpret. In the transition countries, the situation regarding retirement age is also in a state of flux: following the collapse of Soviet rule, the age of retirement was generally raised, creating problems for comparisons over time (see Chapter Five).

Defining the labour force

Calculations of dependency ratios based on the population of working age, as presented in Chapter Two, are further complicated by the fact that not all individuals of working age are necessarily economically active or, in other words, participating in the labour force. For the purposes of carrying out labour force surveys, national statistical offices are expected to follow the recommendations of the International Conferences of Labour Statisticians, convened by the International Labour Organisation (ILO). The ILO guidelines, drawn up at the 13th Conference in 1982, present a common set of concepts and definitions, which have served as a reference point for UN/ECE recommendations for population and housing censuses and surveys, including those for the labour force. The guidelines define the economically active population as "all persons who provide the supply of labour, as employed or as unemployed, for the production of goods and services" (UN/ECE, 1998, § 90). They recommend that current or usual activity status, as presented in statistical tables prepared for international comparative purposes, should include employed and unemployed persons as economically active. Persons attending educational institutions, recipients of pensions or capital income, homemakers and an unspecified category of 'others' should be counted as economically inactive. Eurostat (1996, p 13) labour force survey results show pupils and students separately, but exclude conscripts on compulsory military or community service.

UN/ECE (1998, § 101) classifies apprenticeships and traineeships according to whether they are paid or unpaid. In practice, under the dual system in Austria and Germany, young people in apprenticeships are classified simultaneously as students and workers (European Commission, 2000a, p 31). Job training schemes are considered by UN/ECE as employment if training takes place within the context of an enterprise, or if the trainee retains a formal job attachment. The definition recognises that students may be engaged in paid work, in which case they are counted as employed persons, but the recommendation is that, if possible, they should be identified as a separate category. In the UK, young people on government-supported training programmes are counted as being in employment only if they have an employment contract (ONS, 2003b, p S3).

Economic activity and inactivity rates, as compiled by Eurostat in labour force surveys following ILO definitions, are broader than the employment and unemployment count. The concept selected depends on whether policy analysts are primarily concerned with measuring the size and structure of the economy or the labour market. For studies interested in the relationship between employment and family life, the concepts of economic activity and inactivity are more informative and meaningful, since employment rates for women tend to misrepresent their actual situation in the labour force to a greater extent than do rates for men.

The inactive population covers individuals not classified as employed or unemployed. More specifically, economic inactivity includes those who declare they have not undertaken any work for pay or profit and are not seeking work, and/or are not able to take up employment within two weeks of finding work. UN/ECE recommendations make explicit that:

> 92. Domestic or personal services provided by unpaid household members for final consumption within the same household are **excluded** from the production boundary and, hence, are **not** considered to be economic

activities i.e. production, in the present context. (Examples are: (a) the cleaning, decoration and maintenance of the dwelling occupied by the household, including small repairs of a kind usually carried out by tenants as well as owners; (b) the use, cleaning, servicing and repair of household durables or other goods, including vehicles used for household purposes; 8 [*sic*] the preparation and serving of meals; (d) the care, training and instruction of children; (d) [*sic*] the care of sick, infirm or old people; and (e) the transportation of members of the household or their goods). Persons engaged in such activities may be included among <u>providers of non-paid social and personal services</u>....

(UN/ECE, 1998, original emphasis)

Women who record themselves as homemakers are thus classified as economically inactive, but they can be counted as providers of non-paid services.

According to UN/ECE (1998, § 104c), homemakers are those who, for most of the reference period, were engaged in unpaid household duties in their own home, for example housewives and other relatives responsible for the care of the home. The term 'homemaker' is not used as a labour force status category in Eurostat surveys, but it is found in studies of the division of labour in households, rather than 'housewife' or 'househusband'. Reports on the European Community Household Panel (ECHP) surveys, in the 1990s, use it to describe the person (generally the female partner) in a couple who declares her/his primary occupation as being responsible for the home. This does not mean that s/he does not also work outside the home, but such work is seen as a secondary activity, usually involving short part-time hours. UN/ECE goes on to note that:

> 115. Countries may wish to identify separately the persons who provide social and personal services to their own household, other households or to voluntary, non-profit organizations on an unpaid basis, either for a short reference period or for a longer one. Such persons may be sub-divided either according to types of services provided or according to type of recipient. ...
>
> (UN/ECE, 1998)

Most harmonised datasets do not provide this level of detail. However, it is relevant for the analysis of the family–employment relationship to note that the statistical category for economic inactivity recognises individuals can be engaged in work as producers or caregivers of non-market goods and services, such as unregistered childminding, without necessarily being part of the official labour force. From a gender perspective, the category of inactivity is more encompassing, although individuals who are, by definition, inactive for most of the time may, in some situations, be classified as employed, in line with international criteria, as specified in UN/ECE recommendations:

100. 'Employed' persons comprise all persons above a specified age who during the short reference period of preferably one week performed some work for pay or profit, in cash or in kind, or were temporarily absent from a job in which they had already worked and to which they had a formal attachment or from a self-employment activity such as a farm, a business enterprise or a service undertaking. ...
(UN/ECE, 1998)

The 2001 edition of the European Labour Force Survey defined the employment rate as the percentage of persons in employment in relation to the population of working age living in private households (Eurostat, 2001, p 10). Prior to 1999, this concept was referred to as the employment/ population ratio and was calculated as a percentage of the population aged 15 and above (Eurostat, 1996, p 13). For prime-age men (aged 25-49), the difference between measures of activity and employment rates are relatively minor, since only a small proportion of men are not economically active in this age group. For prime-age women and, even more so, for younger people of both sexes, the difference between the two measures is much greater, because relatively large proportions of persons in these age groups are likely to be classified as inactive.

The UN/ECE definition of employed persons also raises the question of whether women on maternity leave and parents taking parental leave should be categorised as being 'temporarily absent' from their job or economically inactive. Following the 1982 International Conference of Labour Statisticians, UN/ECE (1998, § 101) explicitly recommended that women on maternity leave should be considered as temporarily absent from their work provided they retained a formal link with their employment. Under the provisions of the 1992 European Council Directive (92/85/EEC, *Official Journal* L 348/1, 28.11.1992, article 10) on the safety and health at work of pregnant workers and workers who have recently given birth, women are protected against dismissal during the leave period. The 1996 framework agreement on parental leave (Council Directive 96/34/EC, *Official Journal* L 145/4, 19.06.1996, clause 2.5) provides for reinstatement at the end of the leave period. Women on maternity and parental leave continue, nonetheless, to be conceptualised differently from country to country. For example, in line with EU law and UN/ECE recommendations, women in France in full-time employment are classified as being in employment, but temporarily absent, if they take maternity and parental leave, because they are guaranteed reinstatement at the end of the period of leave. Women who take leave on a part-time basis are counted as being employed part time. In the UK, by contrast, where the conditions for reinstatement are more restrictive, women who take maternity leave may no longer be considered as being in employment. The definition also varies in CEE countries. Women on maternity leave in Poland and Slovenia are included in the employment count, and parents on unpaid leave are considered to be economically active, but in Estonia and Hungary, women on maternity leave and parents on paid leave are counted as economically inactive and excluded from the employment count. However, Estonian and also Latvian women who stay at home to look after children are entitled to receive a childcare payment irrespective of their employment status (Statistical Office of Estonia, 2000, p 206; Frey, 2001; Bite and Zagorskis, 2003, p 35; Stropnik et al, 2003, p 70).

Defining unemployment for statistical purposes is equally, if not more, problematic than defining inactivity, particularly for women. According to the UN/ECE definition for census purposes, which is based on ILO criteria:

> 102. The 'unemployed' comprise all persons above a specified age who during the reference period were:
> (i) 'without work', i.e. were not in paid employment or self-employment...;
> (ii) 'currently available for work', i.e. were available for paid employment or self-employment during the reference period; and
> (iii) 'seeking work', i.e. had taken specific steps in a specified recent period to seek paid employment or self-employment. (The specific steps may include registration at a public or private employment exchange (for the purpose of obtaining job offers); application to employers; checking at work sites, farms, factory gates, market or other assembly places; placing or answering newspaper advertisements; seeking assistance of friends or relatives; looking for land, building, machinery or equipment to establish own enterprises; arranging for financial resources; applying for permits and licenses, etc).
>
> (UN/ECE, 1998)

In 2000, the European Commission revised the Eurostat definition (Commission Regulation (EC) n° 1897/2000, *Official Journal* L 228/18, 08.09.2000). Since the revision, Eurostat specifies that availability for employment should be within the two weeks following the reference week and that persons actively seeking work should include those who have found a job and are due to start work within a period of up to three months. The unemployment rate expresses unemployed persons as a percentage of the labour force (employed and unemployed); the unemployment ratio expresses the percentage of unemployed persons in relation to the population of the same age. When the unemployment rate is compared with the unemployment ratio, the disparity may be very marked, particularly for youth unemployment (Eurostat, 2001, p 10; European Commission, 2002a, p 201).

Again, not all countries closely observe the guidelines. French statistics use a more restrictive definition of unemployment, which excludes unemployed women on paid parental leave (*allocation parentale d'éducation*) on the grounds that they are not seeking employment, even though they are entitled to return to the unemployed status at the end of the period of paid leave. Changes in the conditions for access to paid parental leave can, therefore, affect figures for activity and unemployment, as demonstrated when the right to paid parental leave was extended to women with two children in 1994, after previously applying only to those with three or more children (Afsa, 1996, p 3).

Although the internationally agreed definition of unemployment is widely used for comparative purposes, many countries rely on official registered national unemployment figures taken from sources other than censuses and labour force surveys, which are less likely to be directly comparable. In the UK, for example, the claimant count records the number of people claiming Jobseeker's Allowance and National Insurance credits separately from the unemployment count. National figures from these disparate sources may, therefore, encompass a great variety of unemployment situations, covering persons compulsorily or voluntarily registered, seeking a first job, seeking long or short working hours, in a job with a short-term or short-time contract, entitled to insurance-related benefits or claiming subsistence, available for work a set number of days after registration, or immediately available (Threlfall, 2000, p 327).

In CEE countries, since no official measure of unemployment was applied under the Soviet system for political reasons, no information is available using either ILO or other criteria for the period before transition. Retrospective estimates of unemployment rates are of limited value. The first ever statistics on unemployment in Estonia, using ILO definitions, were, for example, collected in 1994 for the NORBALT Living Conditions Project.

The distinction between unemployment and disability (as well as unemployability) has also become blurred. In the 1980s and 1990s, early retirement was widely used as an alternative to long-term unemployment or extended sick leave. Unemployment may also be 'disguised' when 'short-hours' part-time jobs are taken by those wanting full-time work. Official figures do not generally reveal the full extent of unemployment in cases where workers are 'discouraged' from registering for work. Although the term is not used officially in UN/ECE or Eurostat nomenclature, a record is kept of the reasons why 'inactive persons' are not seeking employment or are unwilling to work. Discouraged workers are people who would like to work and would be available for work if a suitable job became available, but who are not actively seeking work because they do not think they will find a job. They are, therefore, excluded from unemployment figures. The term 'discouraged workers' may also apply to those not in a position to take a job immediately, if offered, because they have family responsibilities and could not make the necessary childminding arrangements.

Another area of work that escapes employment and unemployment counts but would be encompassed in the UN/ECE definition of inactivity, is that carried out within the informal sector of the economy, generally defined as activities and productive work that are hidden from, or ignored by, the state for tax or social security purposes. The informal economy covers both paid and unpaid work, including domestic or voluntary activities. The term used by the European Commission, 'undeclared work', is taken to mean any paid activities that are lawful in nature but are not declared to public authorities. It, therefore, excludes any work that does not have to be declared (COM(1998) 219 final, 07.04.1998, p 2; Mateman and Renooy, 2001, p 1).

Informal and undeclared work is conceptualised differently from one country to another. In cases where the public accepts the need for a high level of taxation as a means of funding universal provision of social services, as in the Nordic states, undeclared work is considered to run counter to the common good and to undermine social solidarity. Where individuals gain rights to social protection through their own social security contributions, as in France or Germany, undeclared work presents less of a threat for the protected population, since undeclared workers do not have access to the same rights. It does, however, create a marginalised population, generally entitled to social assistance, and it represents a loss for state revenues. Where the tradition is for families to have primary responsibility for supporting their own members, informal work may provide a flexible means of supplementing family income but undermines collective solidarity, as in southern European and CEE countries.

Analysts are increasingly interested in the dynamics of family life and transitions between family forms and statuses, as shown in Chapter Three. Similarly, the concept of transitional labour markets is being used to capture the blurring of the boundaries between gainful employment and other productive activities (Schmid, 2000). The 'standard' job, implying full-time, upwardly mobile, lifelong employment with the same firm, is no longer a reality, nor even an ideal, for the majority of workers. As indicated above, most young people will not enter employment when they reach the end of compulsory schooling. Men as well as women will move in and out of the labour market, change jobs, working arrangements and environments. They will undergo periods of retraining, and preparation for the transition into and out of inactivity, including retirement. The problem in trying to analyse these transitions is the limited availability of panel surveys tracking patterns over time and, even less, of comparable data across and within countries.

Defining working time

The working hours of the population in employment are extremely heterogeneous. To be included in the employment count, an individual needs to declare that s/he worked for more than one hour for pay or profit during the reference week. By the same token, the unemployed population is defined as those working less than one hour during the reference week. Such a low level of working time is not, however, helpful in distinguishing between employment and inactivity. Recognising that the one-hour criterion is not a reliable indicator for some of the purposes for which census and survey findings are used, UN/ECE (1998 §§ 100, 116-19) recommendations suggest that information should also be collected on 'time usually worked', including overtime. In the labour force surveys, Eurostat records both time usually worked and actual time worked. Such data are, however, often not comparable for different categories of workers over time and across countries because definitions are not consistently applied.

Actual and usual working hours are particularly difficult to measure in occupations where working time is not regulated by law and where workers are not required to 'clock in' or keep time sheets. Even when time records are kept, the extent to which time spent on the job is productive may be difficult to assess. Unpaid overtime and the long working hours of many professionals may not be recorded. Eurostat (2001, p 12) specifically excludes lunch breaks from the count of the number of hours worked. Practices again differ between countries depending upon whether this aspect of working time is regulated in national legislation, or negotiated at branch or plant level. When the Aubry Laws were implemented in France to reduce the working week to 35 hours, social partners were left to negotiate arrangements for breaks taken during the working day. The overall effect has tended to be the removal of breaks from effective working time. In the UK, the issue of whether comfort and refreshment breaks should be counted in working hours was reopened as more firms banned smoking from working areas, and in the face of claims from non-smokers that they were being discriminated against (for example Weir, 2001).

Despite the European Council Directive on part-time work (97/81/EC, *Official Journal* L 14/9, 20.01.1998), which requires that part-time workers are granted pro-rata rights, disparities may arise due to the way that breaks are counted for part-time and full-time workers. Part-time workers may not, for example, be entitled to lunch breaks, which are generally included as part of the normal (contractual) working day for full-time workers. In addition, part-time work continues to be defined and conceptualised differently from one country to another. In principle, as defined by Eurostat, it involves fewer hours than the norm for a particular type of job. National statistical offices are asked to supply data, based on spontaneous replies from respondents, as to whether they consider they are working part time, compared with statutory full-time working hours (Eurostat, 2001, p 11). The understanding is that part-time work should not involve more than 35 hours, and full-time work starts at around 30 hours. Until 1995, Eurostat presented part-time working hours in labour force survey results in bands, covering 1-10, 11-20, 21-24, 25-30 and 31+ hours. Since 1996, it has recorded only average hours, which means it is no longer possible routinely to identify the concentration of part-time work in terms of short or long part-time hours.

Several countries revised their definitions of part-time work in the mid-1980s, causing a break in time series data. In the Netherlands, for example, a sudden and very marked increase in part-time rates occurred following the change in the accounting system (Anxo et al, 2000, pp 95-6). In France, until 2000, part-time hours applied to workers whose monthly working hours were 20% or more below the statutory number of working hours. Since 2000, all employees working less than statutory hours are classified as part time. In the British General Household Survey, persons who state they have worked more than 30 hours a week, or 26 for occupations in education, are classified as full time. Those working less than 30 hours are counted as part time (ONS, 2001b, p 170).

Although part-time work and other forms of flexibility are defined in terms of the number of hours worked, they may be conceptualised differently from one country to another and also within countries. A distinction is frequently made between voluntary and negotiated flexibility, and working-time arrangements that are imposed and externally constrained (Cebrián et al, 2000, p 6; Wallace, 2003, pp 36-8). Data on the preferences of workers with different working-time arrangements (Bielenski et al, 2002), or on the reactions of workers to the reduction and restructuring of working hours, as in France (Méda and Orain, 2002; Fagnani and Letablier, 2003), provide an indication of how such change is perceived by both workers and employers.

Another concept relevant to an understanding of the meaning of paid work is underemployment, or hidden unemployment. According to the ILO, the population of working age is underemployed if individuals are involuntarily working fewer than the standard number of hours for their occupation, seeking additional work or available to undertake such work. To capture the level of underemployment, or involuntary part-time work, labour force surveys try to establish to what extent part-time workers would take a full-time job if offered (Eurostat, 2001, p 11). Although they may not be classified as economically active, some groups are more likely to be affected by underemployment, namely young people who have not yet formally entered the labour market, women and older people below retirement age, who are economically inactive, working short part-time hours and/or unable to find a full-time job, but who are seeking one.

Although time budget studies consider the totality of time use, less attention has been devoted to recording shifts in the distribution of the unpaid work carried out by men and women in the home. Much of the information available on homemaking and other non-market forms of production associated with family life has been collected in surveys, such as those conducted by Eurobarometer or the European Foundation for the Improvement of Living and Working Conditions (Paoli and Merllié, 2001). Such survey data are problematic due not only to difficulties with sampling, inconsistencies in definitions and inaccuracies in recall, but also to bias in reporting. Men and women often have quite different perceptions of their own and their partners' contributions to the household economy. Changes in the wording of questions further complicate comparisons, making it very difficult to track developments over time and between countries.

Measuring working life

Despite the best efforts by Eurostat and other international bodies to improve the quality and reliability of instruments designed to measure trends in employment, as demonstrated in the previous section, many of the indicators widely used to assess and compare the situation in EU member states must be treated with caution. Eurostat adopted a revised conceptual framework based on ILO guidelines in 1983, which means that time series comparisons cannot be made with earlier data. Although candidate countries are following Eurostat recommendations for indicators of labour market trends as they prepare for EU membership, harmonised datasets are available for new member states only from the point at which they join the Community or Union. Changes in definitions further complicate the situation, as exemplified by part-time work or the use of different age categories and other groupings. In this section, an attempt is made to track and compare changes in the working life of the population in EU15 member states and the 10 countries that joined the Union in 2004. The relationship between working patterns and family life is examined, taking account of the possible impact of new waves of membership on the trends observed, and the distortions and bias created by inconsistencies in data collection methods.

Measuring change in the working population

Across EU15, with the exception of Luxembourg and Sweden, the population of working age, based on the 15-64 age grouping, represented a larger proportion of total population in 2000 than in the 1960s. For the 20-59 age group, the proportion of the population of working age in relation to the dependent population had increased in all EU15 member states (Eurostat, 2002a, tables C-4, C-7). The potential labour supply was, therefore, greater than in earlier decades of the 20th century. However, a number of changes had taken place within the population of working age that were affecting the size and structure of the labour force.

According to Eurostat's harmonised labour force survey results, in most EU member states, compared with the mid-1980s, smaller proportions of young people aged 15-19 were available for work in 2000, generally because they were remaining longer in education and training. The pattern continued, although to a lesser extent, for 20-24 year olds. The proportion of young people obtaining higher levels of educational qualifications had increased commensurably, especially for women. In addition, smaller proportions of the working population were recorded as economically active after the age of 55 and after legal retirement age. In the industrial sector, early retirement had been encouraged from the 1970s in response to the need for economic restructuring and in an effort to reduce the wage bill. Many older people in declining industries were made redundant before they reached retirement age and were unable to find another job. In some cases, they were offered early retirement packages. In others, they were classified as 'unfit for work', rather than being categorised as unemployed. In 1995, across EU15, 67.5% of men aged 55-59 were economically active, and only 32% of men aged 60-64 (European Commission, 1996b, pp 49-50). Data for 2000 do not break down the two age groups, but they do show a small upturn in the employment rate for men aged 55-64 in the late 1990s: from 47.1% in 1995 to 48.6% in 2001 (European Commission, 2002a, p 173). In CEE countries, the rapid transition during the 1990s severely disrupted labour markets, patterns of employment and social life but, as early retirement programmes closed, and retirement age was raised, activity rates of older people began to rise.

The overall effect of these changes in the late 20th century was that economic activity had become more concentrated within the 25-55 age group, coinciding for women with the phase in life when they were most likely to be engaged in childbearing and childrearing, particularly if they postponed having children. Although trends were generally moving in the same direction, the situation was by no means uniform across EU member states. The contrast between north and south, and between east and west, was very marked in terms of the rate, pace and extent of change.

As noted in Chapter Three, women have been postponing family formation, and fewer women are having children in their teens. The reason is not that they are entering the labour market at an early age. Across the Union, young women, and men, are not available for either employment or parenthood because they are taking longer to achieve autonomy (Elias, 2003, pp 22-3). They are remaining longer in compulsory schooling and vocational training as a result of the raising of school-leaving age, and as further education and initial training have become standard practice.

Despite the very marked overall decrease in the proportion of young people entering employment on completion of compulsory schooling, national differences are found in the length of time spent in further and higher education, and in participation rates. More than 80% of young people aged 15-19 were in education and training in the late 1990s across EU15, but the proportion ranged from over 90% in Belgium, Finland, France, Germany and Luxembourg to around 70% in Portugal and the UK. For the 20-24 age group, the EU15 average was close to 40% in the late 1990s, but the range was from 50% or more in Denmark and Finland to under 25% in the UK (European Commission, 1999b, pp 127-42). No breakdown is available for these two age groups for the candidate countries, but figures for 16- to 18-year-olds in the late 1990s show rates of over 80% in CEE countries, but around 55% in Malta (European Commission, 2002e, p 139).

Over time, women have benefited more than men from the extension of educational opportunities. In the mid-1970s, they outnumbered men in upper secondary schooling only in Finland and Ireland. By the late 1990s, they were in the majority in EU15 member states, except for Austria, Germany and Greece. In the 1970s, nowhere did women outnumber men in tertiary education but, by the late 1990s, they were in the majority in all member states except Germany and the Netherlands. The pattern was similar in the candidate countries that joined the Union in 2004. Women were in the majority in upper secondary education except in Malta. In tertiary education, they outnumbered men everywhere except the Czech Republic. Estonia and

Poland reached the highest rates, close to that for Sweden (Eurostat, 1997a, tables G-24, G-25; European Commission, 2002e, pp 120, 139). However, women still more often study social sciences and humanities, law, health and social work, whereas men more often gain qualifications in science and engineering disciplines (European Commission, 2002c, pp 155, 159).

As a result of the extension of education and training, in most EU member states, fewer young men and women in the 15-24 age group are classified as economically active; fewer still are in employment. Datasets are incomplete, and the figures are not wholly comparable for the period prior to the 1990s, but data for the more recent period suggest that, after a dip in the mid-1990s, employment rates for this age group were rising at the end of the decade. In 2000, within EU25, the proportion of men and women aged 15-24 reported to be in employment varied considerably from one country to another. Much higher rates were recorded in the Netherlands and Denmark at over 60%, compared with Italy and Greece, at below 25% (European Commission, 2002a, pp 173-99). The same EU15 countries displayed the highest and lowest rates for men and women separately, as illustrated by Table 4.1.

Differences between men and women within countries were much smaller for this age group than the disparities in employment rates between countries. In Finland, the difference amounted to only 2.2 percentage points, compared with eight or more points in the southern European countries and Austria. Except for Malta, the candidate countries displayed employment rates below the EU15 average for young people aged 15-24. In some cases, the disparities between men and women were very small, particularly in Slovakia, where the difference was less than one point, and only in Latvia did it reach 10 points. In combination with data for education and training, the relatively low employment rates for young people in southern Europe and some of the candidate countries suggest that they are more likely to remain economically dependent on their parents, which would help to explain the delay in leaving the family home, as noted in Chapter Three.

Educational achievement is an important factor in determining subsequent employment rates, but the effect varies between countries. With an equivalent level of education, women in the 25-49 age group consistently display lower labour market activity rates than men but, as the level of education rises, the gender difference decreases. The gender disparity was particularly marked in 2000 for the less well-qualified groups in Greece, Italy and Spain. It was smallest in Portugal and Sweden for men and women with tertiary-level qualifications. Well-educated women in Portugal displayed the highest employment rates in EU15 member states, at 93.1%, whereas the lowest rates were recorded for the least well-qualified women in Italy, at 37.7% (Eurostat, 2001, table 14). By the same token, both women and men were less likely to be unemployed if they had attained higher levels of education, but with the exceptions of Estonia, Latvia and Slovakia, women with tertiary-level qualifications were more likely to be unemployed than men (Eurostat, 2001, table 54; European Commission, 2002e, p 138).

Table 4.1: Employment rates for men and women as a percentage of age groups in EU25 member states, by membership wave (2000)

	15-24		25-54		55-64	
	Men	**Women**	**Men**	**Women**	**Men**	**Women**
EU15	43.7	36.7	87.1	65.9	48.0	27.9
1. Belgium	32.8	25.4	87.3	67.2	36.4	16.6
1. France	32.4	25.6	87.7	70.1	34.1	26.7
1. Germany	48.6	43.7	87.2	71.1	46.3	28.8
1. Italy	30.6	22.1	84.8	50.9	40.9	15.3
1. Luxembourg	35.0	28.8	92.9	63.0	37.2	16.4
1. Netherlands	70.0	67.3	92.2	70.8	50.2	26.1
2. Denmark	68.5	63.3	88.5	79.8	64.2	46.5
2. Ireland	54.5	46.9	88.2	62.6	63.3	27.2
2. UK	59.3	54.7	87.5	73.2	60.1	41.7
3. Greece	32.0	22.4	88.4	52.5	54.9	23.9
3. Portugal	49.0	37.1	90.3	73.9	62.5	41.1
3. Spain	37.6	26.2	85.4	50.7	55.0	20.0
4. Austria	56.8	48.0	91.3	73.8	41.2	17.2
4. Finland	42.2	40.0	84.3	77.3	43.4	40.7
4. Sweden	35.3	34.8	83.8	80.6	67.1	61.8
5. Cyprus	38.3	31.0	92.5	63.8	67.1	31.9
5. Czech Republic	39.3	33.6	89.2	73.7	51.6	22.1
5. Estonia	31.4	23.2	79.5	74.2	50.2	37.5
5. Hungary	37.0	29.2	79.0	66.7	33.0	13.0
5. Latvia	35.2	24.9	75.4	71.8	48.3	25.9
5. Lithuania	30.2	23.2	75.1	76.8	52.2	34.5
5. Malta	55.8	53.3	90.3	33.8	44.5	8.0
5. Poland	26.4	21.9	77.5	64.5	37.4	21.8
5. Slovakia	28.7	27.9	79.1	69.4	35.2	10.2
5. Slovenia	34.7	27.4	85.5	79.6	31.0	14.3

Notes: The numbers in column 1 indicate waves of membership: 1. 1957, 2. 1973, 3. 1981/86, 4. 1995, 5. 2004.

Data for Malta are calculated from national sources.

Sources: European Commission (2002a, pp 173-99); NSO (2003).

Within the Union during the late 1990s, women were progressively taking more of the new jobs created, particularly part-time jobs in the service sector. By 2000, they were obtaining more than half of all new jobs. Consequently, as shown in Table 4.2, the overall gender employment gap for the population of working age (15-64) had narrowed to 18.5 percentage points in 2000, compared with 24 points in the early 1990s (European Commission, 2002a, p 110). The smallest employment gap in 2000 between men and women of working age was 3.8 points for Sweden and the largest

Table 4.2: Employment, full-time equivalent (FTE) and part-time rates for men and women of working age in EU25 member states, by membership wave (2000)

	Employment		FTE		Part-time	
	Men	Women	Men	Women	Men	Women
EU15	72.5	54.0	71.0	45.3	6.2	33.4
1. Belgium	69.5	51.5	70.7	44.2	5.8	40.5
1. France	69.1	55.1	69.2	48.7	5.3	30.8
1. Germany	72.7	57.9	71.1	46.1	5.1	38.2
1. Italy	67.9	39.6	67.0	36.7	3.7	16.5
1. Luxembourg	75.0	50.1	75.9	44.6	1.7	25.1
1. Netherlands	82.1	63.5	74.7	40.5	19.3	71.0
2. Denmark	80.8	71.6	76.9	62.2	10.2	34.1
2. Ireland	76.2	54.1	75.9	45.2	6.9	30.1
2. UK	78.1	64.8	74.4	49.7	9.1	44.6
3. Greece	71.1	41.2	71.5	40.0	2.5	7.8
3. Portugal	76.5	60.3	76.6	57.1	6.2	16.3
3. Spain	69.7	40.3	69.0	36.6	2.8	16.9
4. Austria	77.3	59.6	76.2	51.0	4.1	32.2
4. Finland	70.2	64.3	69.3	60.5	8.0	17.0
4. Sweden	72.2	69.1	70.0	60.2	10.2	36.1
5. Cyprus	78.9	52.5	79.3	49.6	4.4	14.1
5. Czech Rep	73.1	56.8	73.2	55.2	2.2	9.5
5. Estonia	64.3	57.1	64.3	55.6	4.2	9.3
5. Hungary	62.7	49.4	63.6	48.7	2.1	5.3
5. Latvia	62.3	53.5	61.3	51.8	9.5	12.2
5. Lithuania	61.8	58.5	62.4	57.7	7.6	9.6
5. Malta	75.2	33.4	76.0^{e}	29.0^{e}	2.5	17.1
5. Poland	61.2	49.3	59.3	46.9	8.4	13.2
5. Slovakia	61.6	51.1	62.7	50.3	1.0	2.9
5. Slovenia	66.7	58.5	66.1	56.8	4.7	7.7

Notes: The numbers in column 1 indicate waves of membership: 1. 1957, 2. 1973, 3. 1981/86, 4. 1995, 5. 2004.

The employment rate is for the population aged 15-64. Part-time work is a percentage of total employment. Eurostat calculates the FTE employment rate by dividing total hours worked by average annual hours worked in a person's main employment and in any second job. FTE rates for Malta are calculated from national sources.

Sources: European Commission (2002a, pp 173-99), NSO (2003).

was for Malta (44.4 points), followed by Greece and Spain with around 30 points each. While employment rates have generally been increasing for women in EU15, bringing them closer to those for men, in most CEE countries and the east German *Länder*, rates for both women and men fell during the 1990s. Since they generally fell further for men, the gender employment gap, which was previously relatively small compared with EU15, was further reduced (European Commission, 2002a, pp 173-99).

Whereas employment rates for men aged 25-49 vary little between countries, those for women demonstrate much greater fluctuations. Since no comparable data are available for the 25-49 age group for the candidate countries, the employment rates presented in Table 4.1 are for men and women aged 25-54. They indicate that, in 2000, rates for men were, on average, higher for this age group in EU15 than in the then candidate countries, with the notable exceptions of Cyprus, the Czech Republic and Malta, where they were above the EU15 average. Except for Cyprus, Malta and Poland, female employment rates were above the EU15 average. The Nordic states recorded the highest rates within EU15, and the southern European countries, except Portugal, the lowest. Among the candidate countries, Slovenia reached a level comparable with the EU Nordic states, but only in Malta did the level fall below that in the southern European countries. Within EU15, the disparity between male and female rates was widest in Greece (35.9 points) and Italy (33.9 points), falling to the lowest level in Sweden (2.2 points). Within the candidate countries, the largest gaps for this age group were for Malta (55.3) and Cyprus (28.7 points). The smallest was for Lithuania (-1.7 points), which was the only country in the table to report higher rates for women than for men. The other two Baltic states also showed some of the smallest gender gaps across EU25.

The more continuous pattern of employment for women has not yet worked its way through the life span. The generations of women who were reaching retirement age at the turn of the century were characterised by low employment rates. As shown in Table 4.1, in 2000, across EU15, almost 50% of men aged 55-64 were in employment, compared with less than 30% of women. In Spain, more than twice as many men as women were in employment for this age group. The disparity was smallest in Finland where the rate for men was relatively low and that for women relatively high. The gender gap was also small in Sweden, where employment rates were highest for both men and women. France and Belgium recorded the lowest employment rates for men, and Italy the lowest rate for women. The candidate countries displayed some of the lowest employment rates for men in the table, falling to 31% in Slovenia. The rates in Hungary, Poland and Slovakia were also below the EU15 average. Very few women in this age group were in employment in Malta, in particular, Hungary, Slovakia and Slovenia. In CEE countries, retirement age was low during the Soviet era. Since transition, many of the older people, especially women, who lost their jobs during the process of restructuring, have been unable to find work. Nonetheless, the gender gap for this age group falls within a narrower range compared with EU15 countries.

Read in conjunction with the data presented in Chapter Two about gender differences in life expectancy, and in Chapter Three about differential rates of poverty in old age, these figures confirm that, across the Union, women are likely to spend more years in later life than their male counterparts in an economically inactive state, after having also spent a smaller number of years in paid work contributing to a pension.

Employment rates present only part of the gendered picture of activities during working life, not only because women tend to move in and out of the labour force to a greater extent than men, but also, as indicated in the section on concepts and definitions, because they engage in many activities that are not recorded as formal employment. Reliable data on undeclared work are difficult to obtain for obvious reasons. The growth of subcontracting and the increase in the number of activities that have been created by new technologies have contributed to the expansion of informal/undeclared work as the demand has spread for personalised services. Estimates in the late 1990s put the level of undeclared work at 7-19% across the Union (COM(1998) 219 final, 07.04.1998, p 5), whereas other sources have reported figures as high as 23% in Spain and 27% in Italy (Mateman and Renooy, 2001, table 9.1). In CEE countries, illegal activities increased following the end of Soviet rule because of the instability and uncertainty of the transitional period. In Hungary and Latvia, for example, the informal economy is estimated to account for a third or more of GDP (Bite and Zagorskis, 2003, p 7). High taxation and low incomes have encouraged the growth of family firms, which provide additional financial resources while avoiding the burden of taxation. Women are not thought to form the majority of undeclared workers, but they do tend to be in a more precarious situation and are likely to be more dependent on a partner than if they were declaring their work (COM(1998) 219 final, 07.04.1998, p 8).

Measuring the family–employment relationship

Although marriage rates are much less indicative of couple formation nowadays than in the 1960s, Eurostat continues to collect data on marital status for labour force surveys, but it no longer routinely tabulates marital status with economic activity in labour force statistics. For the purposes of analysing the marital status variable, households containing couples with registered partnerships are treated in the same way as married couples. Unregistered, unmarried cohabiting couples are not identified (Eurostat, 2001, p 10). Published statistics for 1986-96 show that activity rates increased during the period for married women in the 25-49 age group, except in Denmark and France, where they were already relatively high in the 1980s. By the mid-1990s, at least 50% of married women aged 25-49 were recorded as economically active across EU15, whereas rates had been as low as 30% in Ireland and Spain a decade earlier. In most member states, the proportion was more than 70%. Over time, the activity rates of divorced women have been increasing in most countries. By the mid-1990s, divorced women (and also widows, although widowhood was relatively uncommon among women in the 25-49 age group) were recording higher activity rates than married women, except in Denmark and the UK (Eurostat, 1988, table 04; 1997b, table 004).

As it became less common for women to leave the labour market when they formed a couple relationship, irrespective of marital status, growth in female employment rates was accompanied by an increase in the proportion of dual-earner couples in the 1990s, again with variations between countries. By the late 1990s, in Austria, Belgium, France, Germany, the Netherlands, Portugal and the UK, two thirds or more of all couples with at least one wage earner were dual-earning couples, compared with less than half in the other southern European countries, Ireland and Luxembourg. The proportion of dual earners ranged from just above 40% in Spain to nearer 80% in the UK. No data were available for the Nordic states. In view of their high female employment rates, they would also be expected to show some of the highest rates for dual earning. In general, the rate in the 12 countries analysed was 20% higher for women with tertiary education than for women with only compulsory schooling. In Italy and Spain, it was more than 40% higher for well-qualified women (Franco and Winqvist, 2002, figure 1, table 3).

Since marriage is no longer a formal bar to employment, data on marital status is less relevant to an understanding of changes in activity rates than is the presence, or otherwise, of children. Information about employment among dual-earner couples during the 1990s suggests that the presence of children is associated with a fall in dual earning in France, Germany, Ireland, Luxembourg, the Netherlands and the UK, but with a rise in Belgium, Greece and Spain. In Austria, Italy and Portugal, the level remains unchanged (Franco and Winqvist, 2002, figure 3). Lone parenthood is also associated with marked differences in employment rates. ECHP data for 1996 indicate that nearly 60% of lone mothers with a child aged under 25 were in employment across EU15, rising to over 70% in Austria, Denmark, France, Germany and Portugal, and falling to 50% or below in Ireland, the Netherlands, Spain and the UK (Chambaz, 2000, table T.02).

Postponement of age at first marriage and childbirth, and the reduction in family size mean that, increasingly, women are able to spend a longer period of their lives – three quarters of their life span – in activities not associated with childbearing and childraising, in theory bringing their availability for employment closer to that of men. However, women's employment patterns continue to be affected to a much greater degree than those of men by changes in living arrangements and family events. In the mid-1980s, it was still not unusual for women to leave the labour market, often for good, when they married and had children. The pattern continued in all except the Nordic states well into the 1990s (Hantrais, 2000b, figure 1.1). By contrast, at the turn of the century, more women were remaining in the labour force and/or returning to it during their childrearing years. Employment rates for the 25-49 age group are, therefore, of particular interest for an analysis of the relationship between employment and family life. While the effective length of working life has been reduced due to later labour market entry and earlier labour market exit, time spent childbearing and childrearing has been concentrated into a shorter period. The impact of women leaving the labour force in the past to raise a family is, however, still being felt in employment rates among the older generations, as noted in the previous section.

Not only the presence of children but also their number and age affect women's employment rates. In the absence of information for the Nordic states, the available data confirm that, during the 1990s, growing numbers of women with young children were in employment. The increase was particularly marked in the Netherlands. The presence of young children had the most depressing effect on the employment rates of mothers aged 20-49 in Germany, Ireland, Luxembourg and the UK. The effect was greater as the number of children rose. By contrast, in France and the southern European countries, especially Portugal, employment rates were much less affected by the arrival of children. Analysis of data for employment rates according to the age of the youngest child suggests that the depressing effect of children is reduced as they reach school age in Germany, France and the UK, but that age makes little difference to female employment rates in Belgium, southern Europe, the Netherlands and, especially, Ireland (Eurostat, 2001, table 11; Rubery et al, 2001, tables A.1, A.2).

Women are also much more likely than men to be inactive because they do not 'want' a job (Eurostat, 2001, table 65). Analysis of the reasons why women withdraw from the labour force completely and become inactive indicates that they do so primarily as a result of family responsibilities. Between the ages of 25 and 54, 28% of women were inactive in 2001, compared with 8% of men. Around 18% of prime-age women were estimated to be outside the labour force due to family responsibilities, and nearly two out of three inactive women had previous work experience. Much higher proportions of women were inactive for family reasons in Greece, Ireland, Italy and Luxembourg (over 29%) than in the Nordic states (below 7%) (Eurostat, 2001, table 65; van Bastelaer and Blöndal, 2003, pp 3-4).

The presence of children not only determines whether or not women are in employment, it also affects the amount of time they spend working. Even if they remain in employment, women are much more likely than men to reduce their working hours and to work part time when they have children. In some countries, most notably the Netherlands and the UK (see Table 4.2), the seemingly greater continuity of female employment and relatively high employment rates have been achieved through part-time work, which continues to differentiate between male and female patterns of employment. In Denmark and Sweden, which reported some of the highest part-time rates in EU15 at the beginning of the 1990s, female part-time rates fell during the decade. In the candidate countries, few women work part time: the highest rates as a proportion of total employment in 2000 were in Cyprus and Malta. Slovakia reported the lowest level of all across EU25.

Figures for part-time work conceal important variations between countries in the hours usually worked by women. In the mid-1990s, when data on groups of hours worked were available for EU15 countries, part-time work was found to be most heavily concentrated in the 11-20 grouping of hours. In the Netherlands, it was mainly concentrated in the 1-10 grouping, and in Finland in the 25-30 grouping (Eurostat, 1997b, table 078).

The average duration of paid working time for men and women combined has been falling across the Union since the mid-1980s, but women continue to work shorter hours than men. In 2001, the average full-time working week for women in the UK (40.7 hours) was the highest in EU15, where the average was 38.8 hours. Women working full time in Italy (36.4) reported the shortest full-time hours. The longest part-time hours were worked on average in France (23.4) and Sweden (23.6), and the shortest in Spain (18) and Germany (18.3) (Franco and Jouhette, 2002, table 2). In most of the candidate countries, part-time and full-time hours are relatively long compared with EU15. In 2001, Latvia recorded the longest full-time hours for women (42.9) and Lithuania the shortest (38.5). Part-time hours were highest in the Czech Republic (25.6) and lowest in Lithuania (21.0) (Franco and Blöndal, 2002, table 2).

While overall employment rates for women appear to have been moving closer to those for men, the greater propensity of women to engage in part-time work and to work shorter hours means that the actual volume of paid work carried out by women is considerably below that for men. The overall gender employment gap was reduced between 1995 and 2000, but the disparity between full-time equivalent rates increased across EU15, except in Denmark and Sweden. In 2000, the disparity was most marked in the Netherlands, where large numbers of women worked part time, and smallest for Finland, which reported low part-time rates and high overall female employment rates. In CEE countries, where part-time rates were relatively low, the difference between men and women was much less marked than in EU15. In the cases of the Czech Republic, Hungary, Lithuania and Slovakia, the male full-time equivalent rate was higher than the employment rate, which may be explained by the number of men with more than one job. The net result is that the gap between the headcount and the volume of female employment is much greater in the Netherlands, UK, Germany and Sweden than it is in the southern European and CEE countries.

When the volume of weekly working hours for men and women with and without children is compared across EU15, except in the Nordic states and Italy, women with children have been found to work shorter weekly hours than women without children. In Italy, they worked the same number of hours whether or not they had children. The difference in hours for women with and without children was greatest in Austria, Germany, the Netherlands and the UK, where part-time rates are relatively high, but the number of hours worked by part-timers is below the EU15 average. Only in Spain did men without children work longer hours than men with children. When working-time preferences were compared with actual working hours, except in the Netherlands where the difference was small, women with children wanted to work shorter hours than they were doing. In Spain, they were looking for a relatively small reduction and, in Denmark, for much shorter hours. Women without children would also prefer to work shorter hours, especially in Austria and the UK (Bielenski et al, 2002, table 25).

Since 1992, labour force surveys have asked about the reasons why men and women are working part time. In response, women seldom mention education and training, illness or disability to explain their part-time working arrangements. In 2000, Portugal was the only country where illness or disability was given as a reason by a sizeable proportion (17%) of female respondents. In Finland, Greece and Italy, the lack of full-time jobs was cited by about a third of female respondents. It was the most frequent response in these three countries, and also in Belgium, Portugal and Spain. In Denmark, France, Luxembourg and Sweden, over 50% of part-time workers stated that they did not want a full-time job. In Germany, Ireland, the Netherlands and the UK, the proportion was over 70% (Eurostat, 2001, table 38).

Data on average hours usually worked, whether full or part time, also conceal the concentration of working time for different age groups. When rates are compared for the 15-24, 25-49 and 50-64 age groups across EU15, female part-time work is found to be concentrated in the peak years for childbearing and childrearing only in Austria. Rather, the highest rates of part-time work were recorded in the 15-24 age group in Denmark, Finland, France, Greece, Italy, Spain and Sweden, and in the 50-64 age group for the remaining EU15 countries. In the Netherlands, the rate for women aged 25-49, nonetheless, reached 69.4%, and it was near or above 40% in Belgium, Germany and the UK in 2000, implying that part-time work was being used by relatively large numbers of women in these countries as a strategy to enable them to combine employment with family life. In Greece, which reports low part-time rates for women at all ages, the rate fell to 6.8% of total employment for the 25-49 age group. Part-time rates were also relatively low for women in the same age group in Finland, Italy, Portugal and Spain, suggesting that, in these cases, women are not resorting to part-time arrangements as a childcare option. Moreover, in Greece, Italy and Finland, relatively large proportions of women in this age group were found to be 'involuntarily' working part time in 2000: 20-29%, compared with only 2% in the Netherlands, and barely 4% in the UK (Eurostat, 2001, tables 34, 39).

Analysis of the working-time arrangements of dual-earner couples confirms the existence of different national patterns. The dominant arrangement, and preference, in France is for both partners to work medium-length, full-time hours, irrespective of whether they have children. In the Scandinavian countries, the pattern is similar. In Denmark and Sweden, where part-time hours are not uncommon, they are most often long part-time hours, and the presence of children does not significantly affect individual working hours. In Austria, Germany and the UK, the model shifts for parents from two long (UK) or medium-to-long (Austria and Germany) full-time jobs without children to long (UK) to medium (Austria and Germany) male hours and shorter female hours with children as a temporary expedient. Working patterns in the Netherlands are characterised by the widespread acceptance of short working hours for both men and women as a lifestyle choice. In Greece, Italy and Spain, where the pattern is either one or two full-time earners or a sole earner, children have little impact on long full-time hours for the relatively small numbers of women who are in employment. In Portugal, where much larger numbers of women are in paid work, the proportion of full-time, dual-earner couples is greater for couples with than without children (Rubery et al, 2001; Bielenski et al, 2002, pp 85-8; Franco and Winqvist, 2002, table 2). In CEE countries, where part-time work is rare, long working hours are the most common arrangement for dual-earner couples, irrespective of whether or not they have children.

Nor does part-time work appear to provide the answer for lone mothers. Data from the 1996 wave of the ECHP show that most lone mothers were working full time, amounting to over 90% in Denmark, Finland, Greece, Italy and Portugal. Their part-time rates were relatively high in countries where part-time working is widely available, namely Ireland (27%), the Netherlands (32%) and the UK (31%) (Chambaz, 2000, table T.03).

Harmonised data by Eurostat from national time use studies for 12 EU member states (including three CEE countries but excluding southern Europe) confirm that women with young children, particularly with children under the age of seven, reduce their paid working hours to devote more time to household tasks and childcare. They may do so either by switching to part-time work or by exiting from the labour market. Except where they leave employment altogether, the reduction in gainful work does not appear to offset the increase in unpaid working time. The total amount of time devoted to paid and unpaid work rises, especially when children are aged under seven. When they have very young children, women in Hungary and Slovenia are found to spend most time, in total, on gainful and domestic work. Women in Finland, Estonia and Hungary experience the largest increase in time spent on domestic work. The presence of older children has less of an effect on time spent on household tasks in all the countries studied, and makes very little impact on the time devoted to gainful work in the three CEE countries, Finland and Sweden. Men also devote more time to domestic and parenting tasks when they have very young children, particularly in Denmark and Sweden, but the time spent in gainful work tends to remain stable or increase (Aliaga and Winqvist, 2003, figure 5).

Whatever their family status or working-time arrangements, women across Europe continue to perform most of the domestic tasks. According to data collected in 2000 by the European Foundation for the Improvement of Living and Working Conditions, over 80% of employed women claimed they had the main responsibility for housework and shopping (Fagan and Burchell, 2002, table 13). When asked about time spent on housework and childcare, 63% of the women questioned stated they spent at least an hour a day performing housework, compared with less than 12% of men. About

41% of women said they spent an hour or more each day caring for children, compared with just over 23% of men (Paoli and Merllié, 2001, table 37).

The pattern appears to vary between countries[1], although this type of data must be treated with extreme caution, since questions may have been phrased and understood differently, particularly when they concern the concept of care. Within EU15, women in Portugal and Italy recorded the highest scores for housework, and women in the Netherlands the lowest. Scores for men were highest in Sweden, with over 25%, and lowest in Greece and Portugal, with less than 5%. Women in Belgium reported the highest scores for time spent caring for and educating children, and women in Finland the lowest. Men in Italy claimed to be more involved in childcare than women in Finland, and men in Greece were least involved.

The range was greater in the candidate countries, with Lithuania reporting the highest rate for time spent on housework by women, and Malta the lowest. Malta also displayed the lowest figure for men, and Estonia the highest. Cyprus recorded the highest rate for time spent by women caring for children, while the Czech Republic reported the lowest rate for men. The gender gap for domestic work appeared to be greatest in Cyprus and for caring in Latvia.

Matching attitudes and practice

Attitudes towards mothers' work outside the home have been evolving in line with changes in behaviour, but to a differing extent across countries, as demonstrated by the European Values Study (EVS). Over time, Europeans have become more accepting of women combining employment with family life. In the EVS 1980 survey, only a minority of respondents in western Europe upheld the traditional role of women exclusively as housewives and mothers, but the symmetrical family did not yet command the support of the majority (Harding et al, 1986, p 146). In the 1999 survey, opinion was more divided across EU15 member states on questions such as whether pre-school age children suffer if their mothers go out to work and whether being a housewife is as fulfilling as a paid job[2]. The views expressed did not, however, necessarily match attitudes towards dual earning and employment patterns. Among the southern European countries, where the gender employment gap was largest, the great majority of Greek and Italian respondents continued to feel that children suffer if their mothers go out to work, while strongly supporting dual earning. Whereas two thirds of Italians believed that being a housewife could be as fulfilling as paid work, the majority of Greeks held the opposite view. Most of the Spaniards questioned disagreed with the proposition that children suffer if their mothers work, and

---

[1] The full dataset was supplied by the European Foundation for the Improvement of Living and Working Conditions, Dublin, in 2003.

[2] This analysis is based on the 1999/2000 EVS dataset supplied by the Zentralarchiv für Empirische Sozialforschung at Cologne University in 2003.

strongly supported dual earning. In Portugal, where the gender employment gap is small, both men and women felt that children with working mothers suffer, but they were closer to Spaniards for the other two issues. Maltese respondents expressed the most conservative views on all three counts.

In the Netherlands and the UK, where the full-time equivalent gender employment gap is large due to the prevalence of part-time work, just over half of female respondents agreed that children with working mothers suffer, and nearer two thirds of Dutch and British men agreed. Respondents in both countries rejected the view that being a housewife can be as fulfilling as paid work, but attitudes towards dual earning were very different, with British respondents largely in agreement, and Dutch respondents opposed to the idea. Although the majority of French and German men and women agreed that children with working mothers suffer, the proportion was considerably higher in Germany, where support for dual earning was lower, and only a third of respondents believed that being a housewife could be as fulfilling as paid work. Respondents in the three Nordic states disagreed with the assertion that children with working mothers suffer but, in this instance, the negative response was much more strongly held in Denmark than in either Finland or Sweden. Support for dual earning was much greater in Sweden than in the other two countries, but only Finnish respondents agreed with the view that being a housewife is as fulfilling as paid work.

The CEE countries, where, under Soviet rule, women were expected to pursue continuous full-time patterns of employment, offer another configuration. Only in the Czech Republic and Slovenia did a majority of respondents disagree with the statement that children suffer if their mothers work. Dual earning was very strongly supported in all eight countries, but only in Latvia did the majority of respondents not feel that being a housewife was as fulfilling as paid work.

Although marital status, childbearing and childrearing no longer constitute an insuperable obstacle to women's employment as they often did in the past, the process of change has not taken place at the same pace or with the same intensity across Europe. Successive waves of EU membership have further contributed to the complexity of the relationship between employment and family life. Data limitations make it difficult to draw any firm conclusions about developments, but the broad patterns identified from official statistics at the end of the 20th century suggest that a variety of strategies may be required to achieve a satisfactory work–life balance.

The overall picture gained from the available data on the relationship between employment and family life in EU25 member states is presented in Figure 4.1. The graph compares different measures of labour market integration (employment and part-time rates for women aged 25-54 and full-time equivalent employment rates for women of working age), plotted against indicators for attitudes and practices with regard to the gendering of the family–employment balance (whether pre-school children with working mothers suffer, acceptance of dual earning, and time spent by men and

Figure 4.1: The relationship between employment and family life in EU25 member states (2000)

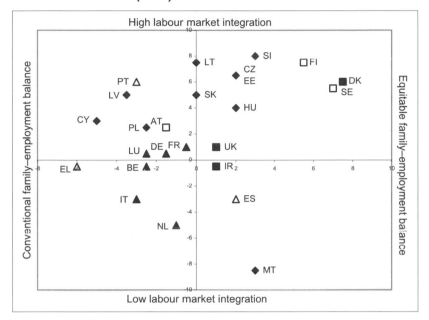

Key: ▲ 1957 members, ■ 1973 members, Δ 1981/86 members, □ 1995 members, ◆ 2004 members.

Notes: No data are available for Cyprus for the attitudinal variables.

For each indicator, the standard deviation has been calculated for the dataset. For each country cell, the deviation of each data point has been calculated from the mean for EU15 (*x*-mean) and has been compared with the value of the standard deviation for each indicator. Positive or negative values have then been assigned according to the number of SDs (0.5 points for ¼ SD, 1 point for ½ SD, 2 points for 1 SD, 4 points for 2 SDs). The scores for each group of indicators have then been added together and plotted on the *x* and *y* axes.

Sources: European Commission (2002a, pp 173-99); European Values Study (personal communication, 2003); European Foundation for the Improvement of Living and Working Conditions (personal communication, 2003).

women on household tasks and childcare). In relation to the EU15 mean, the Nordic states, four of the CEE countries and, to a lesser degree, the UK display the closest match between labour market integration and an equitable balance between family and employment. The remaining CEE countries, together with Austria, France, Germany, Luxembourg and Portugal, also show positive scores for labour market integration, but more conventional attitudes and behaviour with regard to family–employment balance. Greece, Italy, the Netherlands and, to a lesser extent, Belgium display negative scores for both sets of variables, indicating that, in these countries, women are not so well integrated into employment, and that attitudes and patterns of behaviour concerning the balance between family and employment have tended to remain more conventional, compared with other EU25 member states at the turn of the century.

Policy challenges from changes in working life

Since the founding of the European Economic Community (EEC) in 1957, as its original name implies, emphasis has been on the economic dimension of European integration. Despite efforts to move social policy onto the agenda and to place it on a par with economic policies, most European social policy, and more especially that pertaining to family life, has been introduced through measures designed primarily to improve working conditions and support employment (Hantrais, 2000b). Issues concerning work–life balance, which moved onto the agenda in the 1990s, are no exception and need to be understood in the context of the prediction that a dwindling, ageing workforce, and longer, thinner family units will be required to support an inactive, older, dependent population after the year 2010. The active population is expected to produce the resources needed to sustain pensions, health and caring, while ensuring that Europe remains competitive within the global economy. This section examines the debates raised by changes in working life and the challenges they present for policy actors.

Sustaining the labour supply

In a context where unemployment was seen as the major scourge of the 1980s and 1990s, a related issue, increasingly debated at the end of the 20th century, was how to encourage active ageing and foster employability so as to utilise the active population to the full in meeting the needs of a growing dependent population. The issue of labour shortages and underemployment of human resources moved up the EU agenda. Since the mid-1990s, the European Commission (2002d, p 10) has been active in developing policy responses to the predicted longer-term downturn in the labour supply and the need to modernise social protection systems to cope with the consequences of accelerated population ageing. It argued that the potential of the labour supply was not being used to maximum effect because younger and older workers, and women across the age spectrum, were not participating in the labour force to their full capacity (Rubery and Smith, 1999).

This chapter has shown that not all EU15 member states and candidate countries were being affected to the same extent and in the same way by the reduction in the size of the labour force, changing patterns of employment and working arrangements. In some cases, particularly the Nordic states, the labour supply already depended heavily on the contribution of older workers and on women of childbearing age. In others, especially the southern European countries, the potential for women to enter and remain in employment was still largely untapped, and considerable numbers of older women were, technically, available to contribute to the labour force.

For an equivalent level of educational achievement, women have continued to display lower labour market activity rates than men. This raises the issue of how to prevent the labour market and, therefore, the economy losing out on women's skills and training. The 'wasted resources' argument makes the implicit, but debatable, assumption that paid employment is the only worthwhile and productive activity contributing to national wealth, and that time spent outside paid work rearing a family is 'wasted'. While the most affluent and best-educated women have been increasing their economic activity rates and commitment to the labour market by entering full-time, well-paid, highly-qualified employment, poorly-qualified women have been pursuing more irregular patterns of employment corresponding to the male breadwinner model, which raises issues about the divide between job-rich and job-poor families and how to reduce differentials in household income from employment.

The economic advantages of dual-earner families are widely promoted in the literature: family income is increased and, hence, general well being; women are less dependent on male breadwinners; the risk of unemployment and job insecurity is lower; children are protected against poverty; and qualifications are not wasted. To some extent, these arguments assume that families function best with two full-time earners, who readily outsource childcare from an early age to nurseries or childminders. They raise questions about the quality of family life and the sort of upbringing children receive in job-rich, but time-poor, families if mothers seek a return on their investment in education by remaining economically active. They also provoke debate about the role of public policy as a driving force.

Reducing gender inequalities

At EU level, gender issues have long been a focus of policy interest, culminating in the 1990s with mainstreaming. Debate has centred on how to improve equality of opportunity in employment in a situation where legislation at EU and national level since the 1970s does not appear to have achieved the gains anticipated. Even though women are nowadays more often engaging in paid employment outside the home on a longer-term and more continuous basis than in the past, and have been adopting patterns closer to those of men, concern is still expressed in the literature and the media about the persistence of inequalities in working arrangements and conditions. In the context of the European employment strategy (COM(2003) 6 final, 14.01.2003), access to training and employment among women has continued to be a focus for policy measures, aimed at reducing unemployment and improving the quality of employment. EU membership commits governments to introducing national legislation on equal pay and treatment, provision for maternity and parental leave, and improvements in childcare, but concern is expressed about the effectiveness of national laws and the cost of implementation for the state and employers.

The development of more flexible working-time patterns has been associated with the casualisation of employment and segregated labour markets. Across the Union, questions are being raised about the extent to which flexibility in the form of part-time or temporary work, unsocial hours and weekend work, or overtime and additional hours at short notice, are women friendly. When women take part-time and casual jobs because they cannot find full-time work, the jobs offered may not give them the opportunity to choose hours that are compatible with family commitments.

An interesting finding from the comparisons in this chapter is the extent to which gender relations take on a different meaning in the transition countries. While public debate in EU15 member states has focused on issues of equality of opportunity, equal treatment and reconciliation of family life with employment, where women are the main players, transition has brought dramatic changes in labour market opportunities, particularly for women, calling into question their status as workers. While governments in the EU15 member states were addressing the need for measures to assist couples in reconciling paid work outside the home with raising children, CEE countries had moved away from a situation where women were forced by state policy to pursue full-time jobs and to avail themselves of publicly provided childcare services. Transition meant, in the early years, that women were, for the first time, given the choice of whether to stay at home and look after their own children or go out to work. However, their choice was soon to be restricted due to financial necessity, since they needed the income from work to make ends meet. Problems of finding suitably paid jobs and the introduction of charges for childcare and other domestic services transformed the choice into a dilemma for many couples. To a large extent, the situation of women in the post-Soviet era has been made worse by the fact that the traditional distribution of household labour has been perpetuated, if not reinforced, as exemplified by Hungary where the homemaker role of women has been given a fresh impetus (Neményi and Tóth, 2003). The issue is not, therefore, how to assist families in organising childcare, but rather how to create jobs that pay a living wage.

A related question, which has come increasingly to the fore, is the extent to which the individualisation of social rights, for example in taxation and benefits systems, in place of derived rights, can be turned to the advantage of women in a labour market where they continue to operate under different conditions from men, and where the social protection system was founded on a model corresponding to male working patterns. The individualisation of social protection rights tends to be conceptualised negatively in CEE countries. Under Soviet rule, when most women followed full-time uninterrupted employment patterns and contributed to their own pensions, they could expect to receive a reasonable income on retirement. The tight labour market since transition has meant they are increasingly unable to ensure adequate pensions in their own right and have, thereby, lost much of their relative independence.

Combining paid work with family life

As more mothers have entered and returned to the labour force after periods of leave, and when their children grow older, a major issue for public debate across Europe has been the reconciliation of family life and employment and the balance between employment and other activities for both men and women. Although the question had moved onto the agenda of the European Commission in the 1970s, agreement was not reached until the 1990s over specific measures to help couples combine paid and unpaid work (Hantrais, 2000b). The extent to which national governments have sought to respond to the challenge of how to promote a more equitable work–life balance for both men and women varies from one country to another according to whether strategies for reconciling the two areas of activity are seen primarily as a matter for families themselves, the state or other policy actors. It also depends on the legitimacy accorded by different societies to state intervention in family life and the social and economic acceptance of women in the labour market.

In the Nordic states and France, the reconciliation of paid and unpaid work became an issue for governments as early as the 1960s, and women-friendly policies have long been a priority. In Sweden, the debate over parental insurance in the 1970s centred on equality issues. Incentives to encourage men to take parental leave have been advocated as a means of moving away from the male breadwinner concept. In France, an important issue in the debate that took place in the 1980s was how the state could support women's participation in the labour force, while enabling them to maintain their reproductive activity in the national interest. The extension of paid parental leave in 1994 raised the issue of whether benefits might act as a disincentive for women to engage in economic activity.

In more recent years in the Nordic states and in France, interest has focused on how to achieve a more equitable work–balance, on the one hand by enabling women to participate more fully in labour market activity and, on the other, although less explicitly, as a reconciliation issue for families. In France, policy on the reduction in working time has modified the continuous, long working hours model generally adopted by men, with the effect that the working patterns of both men and women are, technically, more compatible with family life and men's participation in household tasks.

In the UK, the starting point in discussions has long been the unquestioned assumption of gender role segregation, based on the male breadwinner model. New Labour challenged the model and relaunched the debate by proposing policies designed to get (lone) mothers and the partners of unemployed claimants back into work, essentially with the aim of reducing reliance on welfare. At the same time, proposals for enhancing the work–life balance have become an increasingly important component in the business case made for retaining highly skilled women (and men) with family responsibilities (Department of Trade and Industry, 2001).

In Ireland, where welfare-to-work schemes have also been actively promoted, negotiations over the supply of household labour have given little recognition to family responsibilities or to the question of how they will be carried out as more women, the traditional household workers, enter employment. Nor has the issue of reconciling paid work and family life been high on the agenda in the southern European countries, where families are left to make their own arrangements with minimal support from the state.

As women have become less available as unpaid carers due to their labour market participation, concern has grown about the inadequacy of care facilities and the impending care deficit. In most countries, questions are being raised about how to pay for care (public and/or private) and ensure that the new domestic service jobs being created do not intensify social differentiation, since they are mostly low-status women's jobs and may not be recognised in the formal economy and social protection system.

Reactions to the extension of flexibility in working time are ambivalent. Flexibility is regarded both as a means of combining paid work with family responsibilities, and as a way of locking women into low-paid, insecure jobs, particularly if they are seen as the only option available for employees, rather than being freely chosen or negotiated. Efficiency gains for employers may mean low incomes and organisational problems for employees. The possible effects of flexible working patterns on career progression and employment-related rights have, therefore, attracted growing attention at EU and national level.

The impact of changing working patterns on the sharing of domestic tasks, particularly care work, is another issue provoking public and political debate in many countries, following the introduction under EU law of entitlement to parental leave for men in Council Directive 96/34/EC and the Recommendation on childcare (92/241/EEC, *Official Journal* L 123/16, 08.05.1992). Consequently, governments are being called upon to introduce measures to encourage more men to become involved in care work.

In CEE countries, high levels of female economic activity during the Soviet era did not result in more equal sharing of domestic labour. Economic restructuring in the 1990s forced women out of the labour market and into the home, thereby pushing care work back onto families and perpetuating gender divisions. The main issue for governments was not how to encourage women back into the workforce as a means of bolstering the labour supply, but how to ensure that families can secure a living wage, thereby enabling them to be both self-sufficient and, at the same time, committed to family life.

FIVE

Changing welfare needs

The challenges posed for societies as a result of population decline and ageing, the spread of de-institutionalised family forms, and changes in the generational contract, working patterns and the family–employment relationship have reopened debates about the role the state can and should play in family life. A question that many governments in western Europe were addressing at the turn of the 21st century was how far to proceed with legislation formalising alternative family living arrangements. Although a major driving force for welfare reform in the 1990s in the 15 member states of the European Union (EU) was the need to meet the criteria for Economic and Monetary Union (EMU) and reduce unemployment, politicians were under growing pressure to respond to public demand for improvements in the quality of life both at work and in the home. The reaction of most governments to EMU was welfare retrenchment and the overhaul of benefits and services, often involving cutbacks in provision for families (Rostgaard and Fridberg, 1998). At the same time, the predicted negative consequences of population ageing were prompting pre-emptive action to ensure that the long-term financial and care needs of older people could be met (Walker and Naegele, 1999). Growing concern about impending labour and skills shortages, in conjunction with welfare entrenchment, was stimulating the development of schemes to shift the recipients of welfare off benefits and into work through more active employment policies (European Commission, 2002d). Coming at the same time as renewed emphasis on equality of opportunity, incentives to encourage women to become economically active were sharpening questions about how to deal with the care needs of younger and older dependants when women were no longer available as primary carers (Rubery et al, 1999; Carling et al, 2002; Mooney et al, 2002). In the candidate countries of Central and Eastern Europe (CEE), which joined the Union in 2004, the social reform process was being driven by the need to adopt the EU's social *acquis* and meet the requirements for EMU in a context where transition had brought far-reaching structural change to the economy, necessitating costly adaptations to welfare systems and labour markets (Ferge, 1997; Berglund et al, 1998; Elster et al, 1998; Pascall and

Manning, 2000; Rys, 2001). The debates surrounding welfare reform in the early 21st century provide a further indication of the relative, although not always explicit, importance of family matters on national policy agendas.

This chapter analyses how changes in family structures and intrafamilial relationships have been taken into account in legal codes and compares the ways in which families as units and their members as individual citizens are conceptualised by public administration. The concluding section considers the extent to which state and family share responsibility for the welfare of dependants in different cultural environments, and it looks at how the interactive process between them is being reconfigured in response to socio-economic change.

Families in law and practice

Civil law and statutes at national level govern marriage and family formation and the legal rights and duties they entail. National legislation reflects differences in philosophical and religious traditions, in the pace and timing of social processes and the level of public support for reform. Analysis of the development of family and marriage law shows that the legal status of family members is a divisive topic. Decisions taken on matters relating to family life are regularly the subject of acrimonious public and parliamentary debate. Most EU member states and candidate countries have experienced the conflicts associated with the introduction of legislative reform to liberalise divorce, to lay down the conditions for custody and maintenance following divorce, and to recognise children born out of wedlock, and the rights of unmarried cohabiting couples. As issues regarding same-sex couples have moved onto political agendas, they have proved to be even more contentious. This section is intended to provide a better understanding of the relative importance of family-related issues in the legislative process by tracking the development of national law and practice with regard to marital status and intrafamilial obligations and duties[1].

Adapting marriage and family law

Across EU15 and beyond, governments have been adapting legislation to reflect changing patterns of marriage and its secularisation. They have recognised the need for couples to be able to undo the ties of marriage if their relationship breaks down, and for the interests of children to be taken into account as the marital situation evolves. An indication of the extent to which marriage has been secularised in EU member states is provided by the

---

[1] Unless otherwise indicated, the material referred to in this section was collected by the partners in a Framework Programme 5 project, funded by the European Commission (see Acknowledgements). Additional information about the situation in the candidate countries is drawn from a series of unpublished social protection reports prepared by national experts for the European Commission in 2003.

fact that it no longer has to be celebrated in a church. Some countries have gone a step further: in Sweden and the UK, for example, weddings can now be conducted in a place other than a registry office. CEE countries have moved on from a situation where church weddings were not officially approved of during the Soviet era: since 1998 in Poland and 2001 in Estonia, church and civil ceremonies have been given equal status in law.

Changes in marriage law can have an impact on statistics, as noted in Chapter Three. In Poland, for instance, a change in the regulations regarding civil status in 1968 meant that religious marriage was prohibited before contracting and registering a civil marriage. The regulation was annulled in 1989 and, since 1998, under the terms of a concordat signed by the Polish government and Holy See, both marriages contracted in a Roman Catholic Church and civil marriages are recognised. During the nine years between the annulment of the regulation and the concordat, many religious marriages may, therefore, have gone unrecorded (Kazimierz, 2000).

Marriage law has traditionally laid down the legal rights and duties of spouses in terms of property, power and authority within wedlock. Progressively, over the postwar period, national law and practice have been adapted to take account of changing attitudes towards equality between women and men within the marital relationship. As average age at marriage has been rising, and equal rights have moved onto the agenda at EU and national level, the legal age of marriage for women has progressively been aligned with that for men at 18, while allowing for marriage at a younger age with parental consent. Across the Union, marriage no longer constitutes a formal bar to women's employment, and marriage law often stipulates that husbands cannot prevent their wives from entering paid work outside the home, from opening their own bank account or owning property. By law, spouses have equal rights and duties within marriage, even if some religious ceremonies still retain references to the duty of the wife to obey (optional in the case of the Church of England). Whether or not they marry in a church, couples are expected to live together, to be faithful to one another and to provide mutual support and assistance.

In several countries, couples are prepared for marriage not only by the church. Despite the traditional resistance in the UK to codifying obligations and responsibilities within couples, preparation for marriage is an area where governments have shown a growing willingness to intervene in an attempt to support family life. In their 1998 Green Paper, 'Supporting families: a consultation document', the British government set out to promote a more responsible approach to marriage, proposing that couples should be encouraged to make legally binding written agreements about the distribution of money and property, and be better prepared for marriage.

In some cases, the law is very specific about the obligations and responsibilities of married couples. The 1918 Marriage Code applied under Soviet rule in the CEE countries laid down precepts that treated women in marriage more equally than in most of western Europe at that time.

Subsequent marriage and family law has upheld these principles. Article 61 of the Polish Family and Custody Code (1994, 1998) states, for example, that spouses have equal rights and obligations in marriage. They must live together, support each other, be faithful and work together for the good of the family they have created. Although the state does not undertake to help prepare couples for married life, the Catholic Church obliges couples intending to contract marriage to follow a programme of lectures offered by parishes. Estonian law affords another example of the binding legal requirements that marriage imposes on couples. Spouses are required to maintain a partner in need of assistance and unable to work. A husband must support his wife during pregnancy and while she is caring for a child up to the age of three, if the financial situation of the obligated spouse permits. As noted in Chapter Three, however, census enumerators in Estonia do not record a person as married unless the legal spouse is living in the same household (Statistical Office of Estonia, 1999, § 39.14).

Under the Family Statute (1952/IV) in Hungarian Civil Law, the rights and responsibilities of married partners are equal. They are obliged to co-operate with one another in all matters concerning family life, including issues related to producing and raising children. Self-assertion and personal autonomy are permitted only under the condition that the 'family interest' is respected. The legal rights and responsibilities of married couples are also laid down. They owe one another faithfulness, especially in the context of sexual relations, and mutual support, involving caring for a sick partner, encouragement in pursuing educational and career opportunities and financial assistance for a partner in need. Spouses are required to use and maintain a common residence, and develop in common property obtained during their marriage, with the exception of items belonging to the partners' own private wealth.

Most national laws recognise equality of status between spouses, but the courts have not legislated to ensure that this equality is put into practice in the division of labour in the home. Exceptionally, the Marriage Act in Sweden does go some way towards laying down guidelines for the distribution of household labour, stating that spouses shall divide expenses and chores between them, and that both spouses, to the best of their ability, shall contribute as necessary to meeting their common and individual needs.

Parental rights and duties are usually made explicit in national family law when it has been adapted to reflect changes in family living arrangements. Most family law includes the right and duty to raise and care for children. As it has become easier, technically, to establish paternity, children have acquired the right to know the identity of their parents, and the legal pursuit of absent fathers has been instituted. The extent to which these duties and responsibilities are shared with the state varies from one country to another, depending largely on attitudes towards the legitimacy of state intervention in family matters (see also Chapter Six).

In some cases, mainly in northern Europe, the legal responsibility of parents for their children ceases when they reach the age of 18, or later if they remain in education. In Italy, by contrast, since 1975, parents are expected to maintain their children for an unlimited period of time. The Civil Code in Lithuania stipulates that adult children, including grandchildren, must maintain disabled or needy parents and grandparents. The Polish Constitution of 1997 sets out not only the duties of parents, including their right to bring up their children according to their own moral and religious convictions, but also the financial responsibility of parents for their children after the age of 18, and until the age of 24 if they remain in education. Hungarian Civil Law (Statutes 1997/XXXI, 1998/LXXXIV) specifies the obligations and responsibilities of parents. They include co-operation with children, respect for their human dignity, providing them with information and advice, enabling them to learn and exercise their rights and helping them to avoid lifestyles that pose a risk to health. The law also lays down the most important obligations of children towards their parents, including the duty to co-operate with them or with official guardians.

The protection of children and of their interests is paramount across the Union. If parents are unable to carry out their parenting responsibilities, regulations lay down the conditions under which children can be taken into care and given for adoption. In all EU15 member states except Greece, children can be formally removed from their home environment if their parents fail to perform their caring duties adequately or put their children at risk. The extent to which the state exercises the right to remove children from the parental home varies considerably from one country to another. In 2002, for example, the organisation Children in Need in the UK reported that some 59,000 children were in care, whereas the French Ministry for Justice put the figure as high as 150,000 in France in 2003.

In the past, adoption was practised largely as a means of ensuring that children who were orphaned or abandoned could grow up in a secure family environment, while also allowing childless couples to experience parenthood. As the number of children available for adoption within EU15 has fallen, governments have sought to tighten up legislation to ensure that the interests and welfare of children are protected, while also scrutinising the criteria for selecting adoptive parents. The state, through it agents, is thus determining who is considered suitable for parenthood. In the CEE countries, the large number of children in care, because they have been orphaned or abandoned, is seen as an indication of the financial and practical problems parents face in raising their children. In Poland, for example, during the 1990s, the proportion of children not living with their families increased by over 10%, the number in foster families rose by more 40%, but the number of adoptions fell (Golinowska et al, 2003, p 84).

In an attempt to avoid such an extreme form of intervention, many governments have responded to family change by instituting classes for parents to help them acquire the skills needed to become good parents. The assumption is that, if they are supported in preparing for their family roles, parents will carry out their commitments to their children more effectively, thus reducing the burden on society. Training for good parenting begins in schools. In Sweden, for instance, all pupils in secondary schools are taught subjects concerned with childrearing and household life, and British governments have become active participants in the debate about the legitimacy of parenting skills in the school curriculum.

Arrangements are also made in CEE countries to help parents prepare for family life. In Estonia, for example, instruction is provided in family skills. Originally, the aim was to help mothers prepare for childbirth and the care of new babies, but the target then shifted towards preparing both the mother and father together for parenthood. Measures introduced during the 1990s were generally intended for parents who were considered to have poorly developed parenting skills, particularly young mothers. In Poland, provision is made for tuition in parenting skills by non-governmental organisations (NGOs) and, especially, by the Catholic Church for couples intending to have a religious wedding. Parenting classes are mandatory in preparation for adoption in Poland.

Adapting divorce law

The rising trend in divorce is contingent on the reform of divorce law. While all countries have long-standing laws regulating the age of marriage and of consent, divorce was not made legal across all EU15 member states until 1996 when the courts in Ireland were given the power to pronounce a decree of divorce. In 2003, divorce had still not been legalised in Malta. In most countries, procedures have been progressively simplified, and recourse to divorce has become more widespread, as illustrated by the statistics presented in Chapter Three. The greater frequency of divorce and the increasing economic autonomy of women have raised issues about the obligations of partners towards each other if the marriage breaks down, particularly if either of them forms a new partnership, which affects maintenance and pension entitlements. Arrangements for pensions after divorce are, for example, being adapted to give former spouses the right to a share of the pension earned during the years of marriage, as explained in the next section.

In CEE countries, the law clearly defines the duties of former spouses. In Estonia, for example, where divorce is regulated by the 1994 Family Law Act, the obligation to support a former spouse, economic circumstances permitting, applies if s/he is unable to work or on maternity leave at the time of the divorce, or attained pensionable age during the marriage. It does not apply if the marriage had lasted less than three years, or if the former spouse remarries. In Poland, the law on divorce dates from 1945, but legal separation for Catholics was not introduced until 1999. Separated couples are expected to continue to be faithful to one another and to provide assistance if needed. The arrangement for maintenance depends upon the conditions under which the divorce was pronounced. A spouse not considered to be at fault is under an obligation to pay maintenance for only five years, and the obligation ceases on remarriage.

Governments have intervened to ensure that changes in living arrangements are also reflected in the provision made for the protection of children after divorce. In most cases, legislators have given priority to ensuring that the harmful effects of divorce or separation on dependent children are minimised and that, wherever possible, parents assume joint responsibility for the custody of their children. Although, in most instances, the preference may still be for women to be granted custody after divorce, increasingly joint custody is being promoted as a way of ensuring that men share day-to-day responsibility for bringing up children.

Such provisions show considerable variations across countries. At the one extreme, every effort is made to ensure that parents share responsibility equitably between them, taking account of the child's best interest. At the other, the mother is almost automatically given custody. Sweden was one of the first countries in the Union to introduce joint custody in 1974. It became the general rule in France in 1993, and in Germany in 1998. Since the 1989 Children Act, custody is resolved privately and informally whenever possible in the UK. In Ireland, the mother's agreement is needed for joint custody to be awarded. Although custody after divorce is generally given to the mother in Spain, parental authority remains with both parents, and they must take decisions together about matters such as the child's education or medical treatment in the case of severe illness. By contrast, in Italy, only negligible use is made of the provision for shared custody and, in Greece, only one parent can have custody. In Poland, the courts decide whether to award joint custody or whether to grant custody to one parent, but in practice women are generally given custody, and the courts decide about the rights and obligations of the father.

As divorce rates have climbed, the issue of maintenance payments once marriage is dissolved has become of critical concern for many governments, particularly in a situation where more complex family structures are ensuing as families reconstitute. Many countries are implementing measures designed to impose a legal obligation on absent fathers to make them provide maintenance for dependent children and their former spouse. In most EU member states, the law requires that children who live with one of their biological parents should receive maintenance from the other parent. Liable parents are usually expected to pay a sum calculated according to the number of children and based on an assessment of their financial means, irrespective of the custodial parent's income. The liable parent's responsibility to provide maintenance continues until children reach the age of 18, or for so long as they are at school.

Some governments, often amid strong public opposition, not least from bodies supporting fathers, have introduced compulsory recovery of maintenance payments and other measures to punish defaulting parents. In

Germany, Finland, France, Hungary, Italy, Sweden and Slovenia, the state acts as a guarantor for lone parents in cases where the absent parent fails to make maintenance payments. The liable parent is generally pursued after divorce or separation, except in Greece, and failure to observe maintenance obligations can result in fines or imprisonment for defaulters. In France, deductions can be made from wages and through the tax office. A prison sentence of three years and a fine can also be imposed for non-payment in cases where a deliberate attempt is being made to avoid liability (article 314-7 of the Penal Code). In the UK, the role of government is seen as enforcing parental responsibility, sometimes using punitive measures as a means of enabling children to gain access to financial support. Beyond the level of financial commitment, however, policy does not clearly define the obligations of parents after divorce, because of political unwillingness to become more closely involved in matters that are seen as belonging to the private domain.

The formal arrangements made in CEE countries are also aimed primarily at ensuring that natural parents (usually fathers) assume financial responsibility for their offspring. Under Soviet rule, the state initiated a search for the defaulting parent. In Estonia, the state no longer intervenes in the process, but maintenance may be deducted from employees' wages without their consent. If former spouses are unable to pay, the lone-parent family becomes eligible to receive social assistance. Under Polish family law, courts decide on the level of maintenance payments, which have to be made by absent parents until their children reach the age of 18, or 24 if they are still in education. Central government pays an advance on maintenance for parents who default, and then pursues them through the courts, resulting in prison sentences for those who persistently refuse to fulfil their obligations. In Hungary, if necessary, the state also intervenes to ensure that absent fathers contribute to the maintenance of their children. If the defaulting father cannot be traced, the state pays alimony for a maximum of three years, which can be renewed. If the absent parent is finally traced, he will have to pay back, with interest, the money advanced by the state. In some cases, the assets of the parent who has fallen into arrears can also be confiscated (Statute 1997/XXXI of the Hungarian Civil Law).

These examples illustrate the extent to which the state steps in to regulate the situation and punish parents who fail to comply with their legal responsibilities and duties to care for family members when formal marital relationships break down. The law is more hesitant about how to deal with cases where partnerships have not been formalised, although the interests of children remain paramount in legislation.

Adapting legislation to alternative family living arrangements

In parallel with the shift in legislation towards greater emphasis on the responsibilities and duties of parents with regard to their children, and the strengthening of the rights of children as individuals, legislators have turned their attention to alternative living arrangements and, especially, to the policy implications of unmarried cohabitation and lone parenthood.

The Nordic states were the first of the EU15 member states to give formal recognition to non-conventional marriage and parenting by introducing contracts for unmarried cohabitees in the 1980s, initially in Denmark in 1989 and then in 1995 in Sweden. A few other EU15 member states have followed the Scandinavian example. In the Netherlands, the registration of cohabitation has been possible since 1998, bringing the legal rights of unmarried cohabiting couples into line with those of married couples. France recognised cohabiting partners as legitimate dependants in 1978 and, in 1999, introduced a formal contract for unmarried cohabiting couples: the *pacte civil de solidarité* (*pacs*) (Festy, 2001). Among other provisions, after three years, couples who register their partnership are entitled to submit joint tax returns, unlike other unmarried cohabiting couples who have to make separate returns. In Germany, the *Lebenspartnerschaftsgesetz*, which was adopted in 2001, gives unmarried cohabiting couples the opportunity to register their partnership legally. In the absence of national legislation, in Spain during the 1990s, several autonomous communities began introducing their own regulations, and mayors in some towns and villages opened voluntary registers for cohabiting partners. As a result, *de facto* couples are afforded the same conditions as married couples in terms of benefits and services provided at regional and local level. In Catalonia, when partners have been living together for at least two years, they are regarded as being in a stable relationship, which opens access to certain specified rights.

Hungary affords an interesting example of the way in which unmarried cohabitation has gained more formal recognition without entailing the constraints of marriage or formal registration. The Family and Custody Code (1964, 1998) does not mention unmarried cohabitation, but cohabitation is codified for couples who are considered to be 'life companions' (Statute 1959/IV of Hungarian Civil Law). To qualify, unmarried partners must form an economic unit and live together in the same household without being next of kin. They must have developed close emotional ties and a sexual relationship, and have raised children together. 'Life companionship' can be compared with common law marriage. It differs from registered partnership in that it provides only limited rights for unmarried couples.

Governments elsewhere have been reluctant to introduce legislation to regulate the relationships between unmarried cohabitees, mainly on the grounds that they do not want to remove remaining differences between marriage and less formal relationships. Where it does apply, legislation on unmarried partnerships has served to regulate the rights to property jointly acquired by cohabiting partners. In Sweden, the Cohabitees Act, which came into force in 1988, contains provision for dividing joint property when the relationship ends. Initially, it applied only to jointly owned dwellings and household goods. In 1999, it was extended to include motor vehicles.

Unmarried couples are still unable to inherit from each other in the event of the death of one party, unless they have drawn up a will. By contrast, legislation regulating community of property for married couples in the Netherlands applies equally to unmarried couples. In Spain, the right of spouses to inherit a rent contract after the death of a spouse was extended to cohabiting couples following a case brought before the Constitutional Court in 1992, which resulted in new legislation to remove the anomaly.

The position in Estonia with regard to property and housing is that an unmarried cohabiting couple can confirm common ownership in a joint statement. When proof has been presented of common ownership of property, the survivor in the event of the death of one of the partners is entitled to inherit up to half the property. If provision for inheritance is made in the will of the deceased, it is not contested. In Hungary, if one of the partners in a life companionship couple dies, the survivor can inherit jointly acquired property. However, in the state housing sector, the survivor must move out of the common rented dwelling, since it is not possible for 'life companions' to inherit the legal tenancy title.

As marital bonds have weakened, and alternative living arrangements have become more widespread, a major concern of legislators has been to ensure that the interests of children are protected. The mutual rights and obligations between parents and children are dependent on filiation, as proven by procedures laid down in law. In theory, parents may, therefore, be expected to have the same duties towards their offspring whether or not they are married. In all EU15 member states and most CEE countries, unmarried parents have an obligation to maintain their children. Usually, parental responsibility is not automatic: the father has to be legally recognised. In France, the parents must be living together. In Sweden, the father has to make an application, and the mother must consent.

Law and practice are in a state of flux with regards to adoption by the new partner of the child, or children, from a previous relationship when they form a reconstituted family. In most instances, such families are ill defined and difficult to measure, as demonstrated in Chapter Three. They therefore tend to be poorly targeted in family law. In many countries, even if the child is not formally adopted, stepparents are considered to be under a moral obligation towards stepchildren. In Sweden, the legal obligations of stepparents in reconstituted families are clearly laid down: biological parents continue to have the right to joint custody. Stepparents can adopt their stepchildren, although custody cannot be granted to more than two people. Under family law in Finland, only natural parents are responsible for the maintenance of their children; stepparents are under no obligation. In the UK, legally stepparents can adopt children from a previous relationship of their partner, but in practice adoption agencies often recommend that children maintain the formal relationship with their natural parents and keep their original surname. In France, following the publication of a number of reports on changes in family law in the late 1990s (Théry, 1998; Dekeuwer-

Defossez, 1999), the government was considering introducing provisions for stepfathers to take responsibility for raising stepchildren. A literal interpretation of article 203 of the French Civil Code obliges a stepparent to maintain only children born within marriage, but case law has led to recognition that the same rights should be granted to children born out of wedlock, whether from a former marriage or partner of one member of the newly formed couple.

Among CEE countries, examples can also be found of the transfer of responsibilities to reconstituted family units. In Estonia, the moral obligation on stepparents to maintain stepchildren can be translated into a legal duty through adoption. In practice, however, few cases are cited in law of biological parents handing over their parental rights to stepparents, and the child can be adopted only if the biological parents relinquish their rights. In Poland, the children of a spouse who remarries are considered by law to be members of the reconstituted family, and the new parents have responsibility for their maintenance and upbringing in accordance with the same rules as those governing parents of the first union. Following the breakdown of marriage in Hungary, many couples prefer not to formalise a new relationship through remarriage, and the legal obligations of stepparents were an area of almost total policy vacuum at the turn of the century.

Countries that have enacted legislation to regulate the relationships between unmarried cohabiting couples have generally extended their laws to same-sex cohabiting couples. The 1999 Cohabitees Act in Sweden replaced a previous act covering same-sex couples. The concept of 'cohabitee' thus refers to unmarried cohabiting couples irrespective of sex. The provisions of legislation on same-sex partnerships introduced in the Netherlands in 1998 have been widely adopted. The *pacs* in France, the *Lebenspartnerschafts-gesetz* in Germany and the municipal registers opened in Spain for cohabiting couples apply to both heterosexual and same-sex partnerships. In Catalonia, in cases where same-sex couples have not drawn up a will, the survivor is, by law, automatically the beneficiary. In Hungary, a decision of the Constitutional Court found that the law (14/1995) limiting partnerships to those formed between adult men and women was unconstitutional. A reform was, therefore, introduced in 1996, enabling same-sex couples to draw up private cohabitation contracts. After six years of debate, a law came into force in Finland in 2002 enabling same-sex couples to register their partnerships, although the rights it conferred were confined to inheritance and property. A bill was passed in the Belgium parliament in 2003, which made it possible for same-sex couples to marry and, thereby, to obtain the same rights as married heterosexual couples.

Adoption by same-sex couples is an area where the law has generally proved to be inflexible, although loopholes exist in cases where single people are entitled to adopt a child. In Sweden, a custodial parent does not lose the right to custody of children if s/he decides to live with a partner of the same sex, but Swedish law does not allow same-sex couples to adopt children. Despite the absence of formal registration for unmarried cohabiting couples in the UK, § 68 of the Adoption and Children Act 2002, which overhauled the 1976 Adoption Act and modernised the existing legal framework for adoption, specified that adoptive parents could be partners of the same sex. Adoption agencies and the courts are left to decide whether, irrespective of sex, a couple is suitable to adopt on the grounds that the partners have a lasting and stable relationship and can provide a loving family environment for the child. The right of same-sex couples to adopt has been accepted in the provinces of Asturias and Navarra in Spain. Elsewhere in the country, they can adopt individually but not as couples, which is also the case in Estonia, for instance.

These examples suggest that the countries where alternative living arrangements are most developed are also generally those where legislation has been adapted to accommodate non-conventional family forms, thereby enabling family members to legitimate their situation. The countries that appear to have gone furthest in liberalising family law are mainly in northern Europe, although Spain affords an interesting illustration of a situation where, in the absence of national legislation, the initiative can come from regional governments. Some municipalities in Italy have also introduced more liberal provisions than are catered for in national legislation.

Administrative definitions and concepts of families

The definitions of family and household adopted in national censuses and surveys, and also in family law, are intended to provide information and a framework that can be used for administrative purposes (see Chapter Three). Governments have an interest in knowing how many and what size of homes need to be built, the number of places required in education, training and employment, and the level of demand for medical and social care. They are expected to plan to meet the requirements for public provision, much of which must be paid for by levying taxes on incomes, goods and services. For the purposes of providing benefits and public services, and for tax collection, the relevant unit may be the legally constituted married or unmarried cohabiting couple, with or without children, or the individual. In determining the liability of family members for one another, public administration may also be interested in more distant relatives beyond the co-resident family or household unit.

Entitlement to benefits often depends upon how relationships within families are conceptualised, and on what is defined as the 'benefit family' (Roll, 1991), which may or may not correspond to changing international statistical concepts. As a result, the same family status and living arrangements may be treated differently from one country to another and over time. This section begins by examining how family relationships are conceptualised for administrative purposes, before going on to explore how families are defined as recipients of benefits.

Changing concepts of family relationships in public administration

When social security systems were being developed in the postwar period in western Europe, the 'preferred' model was that of the conventional family, consisting of a married couple living together with their children, where the husband was the sole or main breadwinner (Lewis, 1992). Women were designated as housewives, and they and their children were entitled to welfare as dependants rather than in their own right. As more women have joined the labour force, and as equality of opportunity and treatment has been actively pursued, the concept of the male breadwinner family has been adapted to become the adult breadwinner model (Lewis, 2002, p 53), but it has not disappeared altogether. In the Bismarckian welfare states, and particularly in Austria and Germany, where benefit entitlement is earned essentially through employment, access to social protection by women and children may still be dependent on marriage and family relationships. Southern European welfare systems were also largely premised on the conservative welfare model, to the extent that they have been described as having an even stronger commitment to the male breadwinner/female carer model than the conservative countries in continental Europe (Guillén and Álvarez, 2001, p 104). Although employment was the mediator for state welfare provision during the Soviet era, in a context of job shortages, a marked trend since transition in CEE countries has been a shift towards conservative insurance-based welfare policies, in which the legitimate role of women is held to be as housewife and mother subordinated to a male breadwinner (Pascall and Manning, 2000; Ferge, 2001b, p 139).

Following the example of the Nordic states, where the concepts of universal rights and equal treatment in social protection have been most actively pursued, the move away from the concept of derived rights to individualised social insurance contributions, taxation and benefits has confirmed the weakening of the male breadwinner model in EU15. Individualisation means that women are entitled to receive benefits in their own right, either as citizens or residents in the case of universal provision, or through their own work in the case of employment-related benefits based on their insurance record[2]. For example, in countries with universal healthcare systems funded from general taxation – Denmark, Finland, Portugal, Sweden and the UK – all residents are covered individually. In systems based on the insurance principle, entitlements for close relatives who are not insured in their own right through employment are determined by the relationship between the contributor and his/her dependants (MISSOC, 2003, table II 4). In the past, women who left the labour force to raise children did not gain

---

[2] The detailed information provided in this section about national social protection systems is taken mainly from annual reports on social protection produced by the European Commission for EU15 member states (MISSOC) and by the Council of Europe for the candidate countries (MISSCEO).

entitlements to pensions on the basis of their own social insurance contributions record. As more women have remained in the labour force, or returned to it after a childrearing break, they are earning entitlement to a pension of their own. In this respect, Malta affords an example of an unusual situation where single women receive the same level of pension as their male counterparts, but where only married men, not women, are entitled to the higher rate of benefit payable to married persons.

Another illustration of the application of individual rights is when women on maternity and parental leave continue to be considered as economically active. Under European law, women who are entitled to reinstatement in their previous employment, or eligible to resume receipt of unemployment benefits after the leave period, are not deemed to have interrupted their employment contract (see Chapter Four). Maternity, parental and childcare leave are thus recognised as periods of activity for the purposes of calculating pensions and other employment-related entitlements. In Italy and Portugal, maternity is treated in the same way as time off work for illness, military service and unemployment (MISSOC, 2003, table VI 4).

Periods spent out of the labour market may be taken into account in the calculation of pension entitlements either as credits for years of service or by reducing the number of years required to qualify for a full pension. Conditions vary considerably from one country to another, ranging from no provision in Denmark and the Netherlands to a maximum of three years for children born after 1992 in Germany, and four years per child in Austria, of which 18 months are counted as contribution periods. Mothers in France are entitled to a credit of two years of insurance per child, and parental leave of up to three years is taken into account in calculating the employment record. The first year of parental leave is considered as a period of effective contributions in Spain. Since 1978, the UK has operated a system of Home Responsibilities Protection: if a minimum of 20 years of contributions has been paid, time spent at home in care work is discounted for a full pension. Similarly, in Ireland, up to 20 years spent out of the labour market in care work can be disregarded for the purposes of calculating pension entitlements. In Greece, women insured before 1992, with children who are minors, are entitled to draw a full pension from the age of 55, or a partial pension from the age of 50, if they have worked for a minimum of 5,500 days (MISSOC, 2003, table VI 3.2, 4). The CEE countries also operate arrangements to cover maternity and parental leave. Periods of six years are credited in Slovakia for women who have raised three or more children, and up to eight years spent out of the labour market raising children are recognised in Estonia and Latvia (MISSCEO, 2002, chapter VI, pp 509-13).

As more women are spending longer in employment, gender differences in the official retirement age are gradually being eliminated, initially on grounds of equality of treatment in social security, although the greater longevity of women compared with men is providing an actuarial justification. In most EU15 member states at the turn of the century, either legal retirement age for access to the standard pension was already the same for both men and women or, as in Austria, Belgium, Italy and the UK, the age for women was being aligned with that for men. In Belgium, it was due to be raised from 63 to 65 by 2009, in the UK from 60 to 65 between 2010 and 2020, and in Austria to 65 by 2033. Under a scheme being introduced in Italy, retirement age for both men and women was set at 57 to 65, but with variations in the level of pension according to age. In Greece, women who began paying insurance contributions after January 1993 will be entitled to receive the standard pension at age 65 instead of 60 (European Commission, 2002d, pp 36-7; MISSOC, 2003, table VI 3.1).

CEE countries have also been following suit. Under Soviet rule, retirement age opening entitlement to the national standard pension was set at 55 for women and 60 for men. Since transition, the aim has been to achieve greater equality, while also reducing the financial burden on the state by increasing the statutory age of retirement, but generally by setting it at a lower age than in EU15. Statutory retirement age for women and men was due to be equalised at 60 between 2003 and 2019 in Slovakia, at 62 in Hungary by 2008 and in Latvia by 2009, and at 63 in Estonia by 2016. In Poland, the aim in 2003 was to standardise retirement age at 62 for men and women, but the proposed reform met with strong opposition on the grounds that women deserved to receive a reward for performing their dual roles as mothers and workers. Consequently, no date was set for implementation. In the Czech Republic and Slovenia, where retirement age was still lower for women, they could retire as early as 56 or 57 if they had brought up several children (MISSCEO, 2002, chapter VI, pp 478-82).

Given that women usually marry at an earlier age than men, a situation can arise where the same retirement age for men and women means that women continue working after their husbands have retired, potentially reversing the dependency relationship and, thereby, creating an identity crisis in societies where the distribution of gender roles in the home is based on the male breadwinner model. In most countries, men and women can continue working after the statutory retirement age for the standard pension and can accumulate their pension and earnings, subject in some cases to conditions such as an earnings limit or a change of employer. In the UK, women who continue working after the age of 60 are exempted from social insurance contributions but pay tax on their combined earnings and pension. In an attempt to provide incentives for workers to remain in the labour force after what may be a relatively early retirement age, in some of the CEE countries, no upper limit is set on earnings that can be received in conjunction with a pension (MISSCEO, chapter VI, pp 533-7; MISSOC, 2003, table VI Accumulation with earnings from work).

Greater individualisation of social protection rights has generally been accompanied by a lessening of the importance attributed to marriage as a qualifying condition for benefits. In countries where eligibility for social security benefits is still subject to marital status, unmarried and married cohabitation may be treated differently. In most EU15 member states, an addition can, for example, be claimed on pensions for spouses. The formula used to calculate pensions in the Netherlands applies equally to married and unmarried persons and also to two men or two women who share a household. Unmarried partners in France, Italy and Spain are entitled to derived rights such as healthcare (MISSOC, 2003, tables II 4, VI 2).

At the turn of the century, all EU15 member states except Greece, which had no general scheme, considered unmarried cohabiting couples as analogous to married couples living together when determining eligibility for minimum income benefits. In Germany, the rules defining the domestic unit specified that "persons living in a quasi-marital partnership may not be better off than spouses" (MISSOC, 2003, table XI 3). Among the candidate countries, only Slovenia made reference to unmarried cohabiting relationships in the calculation of resources, specifying that cohabitees must have been living together for more than a year (MISSCEO, 2002, chapter XI, p 901). To claim social security benefits as a dependant in Hungary, proof has to be given that the partnership lasted for at least 10 years, or that the couple was officially looking after a minor for at least one year.

Few countries extend rights such as survivors' pensions to unmarried couples. Portugal and Sweden are exceptions as far as unmarried survivors are concerned. The rules regarding entitlement in Portugal specify that:

> The person who lived with the deceased during the two years preceding the death in similar conditions as a spouse is regarded as such for the purposes of survivors' benefits.
> (MISSOC, 2003, table VII Entitled persons)

The rules in Sweden are more restrictive:

> A person who lived permanently together with the deceased without being married is regarded as a spouse if they had been married earlier or have had or were expecting a child at the time of death.
> (MISSOC, 2003, table VII Entitled persons)

In the Netherlands, entitlement rules do not specify that partners have to be married, but benefit is conditional on the surviving partner having paid insurance contributions at the time of death. Cohabiting partners in Hungary and Slovenia are entitled to survivor's benefit (MISSCEO, 2002, chapter VII, pp 560, 563; MISSOC, 2003, table VII Entitled persons, 2).

The individualisation of social insurance contributions and benefits has been accompanied by changes in the definition of the basic income tax unit from the couple to the individual (Dingledey, 2001, pp 656-62). The trend towards individualised or separate taxation for couples, irrespective of their marital status, represents a shift away from the concept of a family wage and of the family or household as the primary administrative unit. The family model, where the male partner is held responsible for the upkeep of his wife and children, is thus being replaced by a more egalitarian concept of family life, but without entirely abandoning the commitment to formal marital bonds.

The distinction between married and unmarried households in tax liability has been removed or reduced in the Netherlands and Sweden, by bringing the situation of married couples into line with that of unmarried couples, rather than the reverse. However, marriage may still be used as a criterion for determining eligibility for tax concessions. Married couples may, for example, pay less tax than unmarried cohabiting partners. In the UK, for instance, individual or independent taxation, which was introduced in 1990, removed the disadvantage for married couples of being taxed on their joint incomes. Because the married couple's allowance was maintained in cases where either spouse was born before 6 April 1935, older married couples who are paying tax still have a financial advantage over unmarried cohabitees. In France, married couples can opt to make separate tax returns, whereas unmarried cohabiting couples must each make a separate return. Married partners are entitled to more generous tax concessions than unmarried couples. In Spain, married couples can also opt to make a joint return if it is financially advantageous for them to do so (MISSOC, 2002, p 30). Germany has continued to operate the system of *Ehengattensplitting*, which gives precedence to the definition of the married couple as a unit with a single or male earner. Spouses can choose between separate and joint taxation. If they opt to be taxed jointly, the annual incomes of both partners are added together, divided by two and taxed as two separate incomes, which is advantageous for married couples with a single income, or for couples in which one of the partners earns considerably less than the other (MISSOC, 2002, p 21). A similar system applies in Poland, whereby spouses are allowed to combine their incomes in their annual tax return, which is again to their advantage if one spouse has a high income and the second a low one.

When marriage is dissolved, divorcees usually forfeit most of their derived rights. In some countries, under certain conditions, the benefits of marriage may continue after divorce, unless the divorcee remarries or lives with another partner. In Sweden, for instance, although spouses do not have an obligation to maintain one another after divorce, part of a pension can be transferred to a former partner. The 1999 Welfare Reform and Pensions Act in England and Wales codifies how pensions should be divided up following divorce: divorcees are entitled to half of the full pension benefit accrued over the working life of their partner. Couples divorcing since 1 December 2000 have the option of sharing their pension as part of the matrimonial settlement. Benefit is withdrawn during a period of cohabitation, and the law does not apply to unmarried cohabiting couples that separate. In Scotland by contrast, only the pension accrued during the period of the marriage is taken into account. Pension splitting is not, however, obligatory, and the law allows for couples to make their own financial arrangements. Where such provision is made, it generally ceases if the partner in receipt of maintenance remarries or repartners. In Spain, after separation, divorce or annulment, beneficiaries share the pension between them according to the length of their respective periods of cohabitation.

When a divorced spouse dies, the situation regarding survivors' pensions is also variable. In Austria, a divorced widow is entitled to continue to receive maintenance payments. In Denmark, a widow must have been married to the deceased person for 10 years, if the death occurred before 1992, and be in receipt of maintenance. In Germany, the divorce must have occurred before 1 July 1977 to open entitlement to a survivor's pension. In Ireland, benefits rules specify that the survivor should not be living with another person as husband and wife. Although a new partnership usually brings an end to the payment, in the UK, it is 'withdrawn' during a period of cohabitation and, in the Netherlands, it may be resumed if the subsequent relationship lasts no more than six months (MISSOC, 2003, table VII 2).

In some CEE countries, provision is also made for divorcees to receive a survivor's pension. In Estonia, a divorced widow is entitled to a pension if she was unable to work before or within a year of the divorce, or if she reached pensionable age within three years of the divorce, and the marriage lasted for at least 25 years. In Hungary and Slovakia, entitlement depends on the divorced spouse having received alimony. With the exception of Poland and Slovenia for former spouses aged over 58, as in most EU15 countries, remarriage generally means that pension rights are terminated, although a lump sum is paid in the Czech Republic, and the pension is maintained for a year in Estonia (MISSCEO, 2003, chapter VII, pp 571, 574-7).

These examples illustrate the extent to which principles and practices can vary from one country to another, reflecting differences in the value attached to the marriage institution as the criterion for determining dependency, and in the extent to which rights have become individualised.

Changing definitions of benefit families

Just as the family unit is usually defined, for statistical purposes, by the presence of children, the benefit family can be identified as a unit composed of parents with children. National regulations vary in the ways in which they take account of family or household composition in distributing benefits targeted at children, and this is reflected in terminology. For MISSOC (2003, table IX), 'child benefit', the term used in northern Europe, where the child is the intended recipient, is a subcategory of 'family benefits', which describes the package of benefits paid to family members as a unit. The term 'family allowances' is used in French-speaking and southern European countries, where the family unit is the beneficiary, and the payment is seen as a contribution to family income. In other areas of welfare provision, such as social assistance, across the Union the presence of children can have a bearing on entitlements, except if benefits are attributed solely on an individual basis.

Not all children are, however, assigned the same value within or between societies. In determining the level of child benefit and family allowances, factors taken into account include the rank of the child, the number of children, their ages, the length of time spent in education, and any special needs they may have. Family allowances are not, for instance, paid for the first child in France, although the presence of children, irrespective of their number, is often considered as a necessary defining condition of a family unit. In most cases, rates are progressive for larger families in recognition of the importance attributed to family size in managing household resources. In Austria, Belgium, Denmark, France, Luxembourg, the Netherlands and Portugal, child benefit increases as children grow older. In Belgium, Greece, Portugal and Spain, only parents who are employees paying social insurance contributions are entitled to family allowances. In Italy, Portugal and Spain, adjustments are made to the rate of benefits according to earnings, in line with the trend towards greater targeting (MISSOC, 2003, table IX 2, 3.2, 5.1-3).

The situation in the transition countries during the 1990s is equally, if not more, difficult to characterise, since benefits for children were usually given low priority and were among the first to be cut in an attempt to reduce public spending. At the turn of the century, child benefit was funded primarily from general taxation as a flat-rate payment to permanent residents. Despite its imputed universality, in most cases it was either means tested or income related, with higher rates for large families. Provision reflected confused and shifting objectives, including pro-natalism and a concern about the greater risk of large families falling into poverty. The benefit for families with three of more children in Lithuania was means tested for three children but not from the fourth child. In Hungary, a distinction was made between pre-school age children, who received family allowances, and school age children, who were entitled to an education allowance conditional on school attendance (Ferge, 2001a, p 121).

Just as age is used as a criterion to define childhood but is applied inconsistently in statistics both within and between countries, different age limits are used to define the benefit child. Whereas the age of 18 is widely used as the age of majority at which young people gain the right to vote, few young people are economically independent by that age, as noted in Chapters Three and Four. The normal age limit for child benefit or family allowances is, however, fixed at 16 in Ireland, Portugal, Sweden and the UK, at 17 in the Netherlands, at 20 in France and at 18 elsewhere in EU15. In the fifth-wave member states, the age limit was set at the lower age of 15 in Cyprus, the Czech Republic, Latvia and Slovakia, but at 18 in Slovenia. Across EU25, the limit could be extended for children who were continuing in education and training, or who had a serious disability. In the UK, the extension applied up to the age of 19 for those continuing in 'non-advanced' education. Young people in Austria and Germany who were jobseekers were considered as dependants eligible for child benefit up to the age of 21. In Austria, Belgium, Germany, Luxembourg, the Czech Republic, Slovakia and

Slovenia, child benefit could continue to be paid up to the age of 25, or even 27 in Germany and Luxembourg, for young people in vocational training or further education. The other fifth-wave members states set their upper age limits at 20 or 21. Cyprus was the only country operating a lower age limit for women than for men, at 23 and 25 respectively (MISSCEO, 2002, chapter IX, pp 731-5; MISSOC, 2003, table IX 4).

Children may also be treated differently in benefits systems according to their parents' living arrangements. In Denmark, for the purposes of receiving child benefit, children who share their time between two households following the separation or divorce of their parents are attributed according to where they are reported to be living in the population register, whereas in the Netherlands the benefit is divided equally between the two parents. In Finland, social benefits are based on the situation in the reconstituted household. In the Netherlands, same-sex couples with a child are entitled to receive child benefit (MISSOC, 2002, pp 14, 59, 77).

Children in lone-parent families are often identified as requiring special treatment because they run a higher risk of falling into poverty. Before statistics began recording a steep rise in the incidence of extramarital births, cohabitation and lone parenthood, most countries already made provision for lone-parent families as a result of divorce or bereavement, and unmarried mothers were also catered for, primarily to ensure that their children would not suffer financially from having only one parent. Lone-parent families are recognised as a specific family benefit category only in France and Ireland. In Austria, Denmark, Finland, Italy, Hungary and Slovenia, child benefit is supplemented for lone parents. It is raised in Greece for a child of a lone parent who is a widow/er, invalid or soldier, but no reference is made to provision for divorcees or unmarried lone parents. In Estonia, before transition, lone mothers were targeted as a priority group for housing but, since 1991, they are no longer singled out as a specific category for social assistance. In the Czech Republic, Hungary, Poland, Slovakia and Slovenia, provision is made to guarantee a minimum income for lone parents (MISSCEO, 2002, chapter IX, pp 774-6; MISSOC, 2003, table IX 3).

In the same way that age, income and the number of children determine the level and duration of child benefit, the lone-parent allowances (*allocation de parent isolé*), which was first introduced in France in 1976, takes account of the age of the last child and household income. The level of benefit is calculated on the basis of the difference between the guaranteed minimum income and the income of the parent–child family unit, thus topping up household income (Algava and Avenel, 2001, p 2). In Ireland, the One-Parent Family Payment was introduced in 1997 as a separate and specific means-tested scheme rather than as a family benefit. It was explicitly designed not to facilitate or encourage long-term welfare dependency (MISSOC, 2001, p 26). Similarly, the higher rate of child benefit previously paid for children in lone-parent families in the UK was abandoned in 1998 in favour of the New Deal for Lone Parents, which is a measure aimed at guaranteeing sufficient resources. It was designed to offer a comprehensive package of job search, childcare, training and benefits advice for lone parents to enable them to move off benefit and into work, and was targeted, especially, at those on Income Support (MISSOC, 2003, table IX 3).

In some countries, responsibility for dependent children is taken into account in the calculation of basic pensions. In Austria, Finland, Greece, Ireland, Sweden and the UK, for example, a supplement is paid for children who are dependent on a pensioner. In France, a special supplement is added to pensions for parents who have raised at least three children for at least nine years before their 16th birthdays (MISSOC, 2003, table VI 5.2, 6). No such arrangements are made in CEE countries.

With the exceptions of Greece and Spain, family benefits are not generally subject to taxation (MISSOC, 2003, table IX 1). In Finland and France, parents are entitled to child home care allowances. In Finland, they are taxable, whereas in France, tax deductions can be claimed towards childcare costs for children under the age of seven, and social insurance contributions are covered in full for families who employ approved private childminders and, in part, for those who pay for childcare in their own homes. After 25 years without tax relief for children, a Children's Tax Credit was reintroduced in the UK in 2000 for children under the age of 16, up to a maximum level, which is reduced for incomes taxed at the higher rate of 40%. A Working Families' Tax Credit, established in 1999 and designed to top up the earnings of families on low incomes with children, included a tax credit to offset the cost of childcare (MISSOC, 2003, table IX 2). The situation varies from one CEE country to another and over time with regard to how their tax systems take account of family relationships. In Hungary, for example, tax allowances for children were introduced in the early 1990s, abolished in 1995, then reintroduced in 1999 as a means of supporting larger families on relatively high incomes (Ferge, 2001a, p 122).

Within EU25, France affords a rare example of a country that has retained a family-based tax unit. The *quotient familial* ensures that the responsibility for dependent children is fully recognised as a defining characteristic of family life by reducing the family's tax liability, making it particularly advantageous for high-income earners who have several children. The system provides generous tax relief for children from the first child and at a higher level for three or more children. The taxable income of the whole family is divided into units, or shares (*parts*), according to the number of children. Each parent represents one unit and each child a half unit, except in the case of lone parents, where the first child counts as a whole unit, and, in large families, where the third and subsequent children are counted as whole units.

Differences in definitions of the boundaries to family units mean that the situation is equally complicated for public administration when determining the liability of family members for their relatives. In some countries, members of an extended family unit are entitled to benefits that are usually reserved for spouses and direct descendants. In Portugal for example, under Decree law n° 133-B/97 of 30 May 1997, transfer payments are granted to all unmarried dependants living under the same roof, and to married, separated, divorced or widowed descendants or ascendants, including in-laws, whose incomes fall below a certain threshold (MISSOC, 2002, p 73).

For the provision of healthcare, the definition of dependants may be couched in broad terms. In Austria, for example, parents, grandchildren and stepchildren may be covered by the health insurance of the main income earner in the household. In Spain, dependants encompass not only spouses and children but also brothers and sisters, relatives in the ascending line, their spouses and, in exceptional cases, *de facto* dependants. In Belgium, children under the age of 25 are automatically defined as dependants, whether they are sharing the same residence or not. In Denmark, children under 23 are eligible to receive a housing allowance if they live with their parents, grandparents, adoptive or foster parents (MISSOC, 2002, pp 10, 14, 68; 2003, table II 4).

In Luxembourg, southern European and some CEE countries, rights to survivors' pensions extend to family members other than spouses. Luxembourg includes collateral relatives up to the second degree. In Portugal, parents who were dependent on the deceased are entitled to benefits. Under certain conditions in Spain, siblings, mothers, fathers, grandparents and grandchildren are eligible to receive a survivor's pension and, in Italy, entitlement is granted to parents, siblings and dependent grandchildren. In Finland, foster children are eligible to receive benefits. In the Czech Republic, Estonia, Hungary, Latvia and Slovenia, entitlement may extend to siblings, parents, grandparents and grandchildren, stepparents, stepchildren and, in some cases, in-laws and foster parents (MISSCEO, 2002, chapter VII, pp 566-9; MISSOC, 2003, table VII Entitled persons).

When Council Regulation EEC No 1612/68 (*Official Journal* L 257, 19.10.1968) on the freedom of movement for workers within the European Economic Community (EEC) was introduced in 1968, the assumption was that the then six member states would be able to operate an agreed definition of family dependants, enabling mobile workers to be joined by their families, who would be integrated into the host country. For the purposes of the regulation, the worker's family was described in article 10 in the following terms:

> (a) his [*sic*] spouse and their descendants who are under the age of 21 or are dependants;
> (b) dependent relatives in the ascending line of the worker and his spouse.
> (Regulation EEC No 1612/68, Title III Workers' families, article 10 § 1)

In addition to family relations by blood and marriage, the right to rejoin a migrant worker was extended to household members, broadly defined in the same article to include:

any member of the family not coming within the provisions of
paragraph 1 if dependent on the worker referred to above or living
under his [*sic*] roof in the country whence he comes.
(Regulation EEC No 1612/68, Title III Workers' families, article 10 § 2)

Paragraph 2 also affirms that workers and their families, including non-
nationals of member states, are to be treated in the same way as national
workers with regard to housing, education and benefits.

In theory, the arrangements made in EU member states for defining and
conceptualising dependants for the purpose of distributing benefits and
levying income tax should, therefore, be very similar. The examples
presented in this section illustrate the great diversity of meanings attributed
to family relationships. They suggest that administrative definitions are not
neutral with regard to family life, and provide some indication of the extent
to which public policy is reacting to changing family forms, and attempting
to shape them by opening or closing entitlements for individuals who adopt
non-conventional living arrangements.

Changing responsibilities for family welfare

Before the advent of the welfare state, the assumption was that the primary
responsibility for dependants lay with their families. Intervention was
justified only in extreme cases to assist individuals who were destitute. The
extent to which the state has replaced family members as the purveyors of
welfare has varied considerably over time and space. During the postwar
period and through to the 1970s, the northern European and CEE countries,
although in very different political environments, went furthest in
substituting collective provision for family support in their developing
welfare systems. Since the 1990s, pressures to contain public spending and
the far-reaching societal changes in the wake of the collapse of Soviet rule
have stimulated governments to look for ways of containing costs by shifting
the burden of welfare spending away from the public purse. In countries
where state expenditure on family welfare was already relatively low, and
families were traditionally held responsible for caring for their members, as
in southern Europe, these obligations have been reinforced. Even in
countries where universal provision of social protection is standard practice,
as in Denmark, Finland and Sweden, cutbacks were made to benefits and
services in the 1990s, and charges were introduced for childcare, thereby
shifting part of the cost from the state to families. In CEE countries, the
process of rolling back the state after a period of almost total public
'protection' was forcing families to assume responsibility as individual
providers of welfare for their members.

These shifts were taking place at the same time as governments were
striving to implement EU-driven legislation designed to improve the
conditions under which parenting occurs and to make it compatible with paid

work, while not losing sight of the need to redress the gender imbalance. A major issue for European societies in the 21st century is how to manage the changing relationship between the state, the market, the family and civil society (Daly and Lewis, 2000).

The generational contract of the postwar period, whereby the working age population supported the younger generation of potential workers as well as the older generation of former workers, is being undermined by socio-economic change (Walker and Naegele, 1999; Attias-Donfut and Arber, 2000). Population ageing, in combination with the decline in the number of multigenerational families, the increase in female economic activity rates, the lengthening of the period of dependency of younger people and high levels of unemployment, has raised issues about how to alleviate the heavy demands, in both financial and personal terms, being made on the 'sandwich' or 'pivot' generation (Mooney et al, 2002). More people in their middle years, particularly women, are struggling to meet the competing demands of having their own children still living at home, at the same time as their elderly parents are needing care and attention. As family structure has evolved, increasing attention has been paid to the effects of such change on relationships between the generations. The term 'generational solidarity' has been used to describe the mutual support provided by parents and their children throughout the life of family members (Attias-Donfut and Arber, 2000, p 19). During the 1990s, it became a recurring theme in European Commission documents, as for example in the Communication from the Commission: 'Towards a Europe for all ages – promoting prosperity and intergenerational solidarity' (COM(1999) 221 final, 21.05.1999).

The behaviour of people towards their parents and children involves a complex mix of notions of reciprocity, a moral sense of responsibility and legal obligations, which may change over time in accordance with personal circumstances and public policy (Millar and Warman, 1996, p. 7). This chapter has illustrated variations in the extent to which liability for maintaining relatives is formally recognised and determines the limits of state intervention. Analysis of the ways in which family relationships are conceptualised, defined and implemented in EU member states makes it possible to identify clusters of countries according to the extent to which obligations and responsibilities are shared between different policy actors.

Within the six EEC founder member states, law and practice differed regarding the concept of family dependency and the liability to maintain relatives. Subsequent waves of membership from the north, south and east of Europe have heightened differences. Issues concerning the liability of absent parents and of stepparents in reconstituted families, or the rights of unmarried cohabiting partners, including same-sex couples, have further extended the boundaries defining family and household units.

At the one end of the spectrum are the southern European countries where family obligations are assigned by law to the extended family. Legal obligations exist between family members, in terms of both derived rights and duties. In Italy, Portugal and Spain, family members have primary responsibility for their relatives in law and practice. They are required to provide support for a very wide kinship network. The state makes provision only if other sources of family support have been exhausted, and then only at a minimal level. These are among the countries which, together with Greece, recorded some of the highest old and young age family dependency ratios in the 1990s, in the sense that young people were remaining longer in the family home, and older generations were more likely to be living with their children (see Chapter Three). These are also the countries where, except for Portugal, women were least likely to be combining paid work with childrearing. In Italy, even in-laws and half siblings are required to provide support for family members in proportion to income. The state only takes over as a substitute for family care as a last resort (Millar and Warman, 1996, p 26).

In what are commonly described (following Esping-Andersen, 1990, 1999) as the continental conservative welfare states, Austria, Belgium, France, Germany and Luxembourg, but also in Greece, the legal obligations of family members are confined to close parents and children rather than the wider family network. Adults have a legal duty to maintain both their parents and their children. In Austria, France and the Netherlands, the state can enforce this duty by recovering social assistance payments from inheritance at the death of a recipient of benefits (MISSOC, 2003, table XI Recovery). In Belgium, France and Luxembourg, the state plays a strong supportive role in the provision of services, while in Germany the civil society sector, especially the churches, are heavily involved in delivery.

By contrast, no legal obligations are imposed on family members in the Nordic states, except insofar as parents are responsible for maintaining their children after divorce or separation. The state assumes the main responsibility for care needs on an individual basis. These are among the countries where the age dependency ratio has tipped furthest against the population of working age due to population ageing, or where it is predicted to do so by the year 2025 (see Chapter Two). Public services have long been in place to alleviate the burden on the sandwich generation and 'free up' women so that they can participate fully in the labour market. Both Finland and Sweden make explicit the obligations of municipalities to provide for young, older and disabled people, thereby lessening reliance on family support networks.

Another configuration is found in Ireland and the UK, which are generally characterised by their more liberal welfare regimes. The state does not impose a legal responsibility for caring, and family relationships are not strictly regulated (Ginsburg, 2001, p 174). Families can expect to be supported by the state, but in a situation where the duties of the state are not clearly defined, heavier reliance is placed on the private and voluntary sectors, particularly in the UK, to provide services for families.

In CEE countries, families and their wider kinship network are held legally responsible for their members, but only in Slovenia can social assistance be recovered from the estate of a deceased beneficiary (MISSCEO, 2002, chapter XI, p 930). Although the law usually defines intergenerational obligations, seldom do they become an issue for the courts because the moral obligation to look after family members is so strong. Generational solidarity has become a more meaningful concept in a situation where families can no longer rely on the state and employers for support and where, by default if not by design, governments have largely left families to fend for themselves.

Within EU member states, ties between the generations would seem to be stronger in countries where the law enforces and reinforces family obligations, although the direction of the causal relationship may differ between the southern European and CEE countries. Even in cases where obligations are less formalised, as in the UK, studies of intergenerational transfers suggest that informal arrangements for providing financial, material, physical and moral support are far more enduring than might have been supposed, and that caring, in particular, is still very much socially expected of women (McGlone et al, 1999; Arber and Attias-Donfut, 2000). In a situation where fewer women (traditional carers) are available to look after dependants, and where the state is offloading its provision, family solidarity is being called upon increasingly, and is being translated into contributions both in cash and kind. The extent to which families can be relied upon in the future to assume responsibility for their members is, however, an issue that policy makers across the Union are being forced to address.

SIX

Legitimacy and acceptability of policy intervention in family life

Analysis of socio-demographic trends and the challenges they pose for societies in the member states of the European Union (EU) gives some indication of the relative importance attributed by policy actors to the consequences of population decline and ageing, changing family forms and structures, gender and intergenerational relations, and also the changing interface between paid and unpaid work. When viewed from a distance, many of the trends observed would appear to be converging. Lower birth rates have resulted everywhere in the slowing down of natural population growth. Greater life expectancy and lower mortality rates have reinforced old age dependency, calling into question the generational contract, while the spread of less conventional family forms has created the need for new support mechanisms. Changes in the size and structure of the labour force and the organisation of working life have contributed to the demand for a more equitable sharing of paid and unpaid work, within a context where equality of opportunity and employability are mainstream political objectives at EU level. Closer scrutiny reveals the extent to which governments are adapting national administrative and legal frameworks in response to socio-demographic change. As each wave of membership has brought new clusters of countries and contributed to the overall picture of diversity, family matters have gained greater prominence on the EU policy agenda. However, family life remains an area where the principle of subsidiarity is frequently evoked within EU and national institutions to justify non-intervention, and where the boundaries between state regulation and family autonomy are difficult to establish and maintain (Chester, 1994, p 275; Hantrais, 2000a, pp 109-10).

This and the next chapter explore further the changing relationship between public policy and family life. In an attempt to find out whether family policy matters, they examine the legal basis for government intervention in family life, the perceptions that policy actors in different countries have of their role in responding to socio-demographic change, and the relative importance attributed to public policy in decisions taken about family life. The focus here is the legitimacy and social acceptability of government intervention in family affairs. The first section analyses how the relationship between the state and families is defined, conceptualised and institutionalised at EU level and in member states. The following sections examine the extent to which society considers intervention by political, economic and civil society actors to be legitimate and acceptable in the areas of socio-economic change analysed in Chapters One to Four. In conclusion, an attempt is made to identify the main parameters patterning family policy in the early 21st century and to characterise welfare arrangements in EU member states with reference to their approaches to family policy.

Defining and conceptualising family policy

In the same way that statistical, legal and administrative definitions of families are shaped by political forces and are largely determined by the requirements of institutional users, definitions of family policy reflect the wider policy context and the balance of power between different policy actors. Previous chapters have shown why policy makers, as both producers and users of statistical data, are concerned with tracking shifts in socio-economic behaviour and attitudes. They have mapped the challenges created for policy by changes in family structures and relationships. In seeking to understand whether family policy is a meaningful concept in EU member states, this section begins by briefly reviewing definitions of family policy within the European context before moving on to examine how public policy for families is conceptualised at EU and national level and to assess the extent to which it has been institutionalised across the Union.

Delimiting family policy

Variations in the way families are defined and taken into account in legal statutes, as shown in Chapter Five, reflect persisting differences not only in the principles underlying national family policies, but also in the socio-economic and political climate, political affiliations and policy regimes determining how these principles are formulated and put into operation.

Richard Titmuss's (1974, pp 23-32) overarching definition of social policy may usefully be adapted to family life. Accordingly, family policy can be defined in terms of the principles governing actions directed towards achieving specified ends, through the provision of welfare, minimum standards of income and some measure of progressive redistribution in command over resources, in such a way as to shape the development of families. Following the same logic, family policies, in the plural, can be characterised as policies that identify families as the deliberate target of specific actions, and where the measures initiated are designed to have an impact on family resources and, ultimately, on family structure.

In addition, reference can usefully be made to the need for an institutional framework to implement a coherent set of policies in the form of a government department set up to deal specifically with matters concerning family life (Millar, 2003, p 153). In 1989, the European Commission established a European Observatory on National Family Policies to monitor demographic trends and provide information about the situation of families in members states and the policies being implemented. In one of its early reports, the Observatory adopted a similarly broad definition of family policies. It referred to "measures geared at influencing families", but excluded policies implemented in other areas that had unintended outcomes, or impacts, for families (Dumon, 1991, p 9). A report published by the European Commission in 1994, the United Nations International Year of the Family, bringing together contributions from national experts in 12 of the 15 EU member states, extended the Observatory's definition of family policy to cover policies targeting families as groups rather than individuals. It considered the family impact of all policies, including the family dimension in social and fiscal law, and private sector provision, while acknowledging that the trend was away from family policy and towards "policies for families" (Dumon, 1994, pp 325-6). The Observatory's remit was thus extended to cover labour market and employment policies as well as measures designed to protect children and older people, and prevent social exclusion, implying a holistic approach to family policy development.

Even though the definitions above are couched in broad terms and appear to be all embracing, they are not readily applicable to every member state. Not all governments explicitly identify the family unit as a target for policy or use the term 'family policy'. Few would readily agree that policy should be designed to have an impact on family structure. They do not all have a designated government department responsible for formulating and implementing a set of policies aimed at supporting families. Several countries cannot be said to pursue a coherent family policy agenda or to have a defined set of goals specifically targeting the family as a unit. If the criterion is adopted that family policies should have the family as their target population, many of the measures examined in analyses of national family policies may not, strictly speaking, fall within this policy domain. The Nordic states are notable examples of countries where policy is aimed at protecting and promoting the interests of individuals rather than of families as units. Also, it is difficult to define the boundary between policy measures categorised as family policies and those guaranteeing sufficient resources.

Just as international organisations have issued definitions of families, households and employment that are recommended for use by national statistical agencies, international conventions have been drawn up regarding the rights of families in relation to the state. The Council of Europe's European Convention for the Protection of Human Rights and Fundamental Freedoms, signed in Rome on 4 November 1950, set clear limits on the powers of the state to intervene in family life:

1. Everyone has the right to respect for his [*sic*] private and family life, his home and his correspondence.

2. There shall be no interference by a public authority with the exercise of this right except such as is in accordance with the law and is necessary in a democratic society in the interests of national security, public safety or the economic well-being of the country, for the prevention of disorder or crime, for the protection of health or morals, or for the protection of the rights and freedom of others.
(European Convention on Human Rights, 1950, article 8)

The legal framework for marriage was also laid down in the Convention, but national governments were charged with determining the conditions under which marriage could be contracted:

Men and women of marriageable age have the right to marry and to found a family, according to the national laws governing the exercise of this right.
(European Convention on Human Rights, 1950, article 12)

Governments in member states that have gone too far in using the powers bestowed on them by their national constitution to introduce policies intended to influence family size and structure have come into conflict with the European Convention. Cases brought before the courts have, consequently, helped to clarify the obligation of the state towards families, for example by affording legal protection to children born out of wedlock (Meulders-Klein, 1992, pp 783-4). By contrast, EU member states such as Ireland and the United Kingdom have interpreted article 8 to mean that the state should not interfere in family matters.

In 1999 an Expert Group on Fundamental Rights recommended that articles 2-13 from the European Convention should be incorporated into Community law (European Commission, 1999a, p 23). The text of the Charter of Fundamental Rights of the European Union, finalised at the Nice European Council during the French presidency in 2000 and integrated into the draft Constitution of the European Union in 2003, reproduced article 8 of the European Convention (numbered as article II-7 and headed 'Respect for private and family life'). However, it was couched in gender-sensitive language and employed a form of words more appropriate to the technological age, stating: "Everyone has the right to respect for his or her private and family life, home and communications".

A slightly reworded version of article 12 of the European Convention, confirming the link between marriage and family formation, was included as article II-9 in the Charter:

The right to marry and the right to found a family shall be guaranteed in accordance with the national laws governing the exercise of these rights.
(Draft Constitution of the European Union, 2003, article II-9)

National governments were thus granted discretion in determining their own legislative framework, in compliance with the subsidiarity principle and in recognition of national differences in defining the family–state relationship.

In article II-14, the Charter goes on to delimit the powers of national governments with regard to the education of children:

> 3. ...the right of parents to ensure the education and teaching of their children in conformity with their religious, philosophical and pedagogical convictions shall be respected, in accordance with the national laws governing the exercise of such freedom and right.
>
> (Draft Constitution of the European Union, 2003, article II-14)

The rights of children are clearly set out. In addition to children being afforded the right to receive care and protection and to express their own views, article II-24 of the Charter recognises that:

> 3. Every child shall have the right to maintain on a regular basis a personal relationship and direct contact with both his or her parents, unless that is contrary to his or her interests.
>
> (Draft Constitution of the European Union, 2003, article II-24)

The rights of older people and of persons with disabilities to be socially integrated are recognised in articles II-25 and II-26, but without specifically assigning the responsibility or duty of caring for them to either family members or the state.

The role of the state in contributing to the reconciliation of employment and family life is laid down unequivocally in an article entitled 'Family and professional life'. However, like the Council Directive on parental leave (96/34/EC, *Official Journal* L 145/4, 29.06.1996), article II-33 does not specify that parental leave should be with pay:

> 1. The family shall enjoy legal, economic and social protection.
> 2. To reconcile family and professional life, everyone shall have the right to protection from dismissal for a reason connected with maternity and the right to paid maternity leave and to parental leave following the birth or adoption of a child.
>
> (Draft Constitution of the European Union, 2003, article II-33)

Although the Charter implies that marriage is a prerequisite for family building, it says nothing about the rights of unmarried cohabiting couples and, even less, same-sex couples. The 1997 Treaty of Amsterdam began to address the second of these issues by outlawing discrimination on grounds of sexual orientation (Consolidated Treaty, article 13). Article II-21 of the Charter, entitled 'Non-discrimination', echoes the Treaty provisions and develops further the list of areas where discrimination is outlawed:

> 1. ...sex, race, colour, ethnic or social origin, genetic features, language, religion or belief, political or any other opinion, membership of a

> national minority, property, birth, disability, age or sexual
> orientation....
> (Draft Constitution of the European Union, 2003, article II-21)

The principle of equality between men and women is restated in article II-23 of the Charter, where reference is made to the maintenance or adoption of "specific advantages in favour of the under-represented sex". This was the paraphrase that replaced the reference to 'women' in the Agreement on Social Policy appended to the Maastricht Treaty, when it was inserted into article 141 § 4 of the Consolidated Treaty following the Amsterdam European Council in 1997. Although the equality principle is to be "ensured in all areas", specific reference is made in the Charter to "employment, work and pay" (article II-23), but not to the home, thus setting limits on state intervention in private life.

When it was launched in 2000, the Union's Charter of Fundamental Rights was not a legally binding instrument and was not expected to become a general source of legal rights in the same way as the European Convention on Human Rights. However, the proposal before the European Council in 2003 to incorporate the entire Charter into Part II of Europe's new constitution for the enlarged Union meant that governments may find that national law and constitutions have to be revised to avoid being brought before the European Court of Justice. The introduction of the concept of rights for family members into European law invites greater scrutiny not only of the implementation of policies influencing family structure but also of the procedures adopted for monitoring the impact of policies in other areas, and for setting boundaries in national law and practice that impinge on family life.

Conceptualising policy for families

Despite the fact that social policy has almost always been assigned a secondary role in relation to economic policy at EU and national level, a measure of agreement was reached in the late 1980s over the place of family matters on the European agenda, firstly in a communication from the Commission on family policies (COM(89) 363 final, 08.08.1989), and then in the 1992 Council Recommendation on the convergence of social protection objectives and policies (92/442/EEC, *Official Journal* L 245/49, 26.08.1992). These policy statements identified changing family situations as one of the comparable trends across member states that could lead to common problems, thereby justifying the formulation of common policy objectives. The premises on which welfare states were based in most countries were, it was argued, being undermined as the intergenerational balance was upset, and the stability of marriage and family unity was increasingly disrupted. Although the Recommendation was mainly concerned with family life insofar as it presented "obstacles to occupational activity by parents", it also advocated the development of targeted benefits for categories of families in need (92/442/EEC, p 52).

Most countries would pay lip service to the overall objectives outlined at EU level. However, few, if any, can be said to have consistently pursued wholly coherent family policy objectives at national level and to have made them explicit in policy statements. The existence of family law and the designation of administrative categories for the delivery of benefits, as described in Chapter Five, cannot necessarily be taken as evidence that governments are pursuing clearly defined and consensual family policies.

The lack of an explicit family policy focus may be explained to a large extent by the conflicting demands with which policy makers have to contend. For example, policies that are designed to preserve traditional family structures may conflict with equal opportunities objectives. Policies that target specific categories of families may be incompatible with the concept of universal rights. Given that resources are never infinite, choices have to be made that may involve moral judgements. In their attempts to resolve these tensions, governments in EU member states have sought to meet three main policy objectives, reflecting the different rationales underlying their welfare regimes: income (re)distribution, pro-natalism and equal opportunities. Some member states have pursued all three objectives simultaneously, albeit with different emphases depending on factors such as the political ideology of the government in power and the prevailing economic climate. Others have concentrated on a single issue, or changed course in response to socio-economic circumstances.

Shifts between different policy objectives in the second half of the 20th century can be illustrated by national examples. All governments have implemented measures through taxation and benefits that redistribute resources, either horizontally between families from those without to those with children, or vertically from wealthier to poorer families. In many cases, both horizontal and vertical redistribution has been pursued, either simultaneously or at different times. A terminological distinction is being made at EU level between family benefits policies, which ensure horizontal redistribution, and income maintenance policies, which redistribute resources vertically and provide a minimum safety net, guaranteeing sufficient resources (MISSCEO, 2002, chapters IX, XI; MISSOC, 2003, tables IX, XI). Progressively, the emphasis in welfare systems has been on helping children at risk, rather than the family unit, in line with the child-centred approach adopted in the 1990s. The shift in focus has reopened debates about the relative advantages and drawbacks of targeted as compared with universal provision and, less overtly, about the relative merits of moving away from family policy to social policy.

In their concern about the threat of population decline, several countries have, at some point in their history, attempted to provide incentives to encourage couples to have larger families. Belgium and France pursued this objective in their family policies over the postwar period and made their pro-natalist aims explicit. By contrast, the UK and, until the late 1980s, the Federal Republic of Germany (FRG) are examples of how countries may deliberately avoid formulating policies that might be interpreted as encouraging population growth because of their expansionist connotations. Italy, Portugal and Spain have all been wary of pro-natalist, or population, policy because of its associations with totalitarian regimes. In more recent times, in the countries of Central and Eastern European (CEE) that joined the Union in 2004, concern about population decline has served to justify the promotion of family policy measures to stem the decline in fertility.

The equal opportunities objective has progressively moved up national agendas, for instance in Ireland and the southern European countries as they joined the Union. Further stimulation came from the development at EU level of policies that take account of the need for support measures to help parents, both men and women, reconcile employment with family life, as indicated in the Recommendation on childcare (92/241/EEC, *Official Journal* L 123/16, 08.05.1992) and the framework agreement between the social partners over a Council Directive on parental leave (96/34/EC), concluded in 1996 and, subsequently, extended to the UK in 1998 (*Official Journal* L 10/24, 16.01.1998).

Although the visibility of family matters on the EU policy agenda has increased over the years and was confirmed by the incorporation of the articles cited above in the draft Constitution, the extent to which policies targeting families are made explicit can generally be explained by a society's demographic development. A distinction is often made between countries with explicit and implicit family policies. Explicit family policies have been characterised as far reaching, coherent and legitimated, whereas implicit policies are not overt, legitimated and framed by a designated policy apparatus (Kamerman and Kahn, 1978, pp 3-4; Chester, 1994, p 272). A third category is sometimes added to accommodate a more neutral, or even negative, approach to family policy, in which state intervention is rejected on grounds that family life is a strictly private matter (Schultheis, 1990, p 74).

In the 1970s and 1980s, France and Sweden, as well as Hungary and former Czechoslovakia, were presented as exemplars of explicit family policies, while Austria, Denmark, Finland and the FRG, together with Poland, could be described as having a tradition of explicit but more narrowly focused family policy (Kamerman and Kahn, 1978).

In the early years of the 21st century, France still stood out as one of the few EU member states, with Luxembourg and, to a lesser degree, Belgium, that have most consistently and explicitly supported family policy in its various manifestations, although not without provoking deep-seated ideological conflicts (Neyens, 1994; Commaille et al, 2002, pp 7, 16). Irrespective of their political leanings, French governments do not hesitate to advocate policies overtly aimed at supporting families as a fundamental social unit.

Present-day Hungary can also be said to have continued to pursue an explicit family policy, although critics maintain that, under the conservative, Christian nationalist government brought to power in 2001, the focus of policy was narrowed. The normative definition of the family has changed relatively little since the 1970s and does not adequately cover the range of living arrangements that apply today. As the state has withdrawn its universal support and resorted to a conservative and elitist interpretation of family policy, families, and specifically low-income families, are widely considered to have been the main losers (Ferge, 2001a; Neményi and Tóth, 2003).

Since the 1970s, Germany and Poland have been pursuing more narrowly focused family policies, which are explicit at least in rhetorical terms. Today, the need for state involvement in family affairs is also recognised in political rhetoric in Germany, although emphasis is still on the conjugal relationship rather than the family unit, as exemplified and reinforced by the taxation system (Daly, 2001, pp 96-7). Traditional support in policy for women as homemakers and for marriage as the only acceptable framework within which to raise children has, however, been successfully contested, as demonstrated by the eventual adoption of the *Lebenspartnerschaftsgesetz* in 2001 (see Chapter Five).

The situation in Poland resembles that in Germany in terms of the explicitness of the focus of policy on the conjugal and male breadwinner family. As in many of the other CEE countries, during transition, family policy in Poland was overshadowed by other concerns. During the 1990s, governments maintained their support for traditional family values and pro-natalist measures both in their rhetoric and their actions, but the priority given to economic sustainability led to severe cutbacks in welfare provision at the expense of low-income families.

Among the 10 countries that joined the Union in 2004, eight had shared the experience in the 1990s of the rapid transition from Soviet rule, where the family and private space were annexed to the state. Prior to Stalin's death in 1953, family policy was essentially identified with population policy. Subsequently, policy was aimed at weakening family ties and replacing traditional family solidarity by social solidarity, thereby dismantling the boundary between the public and private spheres. Policy was based on a paternalistic relationship, with the state offering protection in the form of family policy measures in return for subservience (Mezei, 1997, p 220).

Most of the transition countries have not put in place a coherent and supportive family policy. The welfare mix that developed during the 1990s fluctuated between targeting the family as a unit and supporting individuals in need in a context of limited resources (Ferge, 2001b, p 142). As a result, families cannot be said to be a strong focus for policy, either in family benefits or social assistance schemes. Despite the supportive rhetoric, they are expected, instead, to be the main welfare providers.

Although the characterisation in the 1970s of countries according to the explicitness or otherwise of their family policies did not extend to the southern European countries, they could be described as having had explicit family policies under the dictatorial regimes to which they were subjected during the postwar period. The backlash came when democracy was restored in the form of the rejection of pro-natalism. Today, in Spain, for example, the memory of the pro-natalist legacy of the Franco era is still a powerful force restraining the role of the state (Mangen, 2001, pp 150-1; Flaquer, 2002, pp 84-5). Compared with the situation in neighbouring France, family policy in Spain is, therefore, marginalised. In the welfare mix that has developed, explicit reference to family policy measures is strictly limited, not on the grounds that family life is out of bounds for the state but, as argued in Chapter Five, because families, rather than the state, are legally and morally obliged to assume responsibility for their members as primary providers of welfare.

In another configuration, some countries deliberately avoid labelling policies that can have an impact on families as family policies. By the turn of the century, the explicit focus of policy in the Nordic states, for example, had shifted away from the family unit to the promotion of more individualistic values, and other countries were following suit.

The UK is often presented as an example of an EU member state with an implicit, neutral, underdeveloped or negative family policy, in the sense that governments have gone so far as to reject the idea that family policy should be identified as a specific policy domain. During the 1990s, however, British politicians started to become more explicit, at least in their rhetoric. Supportive family policies were presented through the 'back to basics' campaign under the Conservative government led by John Major, and then in New Labour's high-profile policy statements on 'supporting families' in 1998. Although the rhetoric remains stronger than the practice, family matters have thus become a recognised policy domain, with the emphasis on promoting the two-parent family and helping families to become independent of welfare in a culture of self-reliance and a context marked, since the 1980s, by the rolling back of the welfare state (Maclean, 2002, p 64). Like the UK, Ireland is generally categorised as a liberal welfare regime (Ginsburg, 2001, pp 174-5), where the privacy of individual families is a deep-rooted principle. Unlike the UK, however, and despite commonalities in policy development, the rhetoric surrounding the family has been strongly underpinned in Ireland by the teaching of the Roman Catholic Church (Kiely and Richardson, 1994, p 157).

Legal and institutional bases for national family policies

Countries with a long history of interest in family affairs as an explicit area of family policy have often translated their involvement into constitutional and institutional structures. This section provides an overview, firstly, of the status of family policy in national constitutions and, secondly, of the institutional frameworks for formulating and delivering family policy.

Family policy in national constitutions

Despite differences in the ways in which family policy is conceptualised, the constitutions of France, Germany, Greece, Ireland, Italy, Luxembourg, Portugal and Spain all lay down normative institutional frameworks, recognising 'the family' as a social institution founded on marriage, and to which the state owes protection. France, Germany and Portugal, although in different ways, have probably gone furthest in lending institutional weight to the recognition of the responsibility of the state and society as family policy actors, whereas the Nordic states, Ireland and the UK are situated at the other end of the spectrum.

The 1976 Portuguese Constitution presented the family as a fundamental social institution, rather than simply a legal entity, that has the right to be protected by both state and society (Amaro, 1994, p. 256). In France, article 10 of the preamble to the 1946 Constitution conferred on the state responsibility for ensuring that individuals and families are afforded the conditions necessary for their development. In Greece and Portugal, the Constitution was also designed to provide an enabling and supportive framework for family law. In addition, the Greek Constitution of 1926 stipulated that the state has a duty to provide for the special needs of large families and other categories of population at risk (Moussourou, 1994, p 91). The 1949 Constitution in Germany, like that in Luxembourg, provided a rigid and restrictive framework for family law. Article 6 of the German *Grundgesetz* (basic law) covers marriage, family and illegitimate children. It attributes responsibility to the state for protecting marriage and the family, and presents the care and upbringing of children as a natural right and duty of parents, under the watchful eye of the national community, which must also afford protection to mothers. Only if parents fail to fulfil their responsibilities can they be separated from their families, and no distinction is to be made in legislation between illegitimate and legitimate children.

In Italy and Spain, the constitutional status of families was adapted in reaction to authoritarian regimes by moving away from providing a strict normative framework for family life. The 1947 Italian Constitution specified that the family is a natural social unit founded on marriage, in which spouses are moral and judicial equals within the limits laid down by the law to guarantee family unity (article 29). The state has a duty to protect pregnant women, children and young people, and to assist families in carrying out their duties, particularly in the case of large families (article 31). Intervention by the state to protect women as workers is justified by the need to enable them to carry out their essential family function (articles 37). The state is also under a constitutional obligation to remove all economic and social obstacles to equality between citizens, and to ensure that they can exercise their right and duty to work (articles 3, 4). In Spain, the 1978 Constitution promoted a broad concept of the family, whereas the Civil Code only recognised families formed by marriage (Fernández Cordón, 1994, p 110).

By contrast, although the revised Swedish Constitution of 1998 does not refer directly to family structure, it sets out to promote the development of democratic ideas across the whole of society and stipulates that equal rights should be guaranteed for women and men. The Danish Constitution, which was written in 1849 and updated in 1953 to allow for female succession to the crown, makes no reference to families, although it does mention the rights of children, for example in access to education. Nor does the revised version of the Finnish Constitution that came into force in 2000 refer to families, but a reworked section emphasising the fundamental values of individual freedom, democratic participation and personal security stipulates that children should be treated as individuals and allowed to influence decisions about their own development.

In Ireland, although the 1937 Constitution established the state as the guardian of the family founded on the institution of marriage (article 41), this commitment has to be balanced against the recognition of the private nature of the family unit and the need to protect it against outside intrusion, even when children are at risk (Kiely and Richardson, 1994, p 157). Together, the Constitution and the Catholic Church present a force opposed to changing social values, as exemplified by attempts to reform divorce and abortion law. In a context of strong institutional support for women as homemakers, a source of potential conflict within the Irish Constitution arises from the prescription that mothers should not be obliged by economic necessity to engage in paid work outside the home if it means they neglect their duties towards their families (Kiely and Richardson, 1994, p 165). Although British governments are not bound by constitutional prescriptions, with Ireland, the UK has been one of the strongest advocates of the family as a private domain. While admitting that the protection of children is a public responsibility, governments must respect family privacy.

The precepts of family life are also underwritten to varying degrees in the countries that joined the Union in 2004[1]. The official constitutional position of women under Communism was that they were equal to men (Pascall and Manning, 2000, p 245). Hungary's 1949 Constitution, updated in 1989, provides for the special protection of marriage and the family. This does not mean the state should intervene to prevent or hamper the dissolution of marriages that have irreparably broken down. The autonomy and independence of married couples is upheld, but the state reserves the right to act to further the interests of the family as a whole.

The Constitutions drawn up in Estonia and Poland after independence devote attention to the place of the family in society and to the role of the state in protecting the rights of family members. Despite the fact that they were drafted in the 1990s, they continue to emphasise the link between marriage and family formation and the rights and duties that ensue between

---

[1] Unless otherwise specified, information about CEE countries was supplied by the project partners listed in the Acknowledgements.

---

spouses and their children. The Estonian Constitution, which was instituted following a referendum in 1992, presents families as the basis of society and fundamental to the preservation and growth of the nation, justifying protection by the state. The wording used is similar to that found in earlier constitutions of EU15 member states. Article 27 stipulate that spouses have equal rights and that, by law, parents have the right and the duty to raise and care for their children and for family members in need.

The 1997 Polish Constitution affirms that marriage, family, motherhood and parenthood are protected by the state (article 47). It affords women and men equal rights not only with regard to political, social and economic activities but also in family life (article 33.1), specifying that the state must take account of the well being of families in its economic and social policies. Not only large families but also lone-parent families are explicitly identified as having a right to special assistance from public authorities (article 47.1).

Latvia's Constitution lays down the universal right to social security and the duty of the state to protect and support marriage, family, and the rights of parents and children, especially those who are disabled, without parental care or who have suffered violence (Bite and Zagorskis, 2003, p 22).

These examples underline the distinction that can be made between the Nordic states and the UK, on the one hand, and the rest of the Union, including CEE countries, on the other, in terms of the level of constitutional support and protection provided for the family as a social unit. They also offer an indication of the extent to which national constitutions uphold traditional values and act as a restraining force in the reform process.

The institutional status of family policy

References to families in the constitutions of member states are not necessarily translated directly into designated ministerial positions. Within EU15, France and Germany have probably gone furthest in lending institutional weight to the recognition of the responsibility of the state as a family policy actor. During much of the postwar period, both countries consistently gave a high profile to family matters by setting up government departments with responsibility for this policy domain. In the early years of the 21st century, Germany, Ireland and Luxembourg had a designated ministerial department with 'family' in the title (MISSOC, 2003). In France, a dedicated institution, the Haut Conseil de la population et de la famille (originally established in 1939 as the Haut Comité de la population) has played an important role for over 60 years in monitoring trends in family building and structure. Since 1995, an annual 'Conférence de la famille' sets national priorities for family policy.

Elsewhere, the institutionalisation of family policy is more low key, although the Netherlands, for example, gave a high profile to family policy in the 1960s as an essential component of welfare policy through a formal Directorate for Family Policy (van den Brekkel and van de Kaa, 1994, p

225). Although it does not have a separate department for family affairs, the Labour government brought to power in 1997 in the UK set up a Ministerial Group on the Family, chaired by the Home Secretary, and a Family Policy Unit was created in the Home Office to co-ordinate policy across government departments. In 2003, it became part of the Children and Families Directorate at the Department for Education and Skills. Among CEE countries, Hungary, Slovakia and Slovenia had designated ministries for family affairs at the turn of the century (MISSCEO, 2002, pp 25-53).

In accordance with the principle of subsidiarity, national governments usually allow discretion at local level in assigning responsibility for the organisation and delivery of services that directly affect families, including housing, and care services. Regional and local institutions and agencies act as mediators. In France, a specialised non-governmental administrative agency at national level, the Caisse nationale des allocations familiales, works closely with local branches, or Caisses d'allocations familiales, to ensure the provision of a wide range of benefits and services for families, while also acting as fund holders for family allowances and other family-related benefits. Similar agencies exist in Belgium and Luxembourg. In Germany, central government exercises responsibility for family affairs jointly with the *Länder* and, in Austria, offices for family allowances operate within fiscal services at regional level. In Greece, Italy, Portugal and Spain, authority is delegated to local and regional level. In the Nordic states, Ireland and the UK, although policy is decided at national level, local government is given a large degree of responsibility and discretion in dealing with family matters. In Sweden, for example, local administration is left to determine how best to meet national targets. Local authorities are often expected to work in conjunction with the voluntary sector and, increasingly, in partnership with the private sector, to ensure the delivery of services as, for example, in the UK under the New Deal for Lone Parents, which was introduced in 1997, and was designed to optimise the involvement of non-governmental agencies. In CEE countries, responsibility for delivery of family policy is also left to municipalities. In Estonia, for instance, local government has responsibility for the provision and administration of social services, including domestic services, housing and foster care. In Poland, the administrative reform of 1999 redefined the duties and obligations of central and local governments, assigning them joint responsibility for family affairs, covering health, education, housing, and care for children and older people.

In combination, the legal basis provided by national constitutions and the institutions set up at central and local government level to formulate and deliver policies for families offer an indication of the extent to which family affairs have been recognised as a policy domain where it is legitimate for governments to intervene. Analysis of constitutional and institutional frameworks at national level shows how the legal basis for government intervention may constrain their capacity to respond to international pressures and to socio-economic change.

Perceptions of the legitimacy of public policy for families

The Charter of Fundamental Rights of the European Union, adopted at the Nice summit in 2000, reopened the debate about the relative competence and legitimacy, not only of EU and national governments but also of economic and civil society policy actors, to intervene in family matters. Whether or not the relationship between the state and families is described as family policy, and whether or not it has formal status in national constitutions might be expected to have a bearing on perceptions by policy actors of the legitimacy of government intervention in family affairs. It can also be hypothesised that the differences found within and between countries over the objectives of family policy and the institutional structures for formulating and delivering policy measures may be reflected in the extent to which different policy actors are involved in relevant spheres of activity, and in the perceptions they have of their ownership of family policy. This section begins by considering legitimacy in terms of the legal and moral rights bestowed by law and practice on policy actors. It then looks at the social acceptability of their actions, as recorded in surveys of public opinion.

Legitimating intervention in family life

In addition to the rights and duties conferred on the state by national constitutions, which provide the legal basis for policy formulation, an indication of the legitimacy of government intervention in family life can be gained by examining the ways in which different policy actors co-operate in policy formulation and delivery[2]. Across the EU, clusters of countries can be identified in terms of the degree of co-ordination or segregation between policy actors in family policy (Appleton and Byrne, 2003). At the one extreme are the countries that adopt an integrated approach, exemplified by France. Here, legitimacy of state intervention in family matters is a prerequisite for close co-operation between political, economic and civil society actors and goes almost unchallenged. At the other extreme, the three sectors are perceived as separate entities with distinct family policy agendas, as exemplified by the southern European countries. In these cases, co-operation between sectors is minimal, and they may be forced to compete for legitimacy.

In line with the overall coherence and comprehensiveness of the approach, which has been shown to characterise French family policy, political, economic and civil society policy actors in France readily

---

[2] The information reported here about the views of policy actors on the legitimacy and acceptability of state intervention in family life is based on 188 elite interviews conducted with selected policy actors in eight EU15 member states and three candidate countries in 2000-02, as part of a research project carried out under the European Commission's Framework Programme 5 by partners and their research assistants (see the Methods Note in Hantrais, 2003, annex 2, for further details).

acknowledge the legitimacy of state intervention in family life and the duty incumbent on governments, enterprises and non-governmental organisations (NGOs) to take account of family factors The historical consensus among policy actors in France over the legitimacy of state intervention in support of families remains uncontested, despite ideological differences over principles, objectives, content and delivery (Lanquetin et al, 2000; Commaille et al, 2002). France is a country where both economic and civil society actors are strongly involved as partners with government in family policy formation and delivery, and where the family lobby is powerful, highly organised and unified under the Union nationale des associations familiales (UNAF).

In the Nordic states, government intervention in the private lives of citizens is also unquestioningly recognised as legitimate on grounds of equity and equality. The responsibility of the public sector for funding and delivering a high standard of social protection is widely acknowledged, although differences can be found within and between countries in the extent to which the balance has shifted between funding mechanisms and between the family unit and individuals as the target for policy measures (Kosonen, 2001, pp 168-9). The family policy network is also relatively well integrated. In Sweden, for example, economic actors and NGOs co-operate closely with government, but their focus of attention, like that of political actors, is not the family unit. Economic actors are interested in removing the remaining barriers to women's employment and in creating the necessary legal conditions to enable couples to achieve a satisfactory work–life balance. NGOs tend to concentrate their efforts on the well being of children, while older people have established a powerful lobby through which to make their concerns heard. The role of NGOs in implementing policy is limited, however, due to the universal social protection cover provided by the state, which remains the lead partner in the relationship.

In Germany, Ireland and the UK, the exercise of the principle of subsidiarity means that limits are placed on the legitimacy of the state as an actor in family policy, even though it is recognised that family policy has moved out of the private domain and is no longer a matter solely for women. In Germany and Ireland, although government intervention has acquired legitimacy, national constitutions continue to impose limits on their sphere of action. The churches are still key actors in co-ordinating the provision of support for families in areas where the state assumes primary responsibility in France and the Nordic countries. In Germany, federal government subcontracts responsibility for family policy to other policy actors. Although economic and civil society actors play an important part in the delivery of services, their legitimacy is not uncontested. The interests of employers remain distinct from those of trade unions. Whereas employers have been concerned to raise levels of employment by getting more women into work, but without being constrained by regulations on working conditions, trade unions have advocated more regulation to promote greater equality of opportunity for women. The role of non-profit organisations in this context is essentially to deliver services for families. They have a strong presence at local level but are competing for funds against local authorities, which are under an obligation to provide services such as childcare. In addition, the limited involvement of NGOs at national level undermines their legitimacy as policy actors.

In Ireland, where the Constitution sets strict limits on the legitimacy of the state, policy actors in all three sectors remain aware of the need to justify state intervention in family matters. They do so primarily on economic grounds and with reference to labour shortages. As in Germany, NGOs have a policy implementation role rather being involved in policy formulation. In Ireland, however, they have been able to gain legitimacy as an alternative to government in some of the more contentious policy areas, such as abortion (Appleton and Byrne, 2003, p 214).

In the UK, in the absence of institutional recognition of a specific family policy domain, civil society actors were, in the past, left to take the initiative in responding to the needs of families. The late 1990s saw an intensification of efforts to involve economic actors as legitimate participants in family-friendly employment policies. Employers, who had previously shown relatively little interest in their employees as members of families, except in family firms or older paternalistic companies, were encouraged to recognise that family-friendly policy was an important issue in human resource management. They were stimulated by a number of factors, including the tight labour market, growing feminisation of the labour force, concerns over stress at work and the long-hours culture, and the influence of EU policy in areas such as parental leave. Successive governments have used the argument that regulations emanating from Brussels entail more bureaucracy and undue costs for employers to justify their resistance to the imposition of European law in the private affairs of businesses and families. In the absence of a coherent family policy at national level, many of the NGOs established in the UK were set up to deal with families in crisis. They have generally acted as single-issue organisations, as for example with lone parenting or child poverty, which has limited their bargaining power. Nonetheless, they have progressively gained legitimacy and become effective players in a variety of roles from lobbying, disseminating information, providing practical help and advising government (Appleton and Byrne, 2003, p 213).

In the southern European countries, the relationships between different policy actors can be described as segregated. In Greece, Italy and Spain, state involvement in family life was restrained during the second half of the 20th century. While socio-economic change, in conjunction with the secularisation of society, opened the way for greater intervention on the part of the state, legitimacy has proved difficult to achieve. Spain did, however, see a shift in the late 1990s away from the previous government's 'hands-off' stance. The legitimacy of state intervention in family issues has been acknowledged by governing conservative party actors, ministerial officials and the small business confederation of employers, as well as by the main opposition party and the two major trade union confederations. Employers have used their position to persuade government not only to remove employers' social security contributions for employees on maternity and parental leave, but also to avoid paying national insurance contributions if they take on unemployed persons as replacements during the leave period.

Both Italy and Spain afford examples of internal differentiation in the status and legitimacy accorded to public policy for families. In autonomous regions in Spain such as Catalonia and in the north of Italy, local initiatives have been taken to fill the policy vacuum left by central government. Trade unions and civil society organisations are gaining legitimacy as pressure groups, although rarely in a spirit of co-operation with central government. In Italy, NGOs have tended to concentrate their efforts on particular issues or family types, which brings them into conflict with the powerful Catholic lobby but also enables them to work in conjunction with local government as service providers. As in Italy, the constitutional commitment of the Greek state to protect families at risk and the legitimacy it confers have not resulted in coherent action by the state or co-operation with other policy actors, but NGOs do not possess the means or the experience needed to fill the vacuum.

Just as opposition to government intervention in family life in southern Europe can be explained by historical reasons, CEE countries share an aversion to state control over family life as a reaction to the legacy of Soviet rule. In this case, civil society organisations are seizing the opportunity created by the withdrawal of provision by the state and employers to develop organisations to support families. During the 1990s, the Church in Poland played an important role in setting the policy agenda for family issues. However, employers believe that the existing labour code takes sufficient account of the needs of families and protects women as mothers. They see their responsibility as being confined to ensuring the company's profitability in the knowledge that employees stand to benefit from sound management.

Although cross-sector co-operation in policy delivery is being encouraged in Estonia, for example by contracting out public services to civil society organisations, dialogue between the sectors on family issues remains underdeveloped. At the workplace, family matters are regarded as a question for government, trade unions and employees to resolve together, but employers do not consider that their role is to make provision for their employees as members of families. NGOs lack the resources to be effective as pressure groups, and they consider their role to be limited to offering advice and specialised services. The situation is similar in Hungary, where no concerted effort was made in the 1990s to foster co-operation between the sectors, but interest was growing in the early years of the 21st century in the potential for economic and civil society actors to fill the vacuum left by the withdrawal of Soviet-style enterprise welfare.

One of the requirements for EU membership was that candidate countries must have established stable institutions guaranteeing democracy. NGOs are recognised as being capable of making "an important contribution to the development of democracy and civil society" (Prodi and Kinnock, 2000, p 4). Family policy is as an area where the contribution of NGOs offers a convenient mechanism for governments concerned to avoid being perceived as intrusive. At the same time, it provides an opportunity for NGOs to gain legitimacy as policy actors, particularly in situations where family affairs are a relatively low priority on the agendas of governments.

Public opinion on policy intervention in family life

National differences in attitudes towards the legitimacy of outside intervention in family life among political, economic and civil society actors are largely reflected in public opinion, but with variations according to the actors involved, the policy issues and type of provision concerned, individual political affiliations and socio-economic factors[3].

Among the countries for which information is available, state intervention in family life is most strongly supported by the public in France. Here, the state is expected to formulate and deliver responsive and proactive public policies that take account of family change. In the Nordic countries, where public policy provision is taken for granted, the right of the state to intervene in the private lives of individuals to implement permissive and supportive policy measures is undisputed. By contrast, in Germany, Ireland and the UK, the three countries where family policies are partially co-ordinated, the principle of outside intervention receives relatively little support among the general public, particularly when it is considered as interfering and intrusive. The Irish population remains conservative and cautious about state intervention in family life when it is not upholding the *status quo* and, in the UK, government is recognised as having a role to play only when it is providing protection and a safety net for families.

In southern Europe, attitudes towards government intervention in family life are more ambivalent. The state is expected to provide a permissive and enabling legislative framework and to channel resources towards families, but without usurping the role of family members. Moreover, the public, particularly in Greece and Italy, displays a profound distrust of any interference in family life by the state and expects to rely, instead, on family networks for mutual support.

In CEE countries, intervention by the state in family life is, for the most part, considered to be justified and necessary, but the resources devoted to family policy are deemed to be insufficient to meet even minimum needs. Acceptance of policy intervention starts with the provision of jobs, reasonable working conditions, adequate wages and pensions, and extends to support for families that are unable to meet their own needs. Governments

---

[3] The views reported here, except where otherwise indicated, are taken from a small-scale survey carried out in 2001-02 as part of the project referred to in the previous note. Over 3,000 family members were questioned about their perceptions of public policy and its impact on their lives (see Hantrais, 2003, annex 3, for further details).

are also expected to take responsibility for implementing policies designed to guarantee the demographic survival of the nation.

In most EU member states, alternatives to state provision and family solidarity find relatively little public support. Private and workplace delivery of services is generally limited, and nowhere is it considered as an appropriate substitute for public policy, particularly with regard to health and childcare. Employment in the public sector is widely seen as more supportive of workers with families than that in the private sector, which is often regarded with suspicion, particularly over issues such as flexible working arrangements. Despite the agreement reached by the social partners at EU level regarding legislation on parental leave and time off on grounds of *force majeure* (Council Directive 96/34/EC, clause 3), views are divided between and within countries about the extent to which employers should be sensitive and responsive to the private lives of their workers. Employees, for their part, are seeking flexibility that is freely chosen and designed to suit their family needs, thereby serving as a valuable component in the work–life balance. However, flexible labour markets are often seen as a source of economic and, consequently, family instability, requiring more, rather than less, state regulation. When flexibility is perceived as being imposed by employers, as with part-time or temporary work in many countries, or when, as in the informal economies of southern Europe and CEE countries, it offers low wages and little or no job protection, it tends to be rejected as threatening and negative (Wallace, 2003, pp 36-8).

Views on the provision of workplace crèches are also divided. Greater support is expressed for employer involvement in childcare provision in Sweden than in other EU member states. The public is least supportive in Italy, Spain, the UK and Poland. In Spain, workplace crèches are regarded with suspicion on the grounds that they discriminate against employees on temporary contracts or in small firms, and that employers take advantage of the existence of crèches to extend working hours. In most EU15 member states, the opinion was widely held that employers should not be involved in the provision of leisure facilities, possibly due to the fear of employer paternalism, although facilities and services provided by workplace organisations, such as the *comités d'entreprise* in France, or initiatives by trade unions in Germany, are welcomed. In CEE countries, where, under Soviet rule, employers played an important role in delivering welfare services, including housing, employer involvement in the organisation of leisure activities is also more readily accepted.

Despite attempts at EU level to raise the profile of NGOs, little awareness was found among the general public of the role played by the voluntary sector in family life. The sector tends to be generally ill defined and is referred to only insofar as it complements, or is a substitute for, public policy, particularly in the case of families at risk. Even in France, which has a vibrant network of family associations working closely with government, the role of the voluntary sector, as distinct from the associative network, is seen primarily as providing a safety net for families in difficulty. This was also the main role attributed to the sector in the UK, where co-ordination between organisations is less developed.

The voluntary sector in Sweden is considered to make only a limited contribution to policy formulation and is even less involved in implementation. In Germany, by contrast, the sector and, more especially, the churches are recognised for the valuable part they play in the provision of social care. In Ireland, religious organisations occupied a powerful position in the past, but today they tend to be viewed with suspicion, and are being supplemented by secular associations. In the southern European and CEE countries, where the involvement of non-religious organisations in promoting the interests of families is limited, relatively little awareness is found among families of the contribution the voluntary sector has made, or could make, to family well being.

Public acceptability of policy responses

When European families are questioned about their attitudes to the policies implemented by governments in response to the challenges raised by socio-economic change, they are more likely to support policies that are perceived as enabling and permissive rather than prohibitive or proactive. The strength of public opinion varies not only between countries but also within them, according to factors such as age, sex, region, socio-economic status, religion and ethnicity. Previous experience of different living arrangements and policy measures also comes into play. This section examines attitudes towards policy intervention in EU15 member states and candidate countries, with reference to the policy issues arising from the demographic trends presented in Chapters Two to Four.

Acceptability of responses to population decline

Although population decline is presented in the literature as characteristic of the first demographic transition, it is not a problem peculiar to the late 20th century. Nor is policy responsiveness a new phenomenon. Governments in EU15 member states and candidate countries have long intervened with repressive, coercive, permissive and proactive policies to stem the decline in the birth rate and encourage family formation. The acceptance or rejection by the electorate of government action to influence demographic trends varies over time and space, both between and within countries. The repressive measures introduced in the past by governments pursuing the strategic goal of promoting population expansion would no longer be morally acceptable today. In the interwar period, governments in France, for example, introduced harsh penalties for abortionists and banned 'artificial' methods of birth control. In 1942, abortion was declared to be a crime against the security of the state, punishable by the death penalty. The contraceptive pill was not legalised until 1967, and the law did not come into force for another four years. Fascist regimes in Germany and Italy during the war years, and in Portugal and Spain in the postwar period, used repressive and coercive policies in an attempt to control reproduction. Until 1978, article 416 of the Spanish Penal Code imposed fines and detention on anyone facilitating abortion or the avoidance of procreation by whatever means, including advertising. The methods adopted under Soviet rule in CEE countries, which included restricting access to abortion, could also be described as punitive.

In the early years of the 21st century, public opinion in democratic states was strongly opposed to prohibitive and repressive measures designed to promote population expansion. The legacy of the past is such that few governments in western Europe are prepared to acknowledge that their policies have pro-natalist objectives or to describe them as population policies. If governments want to encourage natural population growth, they generally need to adopt less explicit and more family-friendly approaches. Incentives, such as the award of medals to mothers of large families in the Soviet states and in France after the Second World War, have been replaced by progressive cash benefits for large families and other forms of financial support and services, as noted in Chapter Five. With very few exceptions, prohibitive or proactive policies that might be construed as an indication that the state is seeking to influence family size and structure, or decisions about the timing and number of births, nowadays provoke considerable opposition.

As illustrated by the examples above, with its consistently above-average fertility rate, France is one of the EU15 member states that have gone furthest in drawing on demographic data to fire political debate, and in recognising the state as a policy actor in demographic matters. Declining fertility has long been considered as representing a threat to the nation's economic future, thus demanding and justifying government intervention. Whereas public opinion is almost unreservedly in favour of public policy measures to underpin family life, it does not, however, support explicitly pro-natalist measures designed to encourage family formation or to influence family size or the timing of births (Letablier et al, 2003, pp 42-4).

Similarly, in Ireland, with its relatively young and expanding population, and in Germany (postwar), Italy (post-Fascist), Spain (post-Franco) and the UK, which display different demographic profiles with regard to population growth (see Figure 2.1), public opinion is suspicious of governments that seek to intervene directly in demographic affairs, considering that issues regarding reproduction should be a matter for individual choice. Freedom of choice, like government intervention, does, however, have limits. Opinion is by no means unanimous on subjects such as legislation permitting access to abortion on demand, birth control for minors, medically assisted reproduction, surrogate motherhood and euthanasia.

When permissive legislation on contraception and abortion was introduced across the Union in the 1970s and 1980s, the removal of legal constraints on what were already widespread practices was largely a response by governments to popular demand and social pressures. Modern methods of contraception and medically controlled abortion offered a means of avoiding unwanted pregnancies, enabling couples to plan parenthood by exercising greater choice over the timing and number of births. Here, the country that has consistently registered the highest fertility rate – Ireland – is the EU15 member state where legislation has remained prohibitive, and where opinion continues to oppose the liberalisation of the legal ban on abortion. The topic is also divisive in countries such as Poland, where completed fertility rates have remained relatively high, but total period fertility rates were much lower than in Ireland in 2000. Although few people in both countries believe that the state should intervene to encourage parents to have children, religion is a strong force opposing the removal of prohibitive legislation on abortion.

An alternative solution to the threat of population decline, which has become almost a taboo subject in some countries because of its divisiveness, is immigration. Public opinion is far from being united over the action expected of governments in dealing with the question of immigration. Opinion surveys suggest that few Europeans would want to see a complete ban on immigration, but nor would they welcome an open-door policy as a measure to offset the problems associated with negative natural population growth. According to the European Values Study (EVS) carried out in 1999, the EU15 member states most open to immigration and least supportive of a total ban were Spain and Sweden, whereas Greece and the UK were at the other end of the scale. The countries where attitudes were most favourable towards immigration over a battery of indicators were Sweden, Italy, Spain and Ireland, which had quite different profiles with regard to immigration. The strongest opposition came from the UK, Germany, Austria and Denmark, and Greek respondents recorded high scores for indicators of xenophobia. Across EU15, the better educated and higher socio-economic groups were more tolerant of immigration, as were supporters of the political left (Bréchon, 2002, tables 17-19). In the candidate countries, very little support was found for an open-door policy, whereas respondents were much more likely than in EU15 member states to support a prohibition on immigration, especially in Hungary, Malta and Lithuania[4].

Acceptability of responses to population ageing

The necessity, desirability, and social and political acceptability of policy intervention to deal with the consequences of ageing command much greater consensus over government action than do efforts to stem population decline, although opinion has remained divided regarding the most appropriate measures to introduce. Analysis of Eurobarometer surveys

---

[4] Data for candidate countries from the 1999/2000 EVS survey were supplied by the Zentralarchiv für Empirische Sozialforschung at Cologne University in 2003.

carried out in EU15 member states in 1992 and 1999 shows, for example, that Europeans are increasingly aware of the threat to the future of pensions from population ageing. Despite their contrasting welfare systems and differences in the relative proportions of their populations over the age of 60 at the time of the 1999 survey, awareness was especially high in Austria and France, followed by Finland and Sweden. The countries expressing least concern were Greece, Ireland, Portugal and Spain. Greece was, however, the only EU15 member state where more respondents felt optimistic rather than pessimistic about the future viability of old age pension schemes (Walker, 1999, table 3).

Opinion about who should be the main provider of pensions changed very little during the 1990s. In both 1992 and 1999, almost half of respondents thought the state should be responsible. Less than a third believed that employers should be the main providers, and fewer than 14% expected individual workers to make private arrangements with pension companies. The countries where public opinion was most strongly in favour of state provision were Portugal, Belgium, Greece and Spain. Only Finland reported more than 50% of respondents in favour of employers as the main providers. The strongest support for private arrangements was in the Netherlands, followed by Denmark and the UK with around 20%. The lowest level of support for private provision was in Greece, Spain, Portugal and Finland, where it fell to single figures (Walker, 1999, table 6).

Although most Europeans expect to get less in the future in return for their pension contributions, the majority of them do not believe they will have to retire at a later age. Sweden, where the legal retirement age for the standard pension was already the latest in the Union, reported by far the largest proportion (80.5%) of respondents expecting to have to retire later. In Sweden, measures such as restrictions on early retirement and the reform of pension schemes, which were hotly contested in some EU15 countries, have attracted public support. Greece, where men and women could still retire at a relatively early age on a full pension, reported the smallest proportion (5.9%) of respondents expecting to have to postpone retirement (Walker, 1999, table 4). Here, it was hoped that measures being introduced at the turn of the century would have the effect of reducing the scale of contribution evasion.

After a period when early retirement was being actively promoted, the raising of retirement age to 65, or above, has been accepted in most countries as an economic necessity, but Germany and Ireland, like Greece, all recorded diminishing numbers of respondents expecting to have to retire later. A larger proportion of the French respondents in the 1999 survey (60.5% compared with 41.6% in 1992) recognised that they would have to delay retirement. Resistance to reform, nonetheless, remains strong in France for historical and ideological reasons. Retirement at 60 is considered as a social *acquis*. France was the only EU15 country where the age of entitlement to the standard pension was as low as 60 for both men and women in 2003, and where a relatively small proportion of the population was still economically active after the age of 55 (Walker, 1999, table 4; European Commission, 2002d, pp 36-7; MISSOC, 2003, table VI 3.1).

The Eurobarometer reports did not cover CEE countries, where, in a context of relatively low life expectancy, the issue of population ageing was not attracting the same level of public interest, although pensions became an important component of the reform agenda during the 1990s. They were at the centre of the severe financial crisis affecting the welfare system. The reforms being introduced to raise retirement age were often meeting with opposition (see Chapter Five). Despite a common legacy of old-age security, the Czech Republic, Hungary and Poland followed very different pension paradigms during the 1990s. In the first case, the reform process had to contend with the opposition of the trade unions and the electorate, whereas in the other two countries, reform was deliberately and successfully pursued in a pre-electoral period (Müller, 2001, pp 72-5).

Another Eurobarometer survey, carried out in 1998, asked about responsibility for the provision and payment of care for older people. As could be anticipated from the analysis of the legal and moral obligations of families towards their members in Chapter Five, a much larger proportion of respondents in the north – 80% or more in Denmark and Sweden, and over 60% in the Netherlands and Finland – opted for the state as the main source of funding for care. Barely more than 20% supported this solution in Austria, where more respondents than in any other EU15 member state expected children to pay for their parents' care. This was also the preferred solution for 20-30% of respondents in Spain, Portugal, Greece and Italy, whereas 20% of respondents in Germany, Luxembourg and Italy thought that older people should pay for their own care. The lead role in providing care for older dependants was overwhelmingly attributed to the state (national and local government) in 1998, with a score of over 90% in the Netherlands and over 80% in Finland, Portugal, Denmark, the UK, Sweden and France. The lowest scores were for Austria and Germany with just over 50%, and these were the only two countries where the role of associations as providers of care was supported by more than 20% of respondents. Private companies were thought to offer the best solution for more than 10% of respondents only in Denmark, Germany, Italy and Sweden (Walker, 1999, tables 14, 15).

Austria and Germany, the two countries that show the lowest level of public support for governments to assume responsibility for the organisation of care for older people, had both introduced long-term care insurance. A societal consensus developed in the early 1990s over the need for a solution to the long-term cost of caring to relieve the financial burden on the state and families. The political debate did not centre on 'whether' care insurance should be introduced but rather on 'how' it should be implemented.

The issue of the provision and funding of care reflects the concerns of a growing number of Europeans about their future well being. It also highlights the increasing strains that are being felt by the sandwich generation and, in some cases, their awareness that public policy and the state as a welfare provider have their limits. The economic arguments used to justify a shift in attitudes towards old age are gradually gaining support. The business case made by employers, and taken up by trade unions, is that investment made in older people through funded pensions, medical and care services, and the extension of economic activity, will result in higher incomes and a better quality of life in old age, thereby enhancing the spending power of older people. Rather than being a drain on resources, a healthy and wealthy older population is able to create consumer demand for goods and services while also stimulating production (Walker, 1997).

The increasing role of the voluntary and private sectors in the provision of health and social care services and financial planning has yet to result in an acceptance by electorates within EU member states that governments should not be held ultimately responsible for such provision. In the absence of an influential response to socio-demographic change on the part of NGOs, most voters still expect their governments to resolve the problem of paying for, and managing, the care of an ageing population.

Acceptability of responses to changing family forms

Views about the acceptability of policy intervention when it is aimed at influencing family forms vary according to the type of policy concerned and the socio-economic characteristics of respondents. For example, relatively little support is found among Europeans for legislation prohibiting unmarried or same-sex cohabitation. The view of most Europeans is no longer that couples should be obliged to marry when they want to have children. Attempts by governments to intervene deliberately to promote marriage as opposed to unmarried cohabitation, or to make divorce more difficult, are strongly rejected, although religious convictions remain influential in shaping attitudes among practising Catholics. According to EVS data for 1999, 88% of practising Christians disagreed with the statement that marriage is an outdated institution, compared with 49% of non-religious respondents (Lambert, 2002, p 147). The countries where the largest proportions of respondents (between one quarter and one third) claimed that religion was very important in their lives were Greece, Italy, Portugal, Ireland and Slovakia. The figure rose to nearly 45% in Poland and to 66% in Malta. The countries most strongly rejecting the influence of religion were the Czech Republic, Estonia, Germany, France and the UK.

As with abortion, views are divided as to whether divorce law should be prohibitive or permissive. While it is widely accepted that the state should intervene to assist families in coping with the consequences of divorce when it results in financial hardship, consensus is more difficult to achieve concerning the extent to which the absent partner should be forced to maintain children from a broken relationship. In most countries, public opinion is strongly in favour of state intervention through measures to support families in difficulty, whether they are large, poor or lone-parent families, or have a disabled member, either as a last resort or by providing a safety net when families are unable to manage by themselves. Opinion is even more strongly supportive of intervention when women or children are at risk, as in cases of child abuse or domestic violence.

Differences are found between and within countries in opinions about how far the state should encroach on family life and about the form that such intervention should take. In the Nordic countries, as exemplified by Sweden, the omnipresent democratic state is accepted as the universal provider. It does not, however, exonerate individuals from responsibilities towards their parents, partners or offspring. The understanding is that the state should guarantee a high level of universal provision capable of satisfying most needs. The extent to which state intervention in family life is seen as socially acceptable in France is almost universal and is far greater than in other EU member states. The demand for public provision of benefits and services is insatiable. The French public expects the state to support family life, but remains critical of what it sees as an inadequate level of provision and does not necessarily agree with government priorities. Such intervention is, however, welcomed only insofar as it docs not encroach on personal freedom, including the right of couples to decide whether or not they marry (Letablier et al, 2003, p 44). The view expressed in France, that the state should be enabling and offer choice, but without being prescriptive about family forms, is also widespread in countries that are less well endowed with public support for families.

In France, Sweden and, to a lesser extent, the UK, families most strongly support and expect responsive and, in some cases, proactive policy intervention in family life, which they see as a complement to their own provision. In France and Sweden, services such as those for children and older people are, in some cases, interpreted as a substitute for family care. By contrast, in Germany, Ireland and the UK, the state is expected to play a support role but to do so from a distance. In Germany, policy intervention is only accepted as secondary to the support provided by the family and as a supplement to it. However, the state is attributed the main responsibility for ensuring the basic conditions needed to achieve a good quality of family life and is criticised for delegating responsibility to civil society organisations.

In Ireland and the CEE countries, family obligations remain strong, but public perceptions of duties and responsibilities appear to be changing, particularly with regard to older people. The southern European countries have in common that state intervention in family matters is not readily accepted. Families consider that they have primary responsibility for their members and have failed in their duty if they are unable to meet family needs and must turn to the state. Paradoxically, family solidarity, which has long been relied on as the lynchpin of the support system, is weakening, making alternative provision all the more necessary.

In a situation where governments at national and local level are not trusted to deliver services, public provision of benefits may be more readily accepted than services because they raise standards of living and give families the opportunity to choose how to organise their lives. In Greece, for example, the preference is decidedly for benefits, since they are seen as less intrusive than services. The demand for much greater financial support from the state for large, poor and lone-parent families, and also for parents with young children, is extremely high in a context where only salaried workers are eligible to receive family allowances, where benefit levels are the lowest in the EU, and no general scheme exists to guarantee a minimum income. In Italy, the low level of benefits and the poor availability of public services in the south result in greater diversity of attitudes towards the preference for benefits or services. In the wealthier areas in the centre-north, where local government provision of services is more dependable and flexible, they are seen to offer a more viable alternative to private provision than in the south.

The shared experience of Soviet rule left families in CEE countries highly critical of the inadequacy of public policy provision since transition. After a long period of state dependency, politicians are trying to promote a self-help philosophy through the media, but the public still looks to the state to provide for families by delivering jobs, reasonable working conditions, adequate wages and pensions, and support for families unable to meet their own needs. The widespread view is that the state is failing to deliver. People know they cannot rely on central government to provide the level of support required, and they tend to place greater trust in local government.

Reactions of different age groups are largely determined by past experience, particularly in CEE countries. Here, older generations compare the present situation unfavourably with the past. They are more likely than younger people to accept state provision of benefits and services for families and to support conventional family forms. They also expect more support from employers. Elsewhere too, older people are generally more willing to countenance government intervention when policies are designed to support traditional family forms. In Ireland, for example, older people and those living in rural areas are most likely to consider government intervention in family life to be legitimate and to support prohibitive policies, such as more restrictive divorce law. In the UK, the older generation expects the state to underpin the family unit, by making divorce more difficult and encouraging couples to marry. Younger generations more often express liberal views about policy intervention that extends freedom of individual choice. By the same token, they are more likely to oppose policies that limit choice. In the UK, the younger generation is less enthusiastic about family policies in general, except at the workplace.

Differences are also found within countries in reactions to state intervention according to gender. In EU15 countries, with the exception of Germany and the UK, women tend to be more cautious than men about the extent to which governments should intervene in family life. In Spain, women are more willing than men to accept public policy only when the issue is whether support for families should be universal rather than targeted at particular family types. By contrast, in Germany, the UK and CEE countries, women are more likely than men to express positive views about government support for families. In the UK, men are more positive than women about intervention only in cases of domestic violence or child benefits targeted at low-income families. No issue was found where German men were more accepting of government intervention than women. In Estonia, the only areas where men are more likely to express positive opinions are over the imposition of more restrictive conditions for abortion and the introduction of incentives to encourage couples to marry before they have children. In France, Germany, Ireland and the UK, women more often than men believe that employers have a responsibility for creating family-friendly workplaces, especially by offering flexible working arrangements.

Disadvantaged groups are generally more willing than other socio-economic categories to accept intervention by the state in family life. An exception is Spain, where lower-income groups are marginally more supportive than other groups only in the case of incentives to encourage parents to have more children and to make provision for older and disabled people. Higher socio-economic categories in Hungary were found to be more liberal with regard to the type of policies they are prepared to countenance: they were more likely to oppose restrictions on divorce and abortion, and to expect the state to promote gender equality within families.

Political affiliation, like religious practice, still seems to have a bearing on support for policies that underpin traditional (right) or postmodern, solidaristic (left) family values. According to EVS surveys, the disparity between left and right in attitudes towards family values was, however, substantially reduced between the early 1980s and the late 1990s, in line with the marked decline in political participation in many EU member states. The abstention rate stood at a third or more of the electorate in Spain, Ireland, Finland, France, Portugal and the UK in 1999. Very small proportions of respondents in Estonia and Slovenia attributed importance to politics. The country where support for traditional values remained strongest, namely Greece, was also the EU15 member state where the gap between left and right was the most marked (Bréchon, 2002, tables 8, 15, 16).

Analysis of attitudes towards public policies for families suggests that, across and within EU member states, policy measures are more readily accepted if they are provided on a universal basis and are not seen as intrusive or prohibitive. Families want to maintain their autonomy and to be given greater freedom of choice. They acknowledge their moral obligation to look after their relatives but do not want to feel compelled to do so by law.

Characterising policy for families

The examples presented in this chapter highlight the complexity of the factors determining the legitimacy and acceptability of state intervention in family affairs. The southern European and CEE countries, where families might appear to be in most need of financial support, are not generally those where governments have the funds available to invest in support measures. Yet, the state imposes caring duties and obligations on family members, which they are finding increasingly difficult to meet. In some cases, such as Germany, Ireland, the UK, Hungary and, even more so, Poland, public policy seems to be driven by the desire to ensure that children are raised within a two-parent, preferably (or exclusively) married couple. Meanwhile, governments are under pressure to adapt legislation to accommodate alternative living arrangements. They are recognising that new socio-economic needs are being created requiring, and legitimating, government intervention to protect the interests of individual family members and, especially, children. Their willingness and ability to respond are, however, determined to a greater or lesser extent by socio-economic and political factors that often give rise to conflicts over objectives and priorities.

EU member states fall into several clusters in terms of the historical development of their family policy, its legal base and institutional structure. At the one extreme, in the Nordic states and France, policy is highly structured and legitimated. Policy actors are strongly committed to supporting families. At the other, in southern European and CEE countries, policy is more hesitant, lacking in coherence and under-resourced, and its legitimacy is often contested. Between the two extremes are countries, including Germany, Ireland and the UK, where the rhetoric is supportive of families, but where policy actors are frequently reluctant to intervene in the private lives of families.

Irrespective of the level of commitment and provision, responsibility for family policy is assigned primarily to the state rather than economic or civil society actors. In a few instances, as in France, although still state driven, responsibility is shared more equally between all three sectors and co-ordinated so that policies are complementary. Elsewhere, co-ordination is minimal or absent, and policy delivery is uneven. Whatever the criteria used, France stands out among the countries analysed in this chapter as the EU15 member state where state regulation and intervention in family life, and the concept of family-centred policy are most clearly and explicitly defined and articulated. France and the Nordic states are characterised by their family-friendly environment, their coherent and integrated approach to policy formulation and delivery, and their strong ideological commitment to redistributive policy intervention based on social solidarity. They offer a relatively high standard of benefits and services, designed to afford maximum personal choice and flexibility. The de-institutionalisation of family life and greater individualisation of welfare are raising questions about the future shape and form of family policy, and the balance between universal and targeted benefits and services, but they are not calling into question the legitimacy of the state as the primary provider of family welfare.

Another cluster of countries can be characterised as having only partially co-ordinated, coherent and legitimated family policies. In Austria and Germany, family policy has become increasingly explicit and formalised as family matters have moved up the policy agenda. Policy in Germany continues, however, to be more narrowly focused on the conjugal relationship. Civil society makes an important contribution to policy formulation and implementation through the churches and unions.

During the 1990s, the UK shifted from a neutral, implicit or underdeveloped family policy to more supportive rhetoric, but not to the extent that society, and more specifically government, can be said to be inherently friendly towards families, or that family policy became a legitimate and fully institutionalised policy domain. The establishment of the Family Policy Unit, initially within the Home Office, and its subsequent relocation to the Department for Education and Skills, suggests that family policy does not sit comfortably in any government department. Although child benefit continues to be provided on a universal basis, emphasis has shifted increasingly towards means-tested benefits and so-called tax credits, targeting low-income families, and supporting the transition from welfare to work and the notion of employability, implying that social policy is a more appropriate label than family policy. The traditional reluctance of the state to be seen to intervene in family matters has allowed civil society to gain legitimacy as a policy actor in specific well-defined areas. Apart from families at risk, where state intervention has long been legitimated, family members are largely left to develop their own coping strategies through recourse to private sector provision, although with at least moral and rhetorical support from the state. Governments expect firms to be sensitive to the business case in making arrangements to improve the work–life balance and retain older workers, while continuing to argue that over-regulation will harm business interests. The same argument is used to justify opposition to European legislation suspected of intruding into the private lives of families.

Ireland belongs to the cluster of countries where the relationship between state and family is blurred and shifting. Although the Irish Constitution and Catholic Church support women as homemakers and set boundaries on the legitimacy of the state as a family policy actor, the stance of governments towards the role of women in society and towards family life has been changing rapidly. Whereas mothers, especially lone mothers, were previously discouraged from entering the labour market, they are now being actively encouraged to seek paid employment. Divorce and abortion law reform has been strongly opposed on religious and moral grounds, but divorce was ultimately legalised in 1996. Ireland was going through a period of transition at the turn of the 21st century and still lacked a coherent family policy, which reflected the reluctance of the Irish people to accept the state as a legitimate family policy actor.

During the Soviet era, the universal provision of housing, health and childcare and, more importantly, jobs, which were the precondition for receiving benefits and services, meant that families in CEE countries did not have to rely heavily on their own resources to ensure that the basic needs of their members were met. Following transition, government support for families was severely cut back. Child benefit fell well below inflation. Universalistic provision was largely replaced by means testing and targeting, and low-cost facilities for pre-school children and various workplace benefits were generally curtailed. Responsibility for supporting families has shifted away from the state and employers to families themselves in a context where labour market restructuring has left many people without paid work and other resources to enable them to meet even basic needs. An underlying concern is how to rebuild national identity and ensure the survival of the nation in the face of population decline, which is lending legitimacy to pro-natalist policies designed to promote population renewal.

While they shared the experience of socialism and of transition, and were all preparing for membership of the Union in 2004, CEE countries lacked either the vision or resources necessary to enable them to develop a coherent and supportive family policy. They were fluctuating between targeting the family unit with pro-natalist measures to encourage family building and targeting low-income families to protect individuals in need. In a climate where governments are not trusted to deliver family policy, increasingly, the state has been delegating responsibility to local government, the voluntary sector, private initiatives and families themselves. In several instances, the importance of traditional family values has been reinforced. The normative definition of the family has, for example, remained strong in Hungary. At the rhetorical level, emphasis has been on the revival of traditional moral values. In Poland, the focus of policy remains the conventional two-parent married family. Governments have received public support in their efforts to pursue restrictive policies designed to uphold traditional family forms and moral values, while also providing openly pro-natalist financial incentives to encourage family building.

In the course of the second half of the 20th century, southern European countries experienced the transition from authoritarian regimes, which upheld patriarchal values, to democracies committed to a more liberal approach towards family life. They all needed to build up their welfare systems from a low base, but have tended to do so in a piecemeal way, resulting in fragmentary coverage. Today, they have in common their relatively low levels of provision of benefits and support services for families, compared with other EU member states. Family policy is implicit and largely unco-ordinated. The state continues to delegate responsibility for family well being to family members in a context where the legacy of the past has impeded the process of legitimating family policy, and where the preference for benefits reflects the lack of confidence in the ability of governments to provide the services that are most needed to support family life.

SEVEN

Impacts of policy on family life

Policy actors at European and national level generally concur about the need to take account of socio-economic trends when initiating public policy reform. They are less likely to agree about the moral justification of government intervention designed to influence demographic behaviour or about the effectiveness of such action. Nor is it self-evident that any convergence of demographic patterns, standards of living, lifestyles and policy objectives across the European Union (EU) will necessarily result in similar policies being enacted and, even less so, in them automatically producing the same outcomes. Indeed, European law has consistently retained the caveat that social policy implementation should be discharged at national level, in accordance with the subsidiarity principle, to accommodate differences in welfare systems. The diversity of national arrangements for formulating and delivering social protection in EU member states is acknowledged in international legislation, as illustrated, for example, by article II-9 of the Charter of Fundamental Rights of the European Union, with reference to the right to marry and found a family (see Chapter Six).

Judging whether or not a policy decided by EU institutions has achieved the intended outcome at national level requires an assessment of the fit between the objectives agreed and the outcomes observed. The task is particularly difficult in the area of family life, since policy objectives do not always make explicit reference to the family dimension, and because outcomes cannot necessarily be directly attributed to specific policies. In this chapter, the aim is to explore further the relationship between policy and changing family structure by examining cross nationally the process whereby public policy impacts on families and, more especially, the perceptions that beneficiaries themselves have of the influence of policy on the decisions they take about family formation and living arrangements.

Increasing importance is being attached to evidence-based practice as a mechanism for ensuring that policy is rigorously scrutinised in terms of its feasibility, practicality, affordability and public accountability (Davies et al, 2000, pp 2-3). During the 1990s, within a context of cost containment, greater emphasis was being placed in policy analysis on assessing the effectiveness of implementation and the operational efficiency of policy measures. Governments also became more interested in measuring and evaluating the performance of their institutions over time, as gauged by customer satisfaction (Walker, 2000, p 147).

Since few countries, as yet, have in place reliable systems for monitoring family policy outcomes and assessing their effectiveness, the chapter begins by reviewing some of the approaches used to track the policy process and determine whether policies appear to be achieving their intended objectives. The findings from quantitative impact assessments of family policy measures are then examined in conjunction with qualitative analyses, the intention being to identify and compare the possible influence of public policy on decisions taken about family life across Europe. Comparable statistics are often not available for all EU member states for the same data points, as noted in Chapters Two to Four, making it difficult to track trends over time and unravel linkages between policies and outcomes. Qualitative approaches that take account of context specificity and the motives and meanings of actors, therefore, provide a useful complementary tool for fleshing out the possible effects of social policies. They are particularly valuable when they examine the totality of the process from policy formulation through to implementation and practice, as translated into the lived experience of families. This chapter draws on a combination of approaches in an attempt to assess the match between policy objectives and outcomes for families.

Measuring policy impacts

Benchmarking is being used more and more to track and measure the performance of national governments in meeting targets agreed at international level. Governments seeking appropriate policy responses to socio-economic change are being encouraged to compare their performance with that of their counterparts in other countries. The open method of co-ordination (OMC), applied at EU level, makes extensive use of benchmarking to gauge the performance of individual member states against the targets set. The 1997 Luxembourg European employment strategy, for example, required EU member states to meet targets such as raising employment levels among women and older people, and improving childcare provision. The employment guidelines issued by the Council have since become more refined and results oriented, as noted in a Communication from the Commission on the future of the employment strategy, entitled 'A strategy for full employment and better jobs for all' (COM(2003) 6 final, 14.01.2003, § 1.2). The extent to which policy formulated at EU level is effectively implemented in member states remains difficult to ascertain, not only because they are left to choose their own policy mechanisms, but also because effectiveness in monitoring, policing and applying sanctions can vary considerably from one country to another. Legal action may, for example, provide an indication of effective policing and of access to legal services rather than poor implementation, the more so when it is left to member states to decide on the form and method of delivery, as exemplified by differences in national provision in compliance with the framework agreement on parental leave (Council Directive 96/34/EC, *Official Journal* L 145/4, 19.06.1996).

This section begins by examining some of the reasons why the analysis of the relationship between policy objectives and outcomes is difficult to measure before reviewing the changing policy priorities of EU member states in the area of family policy. Take up of family policy measures is then considered as an indicator of their effectiveness in reaching their target users.

Establishing linkages between policy and practice

In the area of family policy, quantitative data, although useful as an instrument for informing policy, may not always provide meaningful indicators of the success, or otherwise, of policy measures. Causal linkages are often sought in the relationship between policies designed to encourage family building and raise fertility rates, but findings appear to be ambiguous, contradictory and inconclusive (Sleebos, 2003). Data showing a high level of family allowances and a high completed fertility rate cannot be assumed to demonstrate a direct causal relationship between policy and outcomes, as illustrated by the fact that two of the EU15 member states with the highest completed fertility rates, France and Ireland, offer very different levels of policy provision for families (see Chapters Two and Five).

A broadbrush analysis of statistical data designed to measure the effects of care provision for children and other dependants in terms of the ability of parents to reconcile work and family life, as required by the 1998 European employment guidelines (*Official Journal* C 30/01, 28.01.1998, annex IV, p 5), might seem to suggest that the demand is being met to a greater extent in the Nordic states than elsewhere (see Chapter Four). Although the provision of childcare places is less extensive in France than, for example, in Sweden, a larger proportion of French women in employment are, however, working full time. By contrast, poor provision of public childcare in Greece, and in Poland since transition, does not prevent women in employment from working full time, whereas high part-time rates are associated with relatively poor public provision for very young children in the Netherlands and UK.

A policy is sometimes said to have worked if 'customers' are satisfied, but satisfaction ratings, like attitudinal data, are notoriously unreliable. In addition, the public may not share the perceptions that political and administrative actors have of the success of policies. Where policy actors have raised expectations during an electoral campaign, it may be difficult for them to meet their promises when they are in power. Moreover, recorded satisfaction may have little to do with the actual services received. What is believed to be an acceptable level and quality of provision in one country may be judged differently elsewhere. People who may be considered, objectively, to have benefited from a specific policy may report that their experience was negative. In France, for example, women complain about the inadequacy of public childcare provision (Letablier et al, 2003, p 29), but in relative and objective terms, the childcare requirements of French parents appear to be much more adequately met than in most other EU15 member states, except for the Nordic countries. Where standards of living are generally low, and confidence in governments to deliver policies is limited, the public may 'make do' with provision that is elsewhere considered to be poor, because of their low expectations.

Another problem in judging whether or not a policy has worked is how to isolate the effects of a specific measure, particularly in retrospect, in situations where policies have multiple objectives, or where the outcome is not necessarily the one intended. High childcare costs are usually believed to discourage labour force participation, whereas low-cost provision or tax credits may encourage participation, and low subsidies may prevent women from leaving employment, although here too findings are inconsistent (Gauthier, 1996a, pp 320-3). Moreover, public childcare provision may not be the only factor, or necessarily the main factor, in explaining above-average, full-time, dual-earner rates. A whole bundle of measures may need to be considered, including time policies, arrangements for monitoring the quality of public childcare, and the availability of public sector employment for women and protected domestic service jobs, in addition to a generous child benefit package and societal norms and expectations supportive of female employment. Similarly, the lack of success of measures designed to force men to take up parental leave may be attributable not only to wage differentials, as is often claimed, but also, and possibly more importantly, to power relations in society, which may require a different set of policies (Bekkengen, 2002).

Another factor making it difficult to isolate the effect of policies is that outcomes may not necessarily be what was sought or intended. Policies designed to redistribute resources vertically may, for example, not be of greatest benefit to those most in need, if take up is limited due to the stigma attached to means-tested benefits, as for example in Greece or in Central and Eastern Europe (CEE), where the process of applying for benefits is considered to be humiliating (Ferge, 2001b, p 145). Enforcement of policies to protect women as mothers and, thereby, support motherhood can have the paradoxical and unintended effect of widening the gender employment and pay gaps, since they make employers in the private sector reluctant to recruit women due to the additional costs involved (Del Re, 2000, p 109). Policies targeted at specific age groups or socio-economic categories may help to create a dependency culture or provoke intergenerational tensions, which are not only unintended but also unwanted outcomes, sometimes described as 'perverse effects' (Field, 1996, p 16).

Just as definitions of family policy are often extended to encompass policies implemented in other areas that may have an impact on families, the need to achieve policy targets elsewhere, notably for employment in line with the European employment strategy, may affect the everyday lives of families and their well being more than policies designed specifically to meet the needs of certain categories of families. The emphasis the strategy places on high employment and employability and, hence, on the need to develop provision for childcare to make mothers available for work, while also promoting parental leave, is a case in point, which may have both positive and negative side effects for families.

Even where policy evaluation is regularly undertaken, it is often difficult to interpret outcomes as marking the success or failure of specific measures. Policies intended to influence birth rates provide an apt example. Interpretations of outcomes also raise the issue of whether a policy can be deemed to be successful if it achieves unintended but positive effects, as illustrated by the reduction in working time in France, which was intended to lower unemployment but had the side effect of freeing up more time for family togetherness (Fagnani and Letablier, 2003, p 7). Alternatively, a policy may be the victim of its own success, as with the care benefit for older people (*allocation personnalisée d'autonomie*), introduced in 2001, which proved to be prohibitively expensive to operate because take up was so high.

The interpretation of outcomes is further complicated by the lack of consensus over objectives. In contrast to policies aimed at family life, it does seem easier to reach agreement over the objectives of employment, pensions or social inclusion policies, as demonstrated by the quantitative targets set for employment, to resolve the impending pensions crisis or reduce poverty.

Analysis of the fit, or mismatch, between objectives and outcomes highlights many of the tensions resulting from competing interests and ideologies between different policy actors, between policy makers and users, and also between and within societies and families. They further complicate attempts to establish direct linkages between inputs and outcomes and make findings difficult to interpret, particularly when they involve the implementation of policies across national boundaries.

Setting family policy priorities

Family life and, consequently, family policy are not easy topics to define or delimit (see Chapters Three and Six). Policy actors do not agree, either within or between countries, about the legitimacy or objectives of family policy, and the distribution of responsibility for formulating and implementing policy. If the success of policies is to be assessed in terms of their ability to achieve the outcomes intended, objectives need to be identifiable. Party politics and ideology clearly do matter in determining both policy objectives and the instruments used to deliver policy measures that have families as their target. The major political transitions undergone by the southern European and CEE countries as they have moved from authoritarian regimes to liberal democracies can be shown to have had an impact on the aims and objectives of family policies, their social acceptability and their outcomes (see Chapter Six).

Another illustration of how politically charged and divisive the topic of family policy can be was provided during the presidential election campaign in France in 2002. Jean-Marie Le Pen, the extreme right-wing candidate, who succeeded in reaching the second round of the elections as the opponent of Jacques Chirac, sought to gain political capital from an assault on three decades of family policy, which he described as a "politique anti-familiale", and designed with the deliberate, although not openly admitted, objective of destroying the family (National Front Manifesto, 2001). His priority was to pursue a pro-natalist family policy targeting 'French' mothers and children born within marriage. To achieve his objectives, he proposed to repeal the law on abortion and rescind legislation enabling unmarried and same-sex couples to sign formal cohabitation contracts. Instead, he advocated a substantial increase in financial support for families, especially large families of French descent, to a level that would cover two thirds of the cost of raising children and, thus, stem population decline. In his rhetoric, explicit pro-natalism was coupled with an outright condemnation of recourse to immigration as an alternative means of sustaining population growth.

The conservative, Christian and nationalist government brought to power in Hungary in 1998, affords a concrete example of a right-wing government pursuing policies aimed specifically at strengthening the middle classes (Ferge, 2001a, p 112). Rather than redistributing resources to all large families to achieve pro-natalist objectives, or to families most in need to relieve economic hardship, the objective was to encourage ethnic Hungarians to produce 'quality' children, a concept used by economists to describe the investment of parents in their children's well being (Ermisch, 2003, p 9).

Pursuit of population growth is an objective that has often been contested as a legitimate aim for family policy. It is, therefore, treated as a covert justification in most EU15 member states. Although few right-wing politicians across Europe adopt such a radical stance as in the two examples cited above, the right tends to prioritise policies involving horizontal redistribution through universal provision of benefits and services, designed to support the conventional family unit founded on marriage. The left, by contrast, bases its platform on vertical redistribution, through policies targeting low-income families, an approach the right sees as a dilution of family policy. In some cases, for example Finland, parties of the right tend to prioritise monetary benefits, while left-wing parties prefer to invest in services for children and families.

The issue of means testing has often been the subject of heated debate in EU member states. Despite evidence that the additional costs involved in administering means-tested benefits may outweigh savings, even right-wing governments have used means testing in an attempt to cut costs and redistribute scarce resources towards the most needy. Frank Field, a former director of the Child Poverty Action Group in the UK and a Labour member of parliament renowned for his free thinking, has described means testing as "the cancer within the welfare state, rotting decent values and overwhelming the honesty and dignity of recipients in almost equal proportions" (Field, 1996, p 9). His view is shared in the UK by critics of different political complexions, who contend that means-tested benefits can produce over-reliance on the state and a welfare dependency culture, trapping recipients in unemployment and poverty and removing incentives to save (Alcock, 1996, p 50). Concern about the perverse effects of means testing has led British governments of right and left to move away from passive policies focusing on income support towards proactive, or activation, policies, designed to 'make work pay'. This phrase has been adopted in the European employment strategy (COM(2003) 6 final, 14.01.2003, § 2.2.2), the aim being to ensure that people are better off in work than on benefits, precisely by eliminating unemployment and poverty traps.

If the primary objective of policy is not to improve the quality of life for all families but, rather, to concentrate resources on certain types of families at risk, it is questionable whether it should be described as family policy. When employment and employability become the main policy priority for governments and are seen as the most effective solution to the demise of the welfare state, as has been the case in the Union since the 1990s, the legitimacy of family issues as a focus for dedicated policies is further eroded. Moreover, the centrality of employment, coupled with cuts in benefits and the introduction of charges for public services, can have the perverse effect of intensifying social exclusion by creating an underclass of the work poor (without work) and the working poor (in work), reinforcing the need for policies that guarantee a minimum income.

Shifts in the dominant political ideology, in conjunction with differences in the rate and intensity of socio-economic change, mean that policy actors vary in their responses and priorities for dealing with change, as demonstrated in previous chapters by the fluctuations noted in the importance given to family policy and its explicitness, or otherwise, in political rhetoric. Among EU15 member states, family matters tend to surface as an issue in election campaigns, only to recede when governments are faced with seemingly more pressing economic problems. Yet, efforts to reduce public spending and make efficiency gains can have a major impact on the well being of families, by both reducing household income and shifting the cost of providing services onto families. The aim of policy intervention is then to bolster family solidarity and self-reliance, and to find cost-effective measures to assist families in coping with the burden of care.

In this context, an economically viable, and politically justifiable, objective for family policy, as compared to employment, gender equality or social policy, is often to help parents combine paid work with family life. The development of reconciliation policy reinforces the need for interministerial and cross-sector co-operation and co-ordination, but it may further dilute the family dimension of policy, ultimately replacing family policy by social care policy, as mediated through, or delegated to, the market, the voluntary sector and families themselves (Daly and Lewis, 2000, pp 282, 292).

At the turn of the 21st century, policy actors in member states in the centre and north of EU15 were inclined to agree that the reconciliation of employment with care for children and older people, or work–life balance as it was called in the UK, was a major issue for the policy agenda. They expected to be judged on their ability to deliver good-quality services to meet the demand. Housing and employment were also relatively high on the policy agenda, particularly where governments were striving to meet EU targets to increase employment rates for women. In southern Europe, where family policy was still regarded essentially as an economic support system and families as a resource, and where entitlements were conditional on employment and low levels of public provision, the stated aim was to raise the level of benefits for all families. For CEE countries, the priority was to raise the standard of living of the population as a whole and not specifically of families as units. The economic and demographic pressures that had forced women out of the labour market and refocused attention on their role as mothers were producing tensions, due to the perceived mismatch between policy objectives and outcomes (Pascall and Manning, 2000, pp 260-4).

Take up of policy measures

An indicator of the impact that policy measures are having on families and of their effectiveness in reaching the population targeted is the extent to which those eligible to receive them take up benefits and services. High take-up rates can be interpreted as an indication of the acceptability of public policy provision, whereas low take up may suggest that policy intervention in a particular area is not widely accepted. Poor take up can also be explained by other reasons, such as lack of knowledge about entitlements and availability, and problems of access.

Take up of benefits is difficult to measure, and few countries – most notably France, Germany, the Netherlands and the UK – have attempted to do so systematically (van Oorschot and Math, 1996). Self-reporting across a larger number of EU member states[1] suggests that access and take up of many of the benefits and services provided by the state is generally good, particularly when the benefits most people receive, such as child benefit or state pensions, are provided on a universal citizenship or residence basis, or as an employment right. Most people also routinely use publicly provided services, such as healthcare and nursery schooling, when they are available on a universal basis, free of charge, or at a low cost for the consumer.

---

[1] Over 3,000 family members were asked about their take up of benefits and services in a small-scale survey carried out in 2001-02 as part of a project funded by the European Commission, covering eight EU15 member states and three CEE countries (see the Methods Note in Hantrais, 2003, annex 2, for further details).

Cross-national and sub-national variations can often be explained by differences in knowledge and awareness, availability, eligibility, access and personal choice. Information about entitlements was found to be most likely to come from social workers and social services, the media and, less often, friends and relatives. Non-take up was sometimes caused by lack of clarity in eligibility criteria, the complex rules and regulations put in place, and administrative red tape. Where officials can exercise discretion or several agencies are involved in co-ordinating a scheme, non-take up may be the result of the way an individual interprets the rules or of administrative inefficiencies (Walker, 2000, p 154). Despite fairly wide availability, low take up of benefits in Hungary, for example, was explained by the fact that the process is so complicated. Frequent changes in the system, associated with the three successive governments in power in the space of 10 years, meant that beneficiaries lost track of their entitlements.

In Greece, Spain and CEE countries, non-take up of benefits was attributed to restrictions on eligibility and the low level of provision. As a result, beneficiaries felt it was not worth the effort of pursuing claims. The deep mistrust of external intervention in the private domain of the family was another factor dissuading beneficiaries from taking up their entitlements. In some cases, in Estonia and Italy for example, non-take up was explained by the desire to remain self-reliant, and avoid dependence on external help from the state or other policy providers. The introduction of means testing in CEE countries was believed to have reduced access to benefits and services. Confirmation was found that non take up was due to the degrading and humiliating nature of the process of applying for benefits, particularly if they are means tested. When entitlement was limited to a small proportion of the population, means testing could have a stigmatising effect.

Sub-national variations in take up can be explained by socio-economic factors. The level of take up may vary between social categories according to the type of benefits concerned. Certain public services appear to be used to a greater extent by higher status and income groups in cases where a financial contribution is required, for instance for childcare. They may, thereby, become inaccessible for middle-income groups, who cannot afford to pay and are not eligible for means-tested exemption, as with healthcare in Ireland. Low educational qualifications and employment status are often associated with low take up, due not only to lack of knowledge and awareness of rights, but also to poor provision and access in rural areas.

Although few people expect employers to provide workplace services for their employees, the most common forms of provision at work are flexible working hours, crèches and leave to care for sick children or relatives. A frequent finding, even in the Nordic states, is that men are failing to make use of their entitlements. Apart from the usual explanation that childcare is seen as the responsibility of the mother rather than the father, whose role is to provide for the family, a reason given in both Estonia and Greece was that men are afraid to take leave because of the fear of losing their jobs.

Benefits and services supplied by the voluntary sector tend to be used least of all. In most countries, services operated by non-governmental organisations (NGOs) are considered as a supplement to provision by the state and, more rarely, as a substitute for it. Occasionally, however, they are the main, or only, form of external services available. In Germany, for example, the voluntary sector plays a significant role in providing kindergarten and childcare places, as well as counselling services for families after marital breakdown. In Ireland, older respondents make greater use of voluntary sector provision, largely because of the lack of publicly provided services, but younger generations tend to be reluctant to have recourse to voluntary sector services, particularly those provided by the Church, because they distrust any form of intervention in private life.

Measuring the effects of policy on families

A substantial body of literature has examined the possible impact of policy on demographic trends and patterns of family formation. Governments pursuing clearly defined and coherent policy objectives, as in France and Sweden during the immediate postwar period, were interested in assessing the efficiency and effectiveness of specific policy measures. Since the 1980s, British governments have monitored and evaluated the impact of various benefits from the policy formation phase through to implementation (Davies et al, 2000). During the 1980s and 1990s, several large and small-scale international studies and state-of-the-art reviews looked at a wide range of social and, more especially, family policy and child support measures across Europe, with a view to comparing the impact of a range of benefits in cash and kind on household income and the quality of life of families (Kamerman and Kahn, 1982; Bradshaw et al, 1993; Gauthier, 1996b). Comparative studies have examined the possible relationship between welfare benefits, family structure and patterns of employment (Gornick et al, 1997). Attempts have been made to assess, among other things, whether benefit levels have an effect on the number of lone parents or may serve as a disincentive for lone mothers to seek paid work (Bradshaw et al, 1996).

Much of the early work that looked at the success of policies in achieving their intended demographic objectives relied on econometric analyses. Economists posited a direct link between household resources and behaviour. Proponents of the new household economics (following Becker, 1981) generally assumed that decisions about the timing of childbirth, family size and the division of labour within households, and between market and non-market roles, are taken on the basis that families or, more specifically, stable household units, seek to optimise their resources by making rational choices as suppliers and consumers of goods and services. Such an approach has been criticised for taking as its premise that families are permanent indivisible units unconstrained by cultural factors, rather than complex organisations that change over time and space (Allsopp, 1995, p 154).

Economists and statisticians have analysed the cost of raising children to assess the extent to which the financial impact of children on families may be attenuated by policy measures (Ekert-Jaffé, 1986; Ermisch, 1996, 2003). They have also set out to assess the influence of labour market prospects and public policies on the fertility decisions taken by women, in an effort to determine what is the 'right' time for women in different socio economic and institutional contexts to have children, and how different welfare arrangements support or discourage mothers' employment and earnings (O'Dorchai, 2003). Such analysis is premised on the assumption that women 'choose' to participate in paid employment and that decisions about fertility depend on their ability to combine employment with motherhood (Meulders and O'Dorchai, 2002, p 2).

The growing interest among governments in activation policies, designed to move unemployed people off benefits and into work, and in joined-up thinking about policy coincided in the UK with the adoption of a multimethods approach to policy analysis (Walker, 2000). Policies for families offer a propitious terrain for multidisciplinary, holistic policy evaluation, since families are at the nexus of labour markets, employment and social policy. This section examines some of the evidence for and against the possible impact of policies on family life in the areas explored in previous chapters. It looks at the extent to which decisions taken by couples are directly or indirectly affected by public policy: whether to marry or separate; whether mothers with young children go out to work; when young people leave the family home; and whether older people live by themselves or with their families. The discussion draws on the findings from both large-scale quantitative studies that have sought to establish linkages between public policies and changing family patterns, and smaller-scale empirical work that has involved asking families about their perceptions of the influence of public policies on the decisions they take about family life[2].

The impact of policy on family formation

As noted in Chapter Six, few Europeans today accept policy intervention that deliberately sets out to stimulate population growth by prohibiting access to effective means of birth control or by making abortion more difficult to obtain. The assumption underlying the conception of family policy developed in France and Sweden from the 1930s was that, by offering generous financial support, governments could persuade, or at least encourage, couples to have more children (Myrdal, 1945; Calot, 1980). Attempts by demographers and economists to test this assumption

---

[2] A total of 465 in-depth interviews were carried out with men and women representing different family types, age groups and socio-economic categories in 11 EU15 member states and CEE countries between 2001-02 as part of the research project referred to in the previous note (see the Methods Note in Hantrais, 2003, annex 3, for further details).

empirically by measuring the correlation between benefits paid to families (as of right and means tested) and fertility rates have produced contradictory and inconclusive findings, as noted above. Statistical analysis of the possible impact on birth rates of legislation providing for family allowances in selected European countries between the early 1970s and 1980s found, for example, that fertility rates fell less steeply in countries that had pursued active family policies than in those where no adjustment had been made. The generous package of family allowances offered in France was credited with explaining about 10% of births in the 1980s (Ekert-Jaffé, 1986, p 345). These findings, like many large-scale multivariate analyses, can be criticised for taking account of only a limited number of benefits, for assuming that the same relationship exists between fertility and welfare across and within countries, and for imputing rather than observing the effects of policy (Gauthier, 1996a, pp 314-17).

Social policy analysts are also sceptical about the idea that family policy, in the form of universal cash payments, can have an effect on demographic trends, and they question whether the decisions of couples to have, or not to have, more children are the result of materialistic calculations. Rather, it is argued, a sustained rise in the birth rate is more likely to be attributable to broader economic, cultural and social forces, and the value society attributes to family building (for example Hoem, 1993, with reference to Sweden).

It may be no coincidence that countries such as France, where the policy environment is overtly supportive of family life, as shown in previous chapters, have maintained total fertility rates above the EU15 average, or that levels have fallen in southern Europe where state support is limited. However, extensive universal welfare provision, as for example in Sweden, would not seem to be sufficient to prevent fluctuations in total fertility rates, a measure that is more sensitive to policy shifts than completed fertility (see Chapter Two). In 2000, total fertility in Sweden had fallen below the EU15 average and was lower than in the UK, where the policy environment was much less supportive of family life.

In EU member states, when they are questioned about the effect of policies on their decisions regarding family life, most people acknowledge that family events are not always the result of rational choices, reached after careful reflection and negotiation. They rarely mention spontaneously public provision of benefits and services for families as a factor influencing their decisions. Public policy is, at best, a secondary consideration in encouraging family formation, although legal frameworks can limit or extend choice. Prohibition of abortion and restricted access to family planning were not cited as reasons explaining unwanted pregnancies. However, a few women, for example in Ireland and Poland, admitted they may have borne more children than they really wanted, because their strong religious convictions prevented them from using effective methods of contraception or resorting to abortion. Prohibition does not prevent Irish women seeking to terminate an unwanted pregnancy from continuing to travel abroad to obtain an abortion.

When women are not constrained by their own moral beliefs, the existence of negative or prohibitive policy measures designed to stem population decline has not been found to achieve the objective of sustaining the birth rate. A married Hungarian man in his late forties, with one child, aptly articulated the widespread rejection of overt pro-natalist incentives, while also calling into question their effectiveness:

> If I'm not enthusiastic about children, if I don't want to have children, then the state can't make me want them. The state should make sure that, in the long run, the country's population doesn't die out, but this is primarily the responsibility of families, of people who want to have children, who feel capable of dealing with the accompanying worries and problems. ... Everybody's grateful for the various forms of support, but we shouldn't rely on them too much. ... Children were born during the 1950s and the war as well; those people weren't thinking about getting subsidies.

While no unequivocal evidence is available to demonstrate that isolated family policy measures are directly responsible for an increase in the number of births, the indications are that the lack of supportive measures and, more especially, of effective economic and employment policies may be contributing to the continuing fall in fertility rates in southern European and CEE countries. In southern Europe, in the absence of generous public policies, a critical factor in decisions about family formation, especially for lower socio-economic groups, is ready access to family support networks.

In the same way that coercive government intervention to promote fertility is almost universally condemned, evidence from interviews suggests that measures aimed at influencing the timing of births by encouraging couples to start raising a family before they feel ready to do so are not well received and are not effective. The rejection of incentives to accelerate the timing of childbirths was illustrated by a comment from a Swedish mother at home with a reconstituted family, in a reference to the premium paid to parents who have a second child within 21 months of the first:

> It should not be social benefits that decide the size of the family or when you have your children. Many people are perhaps not ready to have a second child but feel they must have a second child in order to benefit from the system [speed premium]. The first might not be old enough.

Whereas public policy was not mentioned as a factor affecting the decision about whether or not to have children in the UK or Ireland, the family's economic circumstances were often said to influence the timing of births.

Views differ about the extent to which governments should intervene to reduce the number of teenage pregnancies or discourage the postponement of births, and about the effectiveness of policy measures in tackling the issue. Over the longer term, the number of teenage pregnancies has been falling, although to a lesser extent in the UK than in the Netherlands or Sweden, as noted in Chapter Three. The concern of British governments to reduce teenage births further has prompted international comparisons of policies. Differences have, thus, been identified between the Netherlands and the UK in moral attitudes towards marriage and family life, which are reflected in adversarial politics in the British system and, in turn, feed into sex education to produce an incoherent message. As a result, sex education may be part of the problem rather than the solution (Lewis and Knijn, 2002).

Data on teenage pregnancies and abortions in Estonia indicate that both rates are declining, although the reasons have not been documented, and the trend in teenage pregnancies runs counter to government objectives of encouraging births. In Spain, where the teenage pregnancy rate is relatively low, and age at first childbirth and all births is relatively high, the explanation given for delaying childbirth is not that women are taking account of policies designed to influence the timing of births. An older Spanish woman, who was married with two daughters, aged 25 and 28 living at home, and who was not herself employed, attributed the postponement of childbirth to the lack of independence among young people:

> Now I see that people don't think of having children so soon. I became a mother for the first time when I was 25, and I see my daughter and her friends at that age, and no way! I began to be economically independent when I was 19, and the same was true for my husband. Now people have to depend on their parents for longer, and can't even think of having children.

In her view, this is a situation that can only be resolved by policies aimed at enabling young people to become financially self-sufficient.

The impact of policy on living standards

The resources concentrated on large families to support family building may help to prevent them from falling into poverty, although the contribution of benefits to the cost of raising children would seem to be relatively small. The incentive effect of tax relief and of the child benefit package on family formation is limited, since benefits only partially compensate parents for the cost of children. A study in France in 2001 suggested that family allowances contributed between 18% of income for a household with two adults and two young children on low earnings and 33% for parents with four children on a slightly higher income (UNAF, 2001). While public policy measures may, therefore, do no more than influence the timing of birth, their impact on the living standards of families, which is an important and widely accepted objective for family policy, may also be limited.

Advance maintenance payments following divorce or separation, social assistance for long-term unemployed and lone-parent benefit for never-married mothers are designed to offer a safety net and security for families to help prevent them from falling into poverty, particularly in northern Europe where the level of benefits is relatively high. In the Nordic states and France, while not directly determining decisions to have children, the overall generosity of public policy support for families is widely credited with redistributing income vertically between social groups, thereby raising standards of living and reducing income inequalities. In Germany, policy measures are thought to be more relevant to the ability of families to manage everyday life than to decisions about whether or not to have children. In the southern European countries, by contrast, governments are strongly criticised for the low level of provision, which is considered inadequate to prevent poverty and is no substitute for family support in times of need, as intimated by a well-educated Italian woman from the north-east of the country, who was in her early fifties and had three children:

> Here we make do with what we have because resources are limited. When somebody decides to have a child, or when a birth is unplanned, we don't look to the state to make legal provision or to ensure other forms of provision for maternity and young children. Everybody talks about family policy, but in reality it's very limited.

In CEE countries, the substantial reduction in public policy support and the withdrawal of a number of benefits and services for families since the end of the Soviet era is seen as having had a detrimental impact on family well being by both creating and fuelling widespread unemployment and poverty. The effect of benefits on family income is said to be negligible, and the low level may serve as a deterrent rather than as an incentive to have children. Raising a large family is more often than not equated with poverty, and to contemplate having children verges on negligence, as intimated by a divorced Polish woman in her mid-twenties:

> Wages are low and social assistance is low. How can you even think of giving birth to another human being and be responsible for him or her? ... The child benefit you get will suffice to buy nappies. ... You receive these few zloty from the state and you don't even know what to do with the money.

Since services for families are generally delivered at local level, the uneven distribution of policy provision between regions reinforces internal disparities within countries. In Italy, for example, benefits and services are much more limited in the south, to the extent that an Italian woman from the north, who was living in a reconstituted family with two children, claimed: "I would never go to the south to be cared for".

Hungarian family members provided clear evidence of the continuing disparity in the treatment of different ethnic groups in public policy, as illustrated by the attention given to 'quality' families. Despite the shift in 1998 away from support for low-income families, public perceptions are that

Roma families are exploiting and abusing the system and do not deserve to be supported in their alien lifestyle. The notion of the 'deserving poor' was also mentioned in the UK, although not specifically with reference to ethnic minorities. In Greece and Poland, minority ethnic groups seem to be invisible in society, whereas disparities between urban and rural communities are seen as a continuing source of social inequality. As a result of the shift of emphasis away from social assistance to employment policies, another form of inequality that is becoming more visible across the Union is between work-rich and work-poor families, which can result in heavier reliance on policy provision (Kay, 2003, p 232).

The impact of policy on living arrangements

In most countries, the public accepts the legitimacy of family policy measures when it perceives them to be a response to socio-demographic change but not when they are seen as an attempt to determine behaviour (see Chapter Six). People are also more willing to admit they take some account of public policy in their decisions about living arrangements than they are to acknowledge that benefits and services influence family formation. The alignment of benefit entitlements between married and unmarried cohabiting couples is a case in point. In countries where unmarried cohabitation is widespread, and unmarried partnerships can be formalised through cohabitation contracts, as in the Nordic states, Belgium, France, Germany and the Netherlands, or where solicitors can draw up legally binding contracts between unmarried cohabiting couples, as in the UK, the advantage of contractual arrangements is that they establish rights with regard to property, home ownership, savings and investments (see Chapter Five). Permissive legislation acknowledging non-conventional family forms means that the main factors said to affect decisions about whether to opt for marriage or unmarried cohabitation in these countries are primarily personal feelings about the value of marital status, which may, in turn, be reflected in changes implemented through legal frameworks.

Prohibitive and restrictive legislation limits the number of divorces, but it does not curb the underlying trend towards marital dissolution, as illustrated by Ireland, where judicial separation was authorised before the ban on divorce was lifted, and remains a less costly and simpler solution to the breakdown of marriage. Nor are proactive measures to promote the formal two-parent married couple associated in the statistics with markedly higher marriage rates or consistently lower unmarried cohabitation rates.

In general, couples claim they take little account of benefits and taxation systems when deciding whether or not to marry, although instances were found in France and Poland of younger couples who had calculated the difference marriage would make in benefits and tax concessions, particularly when they were planning to have children. In Estonia, a few couples took account of the fact that joint taxation of married spouses can give access to tax relief, which is not the case for unmarried cohabitees. The view is strongly held across the Union that government policy should align tax and welfare entitlements of individuals living in non-conventional arrangements with those of married couples to preserve freedom of choice, as argued by a young male unmarried cohabitee with one child in France:

> Today, we live in a society that's free. People don't necessarily want to get married. Some people sign a cohabitation contract. Marriage seems to me to belong to another age. When people are really living together, that should suffice.

In countries where de-institutionalised family forms are widespread, particularly the Nordic states, law reform extending rights to unmarried cohabiting couples, same-sex couples, and children born out of wedlock or living in reconstituted families has largely removed the stigma associated with extramarital relationships by legitimising and normalising *de facto* situations. In Greece, Italy and Poland, where moral opprobrium is still attached to unmarried cohabitation and lone parenthood, social pressure, as translated into legislation, can be an important factor determining decisions about whether or not to marry. In Greece, the pressure to maintain conventional living arrangements remains very strong, and the public has little appetite for reform. A representative of the Greek Federation for Large Families expressed concern that: "Single-parent families ... should not become a norm". She commented: "If this is the case, what kind of society will we create? Society can't exist like this".

Lone parenthood is an issue that is often raised in discussion about the possible influence of benefits on never married motherhood. Evidence from comparative studies does not suggest that lone parenthood is preferred to couple parenthood because of the advantages it procures from welfare benefits (Bradshaw et al, 1996, p 71). Although many governments pay a higher level of child benefit or family allowances for lone-parent families, the benefit is unlikely to be seen as an incentive to become a lone parent, since the rate is relatively low, except in France. In this case, the duration is limited to 12 months for children over the age of three (Algava and Avenel, 2001, p 2). Evidence is found to suggest that the level of financial incentives may be a factor taken into account when assessing the cost of moving off benefits into work. In an attempt to make policy more cost effective in the UK and avoid possible incentives for never-married women to become lone parents, the higher rate of benefit was replaced in 1997 by a package of measures in the form of the New Deal for Lone Parents (see Chapter Five).

Public opinion continues to be divided over legal reform to recognise same-sex partnerships, as demonstrated by the heated debates leading up to the introduction of cohabitation contracts in France (*pacte civil de solidarité*) in 1999 and Germany (*Lebenspartnerschaftsgesetz*) in 2001. Attitudes towards same-sex couples are slowly changing across Europe. Estonian society is, for example, tolerant of same-sex relationships, but governments prefer to pretend they do not exist. A Hungarian woman in her early fifties, with two grown-up children, who was living in a same-sex relationship, described her own perceptions in the following terms:

> In short, for me a family is the smallest economic and emotional community that people live in. I don't necessarily think of a family as the traditional daddy, mummy and children. There is also daddy, daddy and children, and mummy, mummy and children. For me this all fits into the concept of family. The family is a community, a place, where you can find refuge from the problems of the world, where there's quiet, and love … a place to start from and come back to, everybody doing their own thing.

Even where law reform has been enacted, as in the UK, same-sex adoption was found to be an area where legislation was ahead of opinion and a response to the living arrangements of a small minority of the population.

The impact of policy on intergenerational relations

The attitudinal data analysed in Chapter Six indicates that societies vary in the extent to which they expect the state to intervene in making provision to care for young children and older family dependants. Cutbacks in public spending on services such as childcare and residential homes for older people, in combination with the growing need for financial, social and medical support in old age, have placed greater pressure on families at a time when women, as the traditional carers, are less available and willing to provide unpaid care. In many countries, the pivot, or sandwich, generation is beginning to question the moral, legal and financial obligation to assume responsibility for their relatives, and some evidence was found of strain on relationships and the demand for more support from the state.

Most people continue to feel a strong moral and social duty to care for their family members. The way in which they perceive their responsibility for relatives seems to be influenced, directly and indirectly, by policy. In the Nordic states, public administration is relied on as the main supplier of services for both children and older people. Grandparents are not expected to provide childcare for their grandchildren, and it is not unusual for younger people still living at home to pay rent to their parents when they are earning an income. Family members expect to supplement public support with practical help and care to make it possible for elderly relatives to continue living at home, but they do not consider they have primary responsibility for caring, as explained by a young Swedish man without a family of his own:

> My parents are helping their parents with shopping and the like. Me and my brother help them with the garden. All the family helps them. There's nothing special in that. To help elderly relatives is natural. But

it's not easy. My grandmother and grandfather have lived in the same house for 57 years. You can't just throw them out. You try to help them as much as possible, but the main responsibility lies with the municipality and the state.

The high visibility of family policy in France is associated with the widespread public provision of childcare, and the expectation that the state will deliver good-quality and affordable services. State intervention in family matters is taken for granted, as explained by a woman working in the catering trade, and who was married to a divorcee:

Yes, the family is a question for the state to deal with. For childcare, crèches, family allowances. Lots of things. Improvements can only come from the state. We can't do anything about it ourselves. It's natural that the state should look after families, crèches and schools. It's natural because children are the citizens of tomorrow. They will be the ones paying taxes. They're the ones who will make the country function later on. That's why the state has to get involved. So, it's natural there should be facilities for children. It's the same with older people. It's natural for the state to look after them.

Although they expect public administration and local authorities to play a strong support role, families feel they have primary responsibility for elderly dependants. The sense of moral responsibility towards family members does, however, seem to be weakening, particularly among the younger generations and in the urban environment, where the majority view is that members of the pivot generation should not feel obliged to take frail elderly parents into their homes when they are no longer able to live independently.

The UK offers another configuration, where parents expect to bear the main responsibility for children when they are young, but not for older relatives. If a mother with young children does not stop work or switch to a part time arrangement, childcare is discharged by resorting to private provision, either by family members or, if it can be afforded, the market. A high incidence was found in the UK, as in most other EU15 member states, of mutual intergenerational dependence, whereby younger family members rely on their older relatives to take care of their grandchildren, for example after school until the mother finishes work, in return for which younger generations provide services for elderly parents. Many people define intergenerational dependence broadly to include daily care responsibilities, but also emotional care and support for relatives, who often insist on maintaining their independence. Family interdependence is not seen as an obligation or as a necessity due to the lack of public provision. Rather, it is perceived as a moral duty, but the expectation is that financial support will be forthcoming from the state to purchase additional care when it is most needed.

Members of the pivot generation in CEE countries also express a strong sense of moral responsibility towards parents who are no longer able to manage by themselves. They either expect to take their parents into their own homes or to support them financially. Such support is not confined to parents, as explained by a Hungarian respondent, who was married with two children and on parental leave at the time of the interview:

> For me, it's self-evident that if you have a relative who needs help, you go to any length of trouble to help them, even if it means them moving in with you. This has always been very important in our family. ... Grandparents, relatives such as aunts and uncles, they're all included in this understanding. ... We have ourselves taken care of an aunt who wasn't even a close relative, but she didn't have any other relatives, so that's why we had to take care of her. ... This is entirely natural.

Similarly, in Estonia, families with young children receive help from older relatives in taking care of their children, and many families care for close elderly relatives (mothers, fathers and parents-in-law) in the widely held belief that children have responsibility for the care of their parents. Support from a close relative can avoid the humiliation of having to deal with state bureaucracy and being made to feel inferior.

Family relationships are often an important factor in decisions about where people live. Public policy may influence such decisions insofar as it determines family obligations and responsibilities and affects the standards and availability of housing and other amenities. In southern Europe, as in CEE countries, respondents would seem to choose where to live primarily according to the proximity of family members, but their choice is also determined by the availability of suitable and affordable housing. Younger people continue to live with their parents until, and even after, they are earning a livelihood, because they cannot afford to pay for their own housing. The pivot generation may move to the same area and, in some situations, move in with the older generation. Parents also expect to be able to secure jobs for their offspring and to assist them with housing rather than relying on the state.

In Greece, Italy and Spain, decisions by adult children about whether to continue to live in their parents' home, or by families about whether older people should live with their children, are also influenced by the legal obligations placed on families to maintain their members, but they depend to a considerable degree on the availability of morally acceptable and financially viable alternatives. In Ireland too, the generosity of public policies to support people in old age is seen as instrumental in decisions about their living arrangements, determining whether or not they can remain independent. To a greater extent than in most other EU15 member states, people in the UK, especially in the middle- and higher-income groups, admit that the choice of where to live is determined by the quality of local services, particularly childcare and education.

The outcome of state benefits for children and older people living in multigenerational families may be interpreted in some countries as a means of keeping families together, which can be viewed either positively or negatively depending on attitudes towards independent living and the availability of support services. Multigenerational living may serve as a safety net for older people and an antidote for heavy reliance on the state. The legal obligation to care can, however, come into conflict with measures encouraging greater individualism, for instance through the benefits system. It may be in the interest of families to live together because of the financial benefits accrued from pensions and care allowances. This was a reason given by social workers in Poland to explain why families may be reluctant to see an older relative placed in an institution, even when it becomes necessary for health reasons. Children are afraid of losing the regular income from their relative's pension or care benefit, which is an important supplement to household resources.

A similar argument applies in southern Europe, where the property owned by older generations and their pensions can mean that multigenerational living benefits the whole family by raising the household's living standards. The conflict between the duty of care and the aspirations of women to be economically active and to have a life of their own is, however, beginning to be expressed more openly in some quarters, for example in more progressive regions in Spain, or the larger towns in the centre-north of Italy. In Spain, grandparents continue to be an important source of childcare support, but this role is being called into question, as intimated by one older women:

> There's a real need to help these young parents in order for them not to be so dependent on grandparents. When I become a grandmother, I'd like to take care of my grandchildren at weekends once in a while, or during holidays, but not as an obligation. I think I would feel trapped. I'd like to be able to relax when I retire.

The most common solution for frail ageing parents in Spain is still for them to live with their adult children in a show of familial solidarity, but here too traditional expectations are being questioned, as explained by a widow in her early sixties, who was working part time and looking after her grandchildren when her daughter was out at work:

> My daughters and sons-in-law all work, and I've psyched myself up to face the idea of living in a home when I'm older. In the past this would never have crossed your or your mother's mind. I looked after her at home. The family atmosphere for the old and young was quite different.

In Greece, parents and children also feel they have a responsibility to provide mutual support. They expect to take older relatives into their homes, but they are increasingly reluctant to see several generations living together under the same roof, implying a greater need for external support.

The impact of policy on the family–employment relationship

The labour market participation of mothers has long been an issue on national and EU policy agendas. Interest within the Union was justified initially by the twin aims of ensuring equality of opportunity and protecting mothers as workers. The question of how to reconcile paid work and family life gained prominence in the late 1990s, as the European employment strategy unfolded. Ever since women began entering the labour market in large numbers, analysts of the family–employment relationship in western Europe have sought to establish what impact public policy might have on the strategies adopted by couples, and especially women, for combining these two strands of their lives and achieving a satisfactory work–life balance.

Econometric studies have produced conflicting findings about the opportunity cost of children for women's labour market participation, and the capacity of public policy to offset the effect of the presence of children (Gauthier, 1996a, pp 320-5). Policy simulation techniques have identified the level of benefits accruing to French mothers who are economically active as a key feature of policy success in France, compared with Belgium, Ireland and Luxembourg (Jeandidier, 1997, p 43). Financial rationality would not, however, seem to be the only factor determining the elasticity of women's labour market behaviour. Other work suggests that a 'shaping effect' can be found only if governments offer a whole raft of co-ordinated social policies to support a particular model of labour market participation for families (Gornick et al, 1997, pp 63-6; Dingledey, 2001, p 653). In the case of lone mothers, evidence from analysis of differential employment rates may not be sufficient to demonstrate a strong causal linkage between policy and outcomes, but it can serve to justify policy intervention to encourage lone parents to seek employment, as in Ireland and the UK.

Qualitative comparative analysis of the possible linkages between policies that support the employment of mothers, including public childcare, paid maternity and parental leave, indicates that the impact of policies is far from being uniform, and confirms that policy measures may have unexpected, unwanted and unintended outcomes. While public availability of good-quality and affordable childcare is widely believed to be one of the most important factors affecting decisions about whether or not mothers enter or remain in employment in most EU member states, facilities for children need to be compatible with working hours, which must, in turn, be flexible and freely chosen. Leave arrangements are less central concerns, except insofar as they enable parents to take time off when necessary to deal with family crises and, in the case of paid leave, provide an incentive for women to stay at home for a longer period than they would otherwise have done.

The countries in northern Europe that have gone furthest in implementing and policing measures to encourage more women to enter and remain in employment are generally those where public support for dual earning is taken for granted. A side effect of public policy measures in France has been to raise the level of expectations that parents have of public service provision and, in many cases, to fuel dissatisfaction with the available facilities. Even though provision is very generous, compared with many other EU15 member states, and some crèches are open 24 hours a day, a French woman with a young baby, living in an unmarried cohabiting relationship, explained how restrictive entitlement rules can have the unintended effect of preventing unemployed women from entering employment:

> I wanted to start work in September, so from April I began to look for childcare, a childminder, crèche. ... But everywhere I was told that I didn't have the right to have a place because I was unemployed. We wrote to the mayor to explain that it was complicated to find a job when you had a child that needed looking after. She agreed but said that was the rule. When you don't have a job you can't find a place. It's a vicious circle.

Views about parental leave were found to be ambivalent in Germany insofar as they can be interpreted as a measure to avoid the need for public childcare provision, and confirm women are primary carers, since they are much more likely than men to take leave. The taxation system is perceived as favouring the male breadwinner model and providing a further disincentive for women to remain in employment.

In the southern European and CEE countries, decisions about whether or not women with young children undertake paid work are affected to a much greater extent by the ability of employment policy to deliver suitable and secure jobs, compatible working hours and a reasonable level of pay than by policies on leave and childcare. Families also take account of the overall level of support in the community at large. In the absence of state provision, particularly in rural areas, the availability of family care is the most usual arrangement making it possible for women to enter and remain in the workforce, although it is not necessarily seen as the most satisfactory solution for reconciling paid work and family life.

Public opinion does not always agree with state intervention to support mothers in employment, even on equality grounds, if the aim appears to be to force everybody into work. Pressures on women to take up employment are creating tensions in countries such as Ireland where women were, in the past, expected to concentrate their energies on their mothering tasks, as reported by an Irish mother of three in her early thirties:

> Women have in many ways been actively discouraged from participating in the labour market for quite a period of time. Now we've had a very dramatic flip in the situation where we have labour shortages and now it's like 'come on, work, you need to work'. That is causing an awful lot of strain on parenting. People find a huge tension combining the two.

The public sector is widely seen as an attractive employer for women because it is gender aware. However, public sector employment is found to reinforce gender segregation in employment and disparities in pay, since the available jobs, while more secure, are usually less well paid, and it is almost exclusively women who avail themselves of opportunities to adapt their working patterns, as pointed out by an Irish economic policy actor:

> The civil service … have huge family-friendly programmes: job sharing, term-time work, work sharing. All the figures show that 96% who take these are female and just 4% are male.

Private sector employers in countries with effective systems for monitoring, policing and sanctioning gender discrimination in recruitment, training and employment are likely to be aware of gender policies and do generally implement them. In France, where working arrangements are tightly controlled, some employers recognise that they have an interest in being sympathetic to the family needs of their employees. A French women in her early forties, who was married, had brought up three children and was herself an employer, aptly summed up the views shared by many French families about the role of employers as providers of family-friendly policies:

> That's not the role of an employer. An employer is an employer, not a mum and dad. Of course, if you have a large company, you can provide a crèche. But in absolute terms, it's not their role. But employers aren't stupid either; it's better if they improve the working conditions of their employees. There should be crèches available. It's not the job of employers to provide them. But it's true that, if a firm is employing thousands of workers, then why not provide a workplace crèche? It makes life easier and better. It's more practical. Why not? People work better. It helps improve working conditions.

Even where, as far as European law is concerned, policy seems to provide reasonably good protection for working mothers, implementation and monitoring may be uneven. In Spain, for example, legislation is not necessarily matched in practice, as explained by one female respondent living in a cohabiting relationship:

> In January 1998, I started work as a sales assistant in a company. I signed a provisional contract for three months, which they renewed for a further six months. In July, I happily informed the company that I was pregnant and, on October 19, my boss informed me that they would not be renewing my contract. A few days earlier the front pages of the newspapers had been talking about a European Union directive that 'protects' pregnant women. From what?

The effect of the imposition of strict regulatory frameworks to control leave arrangements and working practices has meant that employers in some countries have developed avoidance strategies, which militate against the achievement of greater gender equality in work–life balance. As argued by a representative from the general workers confederation (Cgil) in Italy, preference is given to male workers since they are seen as more adaptable:

> Employers tend to prefer to take on male workers because they expect them to be able to guarantee their presence at work and adapt to meet the needs of employers.

When employers are able to offset the costs of maternity against social insurance concessions, they are likely to be less hostile towards the employment of women. When this is not the case, particularly in CEE countries, instances are found of blatant discrimination. An equal opportunities representative in Estonia was pessimistic about the impact of legislation to protect women as working mothers. Rather than leading to a more equitable work–life balance, it may restrict women's opportunities:

> I think that the protection of maternity rights has put women in a worse position in the labour market, where they are seen as less valuable workers. …the stereotypical gender role of the father as breadwinner and provider for the family has been detrimental overall.

An Estonian economic policy actor described a not unusual experience, now outlawed in European legislation:

> I've attended an employment interview where a male candidate for the post of chief accountant was offered a higher salary than a woman. On asking why this kind of discrimination had occurred, the answer was: men need more for spending.

A number of cases of discrimination were reported in other CEE countries. A trade union representative in Hungary recounted instances that could have resulted in court cases in EU15 member states:

> In a lot of places, at the job interview, young female applicants are faced with the question whether they want to have children or not. In this success-oriented world an employee's wish to have children is bad news.

A Polish trade unionist painted an even bleaker picture of a situation where:

> A young woman about to get married is warned that pregnancy means the end of her career, that her child's illness is no excuse for one of the parents taking leave of absence, that family commitments cannot constrain the parent's availability for work.

The accounts of Polish women provided further evidence of discriminatory practices at the workplace. According to a young divorced woman:

I knew if I was married, ready to have children, this would be seen as a disadvantage. I was afraid my potential employer might say "you're at such an age, you have a husband, it's high time for you to have children, so we won't give you a job". … It's easier for me to find a job now. No one fears I will have a baby. It's awful, but the first question you're asked by an employer is: "Are you going to have children and when?" We're discriminated against as women, as far as employment goes. When I say I'm single … it sounds better.

Another Polish woman, married with two children, described how the situation had deteriorated since transition from the Soviet era:

A woman takes sick leave and people at work frown at her. In the 1980s, it wasn't that bad; it wasn't taken into account when you were taken on, there was plenty of work. If a woman went on sick leave for a month, it didn't count against her. Nowadays, when a child is ill and a woman takes leave, she can be sacked. Again, when a woman goes back to work after having been on childcare leave, she works for a month or two and there's a job cut, and she's the first to be sacked.

A widespread demand among women who have secure employment, a guarantee of reinstatement, leave entitlements and publicly supported childcare is for time policies designed to help parents reconcile employment with family responsibilities. The reduction of working hours in France was found to have the beneficial side effect of making paid work and family activities more compatible for both men and women. According to a French divorcee with two children, who had taken early retirement and was living in an unmarried cohabiting relationship:

The state can offer an encouragement by promoting working hours that enable families to have a harmonious family life without too much stress. In this respect, the 35-hour week is ideal.

Surveys in France show that the majority of workers feel they have benefited personally from the reduction in working time and its restructuring. Parents with young children and with regular secure jobs are among the most satisfied. They claim they are better able to match their working hours with childcare and school hours, and share childcare (Fagnani and Letablier, 2003, p 7). By contrast, in Germany, the ability of women to take employment is affected by both poor provision of public childcare and incompatibility of opening hours, even for part-time workers. A married mother with two children described her predicament in the following terms:

I wanted to have a place in a crèche for my children or any kind of care facilities for them before they were able to go to a kindergarten, but there was no provision of crèches in my region. Now, they're in a kindergarten, and they can stay there from 7.15 in the morning till 1 o'clock. I'm working part time and I don't have much time between finishing my work and picking up the children. But since last summer, the kindergarten stays open till 2 o'clock, and the children can have lunch. That makes it easier for me.

In southern European countries, despite their limited availability and restrictive conditions, public childcare strategies are credited with enabling more women to enter and remain in employment when they have young children. A frequent complaint, in these cases as well, concerns the mismatch between working hours and the opening hours of crèches and nursery schools, which the state is expected to remedy, as explained by a lone mother in Spain with a six-year-old child:

> We complain today because a lot of kids end up with nothing to do really early in the day, like 12 or 1 o'clock in the afternoon, and no one seems to know exactly what's to be done with them. This requires full-time commitment to children, or hiring private help, but that is very expensive, and most people can't afford it. After all those years of intensive work as a mother, re-incorporation into professional life may be difficult; that is if it ever really takes place properly. Why doesn't the state solve this serious problem of short school or crèche hours?

In Greece, inadequate public support to help parents combine work and family life is still seen as a major issue for couples in the organisation of their daily lives and as a source of gender inequality, reinforcing the traditional distribution of roles, as illustrated by an older Greek respondent in a farming community:

> The mother has always been responsible for household tasks, for the care of children, for all tasks in the house. For the rest, all tasks outside of the house, work and everything else, it's the father who's responsible.

In some cases, the gendered distribution of household labour is contested, resulting in conflict and bitterness, as recounted by a divorcee in Estonia:

> Housework was mainly my duty. My husband came home from work, he was tired and impatiently demanded dinner to be served ... but that I also worked and the children were small, really meant nothing to him. This worn-out working man came home and wanted to have what he had deserved. Every situation has its limits. I couldn't tolerate the situation any longer. We got divorced, and I moved back in with my parents.

The overwhelming impression given by these comments is that, if policy is to be successful in making it possible for couples to combine employment and family life, it needs to make couples, and more especially women, feel they can choose whether or not to enter or leave the labour market when they have children. Their expectation is that the state will make available different options that are not constrained by cost.

Matching policy with outcomes for families

Despite the immense socio-economic and cultural diversity across the Union, similarities can be found among the opinions expressed by European families regarding the influence policy has on decisions taken about family life. Most people believe that it is not the level of benefits that determines whether or not they decide to raise a family, but rather the wider socio-economic climate and their personal circumstances. In any case, benefits for families are pitched at too low a level to replace income from work as the main source of family livelihood or, particularly in the southern European and CEE countries, to prevent them from falling into poverty. Although a few examples can be found of couples marrying to gain entitlement to social benefits and services, family members are rarely responding to isolated policies in a calculating way. Whereas individual family policy measures may have only a limited impact on decisions about family formation or living arrangements, bundles of supportive policies would seem to contribute to the creation of a family-friendly society conducive to family building.

Attempts by the state to regulate living arrangements and relationships within couples are found to have very little influence on personal decisions about whether or not to contract a formal marriage, or on the success of marital and consensual partnerships. It is widely agreed that government intervention is most effective when it seeks to accompany changing family structure and responds positively to social change. Even though it may reflect a substantial body of public opinion, as in Ireland and Poland where religion is still a powerful force restraining change, prohibitive legislation does little to prevent the breakdown of the marital relationship or encourage family building. Since the public rejects state intervention designed to shape patterns of family formation and prevent the spread of de-institutionalised living arrangements, policy appears to be more effective when the aim is to deal with the financial and physical consequences of family breakdown. Permissive or reactive policy responses that recognise *de facto* situations may come nearer to achieving their objectives, for example by extending the rights of married to unmarried cohabiting couples and, thus, removing discrimination between children born in and out of wedlock.

Just as family life is generally subordinated to economic imperatives at EU and national level, decisions couples take about family formation and living arrangements are frequently determined by economic factors other than income from family benefits. Although economic rationality is not the primary driving force, a precondition for embarking on family life is economic security, which the state is expected to deliver by ensuring a high level of employment and by guaranteeing a living wage or minimum income through work that pays. The lack of economic security is seen as a factor preventing family formation, particularly in CEE countries. Labour market and employment policies, therefore, appear to have a greater impact on family decisions than policies specifically targeting family life.

Similarly, whether mothers enter paid work and remain in employment would seem to depend less on the availability of public care provision than on access to suitable jobs and flexible working arrangements. The amount and quality of public care facilities and other forms of support for children and older people are cited as factors influencing the strategies adopted by couples for combining paid work and family life, rather than decisions about whether or not to work. In CEE countries, despite the strong attachment to family values, women need to be in employment to ensure a decent standard of living for their families, but they have little choice because so few jobs are available. The 'enforced' choice of working motherhood under Soviet rule is considered to have offered women greater security through their attachment to the enterprise. Today, by contrast, women are forced to turn to family networks for the resources needed to replace the support they have lost.

Deciding how to organise and manage family life implies that different options and choices are available, but choice is a relative, complex and 'contingent' (Glover, 2002, p 263) concept, which is heavily influenced by cultural norms and practices, and personal factors. Public policies and working regulations can both facilitate and obstruct choice. Women's choices about living and working arrangements are clearly more constrained than those of men by family factors, and in some countries more than in others, as demonstrated in Chapter Four. Here, it has been argued that, even among women who, objectively and from a comparative perspective, appear to have a high degree of individual choice, as in France, a recurring theme is the demand for more sensitive public provision to extend options.

Analysis of the impact of policies designed to enable both men and women to achieve a more equitable balance between employment and other activities reveals tensions between policy objectives and within families. Women are under growing pressure to increase their labour market participation, while at the same time being expected to bear children, stay at home to raise them in their early years and then subcontract childcare as they grow older. Men are under pressure to become active fathers, to share household tasks and maintain children financially if the couple relationship breaks down. Policies that seek to promote the economic activity of parents may divert attention away from the best interests of children. Paid parental leave seems to offer parents a choice about whether they care for their own children when they are young, and it can be seen as a form of social recognition of the value of parenting. Since take up of leave by men is so limited, it can also be interpreted as confirmation of women's homemaker role and a means of restricting their employment opportunities. Either way, it is not gender neutral, and choice may be illusory.

Reductions in working hours for parents and short full-time working hours may be a helpful solution to the problem of juggling the schedules of family members, but such arrangements confirm the traditional gendered distribution of caring and household tasks. They appear to be effective only if they include the synchronisation of opening times of schools, shops and other services, as well as appropriate provision of public transport, implying the need for joined-up, or lateral, policy thinking. Efforts to involve men more centrally in childcare through legislation on parental and paternity leave are contingent on a more fundamental shift in attitudes and power relations, both at work and in the home, than can be achieved through family policy alone.

Too much family friendliness and too great an emphasis on active parenting may, however, exert undue pressure on individuals to conform, thereby contributing to the refusal of parenthood and family responsibilities. Where family-friendly and equality legislation is seen by employers as costly to implement, it may have negative side effects for women, by leading to discrimination against them as actual or potential working mothers.

Individuals differ in what they feel they have a right to expect from society and, more specifically, state, enterprise and family. A recurring demand across countries is for the state to deliver a combination of shorter working hours, less rigid working arrangements and longer opening hours for public services as components in a package that would facilitate their arrangements for managing paid work and childrearing, while also improving the quality of everyday life. However, findings from European comparisons of households, work and flexibility point to a paradox between objective situations and subjective perceptions. EU member states with a long history of policies to help balance work and family life, and which report the greatest degree of sharing of domestic labour, have been found to be those where the family–work conflict is felt to be most difficult to manage. Because they have no expectations of equality, respondents in CEE countries do not, on the whole, claim to experience family–work conflict, although they are working the longest hours (Wallace, 2003, pp 38-9).

In the final analysis, individuals expect to be able to choose how they manage their lives. Policy may seek to prevent, reverse or accompany social change. People look to the state to provide conditions that allow them maximum choice without creating further dilemmas and tensions. Nowhere is the public prepared to accept heavy-handed intervention in matters concerning family life. Prohibitive and proactive policies are overwhelmingly rejected in favour of a more conciliatory stance that goes with the grain of socio-economic change, complementing rather than usurping family responsibilities. Instead of imposing conditions, public policy is expected to be responsive to changing needs and non-intrusive to enable maximum choice. The need seems to be for a more holistic and integrated approach, extending across employment policy, working practices and time structures for all individuals throughout the life course, which family policy, narrowly defined as designated family benefits and services, would seem ill equipped to deliver.

EIGHT

Responses to socio-economic change

Underlying European Commission documents on social policy is the assumption that, as a result of common demographic trends, particularly population ageing, family and household change, all member states in the European Union (EU) are facing similar problems, for which they might be expected to adopt similar solutions through a process of policy learning and diffusion. Demographic trends are said to be driving policy (European Commission, 1995, 2002d, 2003). The 1994 White Paper on European social policy, which set out to offer a response to Europe's need for "a blueprint for the management of change", explicitly recognised that "demography ... will impact on and interrelate with social and economic policy", acknowledging that "comparable trends ... lead to common problems and challenges", and hence to the need to develop common policy responses (COM(94) 333, 27.07.1994, pp 7, 47). At the heart of the 2000 social policy agenda was the modernisation of the European social model, which had the overall aim of strengthening the role of social protection as an effective tool for the management of change, thereby converting the political commitments made at the Lisbon European Council in 2000 into concrete action. Modernisation and improvement of social protection were central components in the response to the advent of the knowledge economy and to changing social and family structures, in a context where the quality of social policy was said to depend on social protection serving as a productive factor (European Commission, 2000b, p 19; 2002d, p 10).

Demographic trends are not, however, the only motivation for modernising social policy. A justification for introducing supportive public provision in the form of family allowances during the interwar and immediate postwar periods was to contain wage inflation. The early maternity leave schemes at the turn of the 20th century were primarily concerned with safeguarding the health of mothers and their children. The same argument was evoked in 1992 when maternity leave was incorporated into European law as a health and safety measure (Council Directive 92/85/EEC, *Official Journal* L 348/1, 28.11.1992). In the 1990s, a powerful incentive for governments to review their social policies was the need to control public spending if they were to meet the criteria for Economic and Monetary Union by reducing public sector borrowing without raising taxation. At the end of the century, an additional incentive for modernising social protection systems was the need to realise Europe's full employment potential, in a concerted effort to offset predicted labour shortages while reinforcing equality and fundamental rights. Not least, the prospect of enlargement presented a major challenge to the Union's social *acquis*, requiring more innovative policy responses.

A number of tried and tested instruments were available for delivering social quality and social cohesion, which were key objectives in the plan to modernise social policy. The open method of co-ordination (OMC), officially launched at the Lisbon European Council in 2000, offered a more flexible and softer alternative to the legislative route. After being applied, firstly, as a tool in the employment strategy, OMC was extended to the areas of social inclusion and pensions, with the aim of encouraging member states to improve their performance through benchmarking and by learning from the experience of their neighbours within the Union.

The chapters in this book have combined scrutiny of definitions, concepts and measurements of socio-economic change at EU and national level with an analysis of the policy responses of governments and their impacts on families, as experienced by individuals in their everyday lives. The policy process has been examined not only in long-standing EU member states but also in the candidate countries, especially in Central and Eastern Europe (CEE), which were preparing for membership of the Union when the materials were collected. This final chapter draws together the various strands of the analysis. It sets out to show how the trends identified at macro level are translated into policy in very different institutional settings, reflecting the diversity of policy styles, cultural traditions and social expectations. It goes on to explore the potential for lesson learning and policy diffusion based on the comparative performance of governments, as they respond to changing family structures, within the framework of an enlarging Europe premised on a consensual approach to public policy.

Commonality and diversity of socio-economic trends and policy responses

Chapters Two to Five show that, while the trends characteristic of the first and second demographic transitions could be identified across EU15 member states and candidate countries, the timing, rate, pace, intensity and, in some cases, the starting point and direction of change differ markedly between and within countries, as do reactions to it among policy actors. This section provides an overview of the situation within EU25 and looks at the ways in which socio-demographic trends and policy responses have been shaped by national policy contexts.

The first demographic transition, which began in the late 19th century, entailed a fall in fertility and mortality rates, resulting in population decline and ageing, except where large-scale inward migration served as a compensating factor. The analysis in Chapter Two identified Italy, Greece, Austria and Germany as the EU member states most affected by the combination of population decline and ageing in 2000 in relation to the EU15 mean. Spain and Sweden were also experiencing above-average population ageing, while Ireland and Cyprus were outliers due to their younger and expanding populations. Only Luxembourg was ensuring continued population growth that could be attributed primarily to high net migration. A striking feature of the situation at the turn of the 21st century was that the CEE countries that joined the Union in 2004 were experiencing negative natural population growth but, compared with EU15 member states, they were not yet suffering to the same extent from population ageing.

The hallmark of the second demographic transition, which had begun in the 1960s and was still gaining momentum at the end of the 20th century, was the de-institutionalisation of family life, involving high levels of divorce and growing rates of unmarried cohabitation as an alternative to marriage, entailing rising levels of extramarital births and lone parenthood. The analysis in Chapter Three identified Denmark and Sweden as having gone furthest by the end of the century, in relation to the EU15 mean, in delaying family formation and adopting de-institutionalised family forms. Italy, Spain and Ireland combined the postponement of family formation with more traditional family forms. The picture was also diversified for the CEE countries, although none was characterised by delayed family formation. Poland and Slovakia were the countries most prone to combine conventional timing of family formation and traditional family forms, a characteristic they shared with Portugal, Slovenia and the two island states of Cyprus and Malta. The other six CEE countries had not postponed family building to the same extent as EU15 member states, but in relation to the EU15 mean, they had all gone further in developing alternative family forms.

As demonstrated in Chapters Two to Four, statistics are not neutral. They are produced at the behest of policy makers and cited by them to justify and legitimise policy intervention. They provide indicators that are used to compare and benchmark performance over time and across countries. Analysis of the cumulative effect of family de-institutionalisation in a context of population decline and ageing has called into question a number of the assumptions underpinning policy development, creating the need for a shift in policy focus. The decline in fertility and the reduction in the time devoted to childbearing and childrearing, theoretically, make women less dependent on the formal marital relationship for their livelihood. The instability of marriage and non-marital cohabitation may, in turn, accelerate the reduction in fertility levels and result in smaller family size and an increase in the incidence of lone parenthood, which is often associated with financial hardship. Repartnering can lead to more complex family living arrangements. Longer life expectancy and population ageing may provoke changes in attitudes towards multigenerational living, and destabilise the contract between the generations.

As argued in Chapter Four, it is difficult to understand the impact of population decline and ageing, changing family forms and structure without examining changes in the relationship between family life and paid work. Demographers and policy analysts identify two related issues that are central to an understanding of policy development. Firstly, a major problem ensuing from the combined impact of population decline and ageing is how to sustain the labour supply, and ensure an equitable balance between the population of working age, who are producing goods and services and contributing to the social protection budget through their taxes and insurance contributions, and the inactive older dependent population, who are primarily consumers of pensions, social and healthcare services. The second issue is the extent to which the greater propensity of women to enter and remain in employment is affecting their availability to carry out the caring roles traditionally assigned to them, and calling into question the long-established inequitable distribution of household labour. While de-institutionalisation of family life and the growing participation of women in the labour force is welcomed as part of the solution to the problem of the age imbalance in the population, it is also seen as part of the problem, by making women less available for childrearing and contributing to the deficit in family caring.

Just as analysis of trends in population decline and ageing, the timing of family formation and development of alternative family forms highlights differences in the extent to which the two demographic transitions have affected the age distribution and living arrangements of the population in EU member states, different patterns can be identified in the relationship recorded in the statistics between employment and family life. Compared with the EU15 mean, the three Nordic states combine a relatively high overall level of labour market integration for women with what is considered to be a more equitable family–employment balance. At the other extreme, Greece, Italy and the Netherlands display low rankings for both indicators. The situation in the CEE countries again distinguishes them from most EU15 member states, due to the relatively small gap between male and female employment patterns and, with the exception of Latvia and Poland, their stronger commitment to working mothers in both attitudes and practice.

The distinction between waves of EU members is further reinforced when reference is made to the direction of change. Whereas EU15 member states saw an overall growth in female employment rates during the 1990s, particularly among women aged 25-54, in the CEE countries, female (and male) rates fell steeply as women were forced out of the labour market and back into homemaker roles. From a situation where a larger proportion of women in the CEE countries, compared with EU15, had been in employment at the same time as they were raising children, a stage had been reached where jobs were in short supply. Couples could ill afford to have children, both for financial reasons and because motherhood would further reduce women's chances of finding a job or remaining in work. In EU15, family responsibilities helped to explain why more prime-age women were not economically active, particularly in Greece, Italy and Luxembourg (van Bastelaer and Blöndal, 2003, p 3). By contrast, women in the CEE countries, especially women with children, were more likely to be inactive because they were being denied access to jobs (Pascall and Manning, 2000, p 248). It can be argued that, if they do seek to establish a balance in their lives, it is more for 'self-preservation' than out of 'self-interest' (Glover, 2002, p 262).

These differences in the direction of employment trends imply that policy actors are not facing the same challenges. In the Nordic states, and to a lesser extent in France, the main issue for governments is how to promote greater gender equality in working conditions and pay, while ensuring a more equitable distribution of caring tasks in what are, in comparative terms, women and family-friendly societies. The question that policy actors are mainly concerned with elsewhere in EU15 member states is how to improve the quality of work and make employment more compatible with family care, so that larger numbers of women are willing and able to enter and remain in the workforce, and can find jobs that pay a living wage, thereby bolstering the labour supply, without foregoing motherhood or neglecting family life. The CEE countries, for their part, are contending with a situation where their top priority must be to improve job security and pay, with a view to raising the living standards of families and developing alternatives to the occupational welfare that was assured under the Soviet system, while at the same time safeguarding the demographic future of the nation.

Although it is not difficult to find lowest common denominators in the underlying socio-economic trends and concerns of governments, clearly not all the countries in the enlarged Union are starting from the same base. They are not all advancing at the same pace, and nor do they all have available the same financial, technical and political resources with which to respond to socio-economic change.

In democratic societies, politicians have to carry their electorates with them if they want to remain in power and be in a position to implement policies that will influence prospects in the longer term. They are, therefore, interested in tracking public reactions and expectations, and monitoring and measuring outcomes. The benchmarking requirement of the OMC has exposed governments to greater external scrutiny and placed them under an obligation to meet internationally agreed performance targets and criteria.

The findings from surveys of public opinion reveal that shifts were occurring in the value systems and attitudes of Europeans in the latter part of the 20th century. Although the importance attached to family life remained by far the dominant value across Europe, and had grown considerably during the 1990s in some countries, most notably Portugal and Germany, a distinctive characteristic of attitudes in Europe was the movement away from collective responsibility and duties towards what has been described as a post-material conception of individual rights and personal autonomy (Lesthaeghe, 1995; Coleman and Chandola, 1999; Herpin, 2002; Abela, 2003). While governments were giving increasing priority to employment and labour market policies during the 1990s as a result of the European employment strategy, Ireland, the Netherlands and the UK shared with the Nordic states the declining value attached to work, generally in favour of friends, relations, and leisure[1]. Respondents in Malta, Poland, Latvia and France recorded the highest scores for the significance of work in their lives. Religion was of diminishing importance for Europeans, and remained a central value only in Ireland, Italy, Portugal and, more especially, Malta and Poland. Only in Austria, the Netherlands, Sweden and Malta did the scores for the importance attached to politics reach double figures, confirming the low level of confidence that most Europeans, particularly in Estonia, Slovenia and Finland, have in the ability of politicians and public administration to deliver a high standard of benefits and services.

An additional complication in any assessment of policy responses to issues involving family life is that no universally agreed definition of family policy can be found, and no clear criteria can be established to determine the boundaries of the legitimacy and acceptability of intervention by the state either across or within societies, as demonstrated in Chapters Five and Six. Policy may be more or less explicit, comprehensive and coherent. Policy formation, development and implementation may be more or less closely co-ordinated by political, economic and civil society actors. Objectives and priorities may vary, as do the instruments used to achieve them, coverage of benefits and services, and the perceptions that people have of their value for families.

The efficiency and effectiveness of policies are particularly difficult to assess, since outcomes may be intended or unintended, wanted or unwanted, direct or indirect. As argued in Chapter Seven, a policy measure may serve as a catalyst or trigger, but it is difficult to isolate the impact of a particular measure or determine whether policy in another area is producing any effects observed. The many attempts to measure policy outcomes have shown that it is not sufficient to note the presence or absence of a particular policy measure; it is also important to assess the level, standard and quality of provision, access and take up, and the extent to which policy is perceived as having an impact on the standard of living of the intended recipients. Finally, politicians are not immune to pressure, and it is not usually the most vocal groups in society that have the greatest need or the disadvantaged groups that have powerful lobbies acting on their behalf. Although family associations have long played an active role in some countries in protecting the interests of families, this tends to be the exception rather than the rule.

---

[1] According to 1999/2000 European Values Study (EVS) data supplied by the Zentralarchiv für Empirische Sozialforschung at Cologne University in 2003. See also Bréchon, 2002, table 13; Bréchon and Tchernia, 2002, table 1.

Characterising the family–policy relationship

In assessing the commonality or diversity of policy responses to the challenges facing policy actors as a result of socio-economic change, Chapters Five to Seven embarked on the task of identifying clusters of countries according to the ways in which the family policy process operates and the factors influencing its development. An important aim was to identify the impact that policy is believed by those concerned – the providers and beneficiaries of policy – to have on decisions taken about family life. A picture emerged from the analysis of the generosity, or otherwise, of the provision made for families, the extent to which the male breadwinner model and gender regimes have been modified, and to which individuals can maintain a socially acceptable standard of living without having to rely unduly on family support, a process described as 'defamilialisation' (McLaughlin and Glendinning, 1994, p 65; Lister, 1997, p 173; Esping-Andersen, 1999, p 45).

The approach adopted in this book differs from that found in many accounts of the family–state relationship in that an attempt has been made to capture the complexity of the policy process as a form of social interaction between policy actors with different agendas and interests that change over time, as they react to a variety of socio-economic and cultural pressures, family and household events. The starting point for the analysis was the changing structure and meaning of family life, which have been examined not only by drawing on large-scale demographic and attitudinal data and situating them in relation to the wider policy environment, but also by questioning political, economic and civil society actors about their input to policy formulation and implementation, and by asking family members about their perceptions of the impact of policy on their lives. Like many other studies, the present book identifies clusters of countries that share similar characteristics with regard to the relationship between family, state, market and civil society. In this respect, the findings for the EU15 member states do not depart significantly from those by authors who have sought to overcome the incompleteness of economic theories by taking account of socio-historical factors (for example Lesthaeghe, 1995, p 51), and "the blindness of virtually all comparative political economy to the world of families" (Esping-Andersen, 1999, p 11), or who have undertaken "to theorise and analyse the ways in which culture, institutions, structure and social action are interrelated" (Pfau-Effinger and Geissler, 2002, p 77).

Drawing on the combination of methods and findings reported in this book, Figure 8.1 distinguishes between four clusters of EU25 countries, which are then further subdivided, according the way in which the family–state relationship is constructed and enacted. Depending on the variables used, individual countries may shift from one cluster to another, as suggested by the fuzzy and broken boundaries in the figure. The countries within each cluster share a number of characteristics in terms of the design and structure

Figure 8.1: The family–policy relationship in EU25 member states

1 DEFAMILIALISED		REFAMILIALISED 4	
explicit		implicit/indirect	
coherent		rhetorical	
legitimised		pro-natalist	
co-ordinated		semi-legitimised	
supportive of working parents		unco-ordinated	
universal/residence		institutionalised	
tax funded	mixed funding	transitional	
individualised	family centred	underfunded	
service based	institutional	**Estonia**	**Czech Rep**
Denmark	**France**	**Latvia**	**Slovenia**
Finland	**Luxembourg**	**Lithuania**	**Slovakia**
Sweden	**Belgium**	**Hungary**	**Poland**
Ireland	**Austria**	**Greece**	**Cyprus**
UK	**Germany**	**Italy**	tax funded
Netherlands		**Portugal**	**Malta**
marketised	delegated	contributions	contributions
mixed delivery	institutional	**Spain**	religion
tax funded	mixed funding	tax funded	marketised
residence		underfunded	
partially co-ordinated		unco-ordinated	
partially legitimised		weakly legitimised	
rhetorical		non institutionalised	
implicit/indirect		fragmented	
2 PARTIALLY DEFAMILIALISED		FAMILIALISED 3	

of their policy for families, and the level of commitment of state support for family life. They command a similar degree of legitimacy and have in common a more or less co-ordinated approach to the involvement of political, economic and civil society actors in the policy process. The subgroups reflect differences in funding mechanisms, vehicles for delivery, the target population and the overall impact of policy on family life.

In all the countries in the first cluster, governments have long been explicit in their efforts to minimise the reliance of individuals on their families. State intervention in family life is legitimised and commands public support, even when, as in Denmark, governments may not claim to operate an official family policy. Public administration is committed to underpinning family life, and more specifically working parents, to the extent that the responsibility for family matters can be said to be defamilialised, and the state can be described as family and women friendly. Their strong ideological commitment to redistributive policy intervention rests on social solidarity and collective responsibility. Policy actors co-operate with one another to achieve agreed objectives. They offer a high standard of benefits and/or services, with access based on residence and/or citizenship, with the exception of Belgium. In relative terms, their welfare systems are designed to maximise personal choice and flexibility. In most of these countries, the development of alternative family forms has not, therefore, been considered as a problem for society.

The two subgroups within the cluster differ with regard to their historical development, which has shaped the logic and content underlying family policy, its institutional structures, funding and delivery mechanisms. In the Nordic states, regulation of family life is firmly grounded and institutionalised historically. In Sweden, policy has a long association with pro-natalism. However, family policy in Scandinavia has been influenced to a greater extent than in the countries in the second subgroup by social democratic values, and has been incorporated within labour market and gender equality policy, resulting in more individualised support for family members and greater pressure on men to become active fathers. With a few exceptions, social benefits and services are a universal citizenship right paid for by high taxes, levied on the whole population, without a dedicated family policy funding mechanism or agency, and where the family or household is not identified as the primary benefit unit. Emphasis is on the collective provision of good-quality services rather than benefits, with the aim of making paid work and family life compatible for both men and women.

In France, Luxembourg and Belgium, family policy is presented and funded as a dedicated policy domain. At the end of the 20th century, the proportion of social protection spending and of GDP devoted to family benefits was relatively high and above the EU15 average (European Commission, 2002d, table 2; Abramovici, 2003, table 1). National social security systems were based traditionally on employment-related insurance contributions, administered by a multiplicity of schemes. By contrast with other areas of social protection, employers in France were, originally, the sole contributors to the family allowance fund, and family benefits and services were built upon their contributions. Today, in the three countries in this subgroup, family allowances are funded by a combination of employment contributions and taxes, and administered by specialised agencies, but the link with employment has not been broken entirely. Family allowances in Belgium, for example, are contingent on parents being in work or unable to work. Although traditionally grounded in a strong right-wing ideology that saw the family as the cornerstone of social order, patriarchy and pro-natalism, family policy, as exemplified in France, has progressively been tempered by left-wing concerns with vertical distribution, equality, social solidarity and liberal values. Families continue to be supported by a strong lobby of family associations, which strive to keep family matters on the policy agenda. More so than in the Nordic states, the de-institutionalisation of family life and the individualisation of entitlements are raising questions about the future shape and form of family policy, and the balance between universal and targeted benefits and services. The level of benefits and rights, when paid parental leave, childcare and other allowances for family members are included, is more generous in France and Luxembourg than in Belgium, which brings it closer to the countries in the partially defamiliarised quadrant.

The five countries grouped together in the second cluster have in common that government rhetoric is supportive of families, but policy actors are reluctant to intervene in private life, resulting in a more implicit and indirect approach to policies for families. Co-ordination between policy actors is weaker, and policy tends to be less coherent than in the countries in the first cluster. Family matters periodically move up the political agenda, but policy intervention does not command the same level of legitimacy, or result in the same degree of co-ordination among policy actors, to the extent that society, and more specifically governments and employers, cannot be said to be inherently friendly towards families.

The two subgroups are distinguished by their funding mechanisms and underlying welfare principles, with the Netherlands straddling the boundary between them. Austria and Germany form a subgroup that is, in many respects, close to the second subgroup in the first cluster. They both have formal institutional structures for preparing and delivering family policy. They share a similarly high level of financial commitment to family policy measures, as a proportion of social protection spending and in relation to GDP. They provide support for childrearing, but it is premised on the expectation that mothers will assume the main responsibility for young children in the two-parent family and will fit employment around family commitments, rather than the reverse. They differ in that families in Germany rely more heavily on the voluntary sector for childcare support than in Austria. The Netherlands is close to the subgroup with Austria and Germany for the importance of employment-related social insurance as a funding mechanism but, in other respects, it is nearer to Ireland and the UK.

Like these two countries, the Netherlands does not have a dedicated institutional structure for delivering family policy measures, nor an explicit and coherent family policy. The level of spending on families and children is above the EU15 average in the UK, but much lower in the Netherlands. Ireland devotes a high proportion of its social protection spending to the budget head for 'family and children', but the proportion of GDP is close to the EU15 average. All three countries fund child benefit from general taxation, as in the Nordic states, but none of them makes provision for paid parental leave. They all expect families to bear the main responsibility for organising care for children and older people. As in the Nordic states, family members are not under a legal obligation to provide mutual support. In the absence of extensive public provision of care, part-time work is an important strategy, adopted in the Netherlands, especially, and in the UK, for combining childraising with paid work. A primary objective of policy in all three countries is to encourage mothers to participate in the labour force, but only insofar as their employment does not bring the interests of business and motherhood into conflict. The UK shares with Ireland the emphasis on measures to protect families at risk, often involving a combination of means testing and welfare-to-work policies, together with reliance on the voluntary sector. Families not considered to be in need of support and protection are expected to turn to the private sector for services, which may be provided in a partially defamilialised form through state–market partnerships.

The southern European countries in the third cluster have in common their fragmented and largely unco-ordinated approach to family policy, which is not administered by a dedicated institution. The state delegates the responsibility for family well being to families themselves, who are under a legal obligation to look after their members. In this case, family welfare can be described as familialistic. In the course of the second half of the 20th century, the four EU15 member states in the cluster experienced the transition from an authoritarian regime, which upheld patriarchal values, to a democracy committed to a more liberal and non-interventionist approach towards family life. They all needed to build up their welfare systems from a low base, but tended to do so in a piecemeal way, resulting in fragmentary coverage for families and children. By the turn of the century, they were all recording a relatively low level of provision of benefits and support services for families, compared with other EU15 member states. Their social security systems are fragmented along occupational lines, especially in Greece, and family benefits are contingent on employment, often with an earnings limit. Means testing is used extensively for low-income families. Childcare provision is also relatively underdeveloped, although nursery schooling is widely offered as part of free education. Reliance on family networks extends to employment and housing, and is reflected in the high proportion of self-employment and the large number of informal family helpers. Another aspect of fragmentation arises from the delegation of provision of benefits and services for families to local authorities, resulting in marked regional discrepancies in access and quality.

The two small island states share with the four southern European countries geographical and cultural proximity, although the internal cultural diversity within Cyprus and the legacy of British rule mean that it only partially recognises its affinity with Greece. Both countries have in common with southern Europe their strong reliance on extended family networks. Malta has been at the confluence of many civilisations and is, today, characterised by the high value Maltese people place on family life and religion, which brings it close to southern Europe. Although state intervention in family matters is considered to be legitimate, family allowances are funded by contributions and paid to resident Maltese citizens.

They are means tested, and services such as childcare are limited and not freely available (MISSCEO, 2002, chapters I, IX, pp 99, 733). Governments in Cyprus have pursued policies designed to promote population growth, by providing generous benefits for large families, funded from general taxation, and by encouraging repatriation. The private sector plays a major role in the delivery of healthcare and pensions, and social insurance is seen as a disincentive to undertake formal work (Pashardes, 2003).

The fourth cluster of countries groups together the remaining eight CEE countries that joined the Union in the fifth wave of membership in 2004. During the Soviet era, the universal provision of housing, health and childcare, and more importantly jobs, which were the precondition for receiving benefits and services, meant that families did not have to depend heavily on their own resources to ensure that the basic needs of their members were met. Transition from Soviet rule entailed the dismantling of the enterprise-based welfare support system for workers and their families, a shift towards a minimalist state and the dominance of the open market. Responsibility for supporting families moved away from the state and the enterprise to families themselves, at a time when labour market restructuring had left many people without paid work and the resources required to meet even basic needs. Traditional family values resurfaced as women were forced back into family care work, while child poverty became a major concern for governments. Family policy can be said to have been refamilialised. This does not mean that formal institutional structures for managing family policy are non-existent, or that they are not legitimised. It does mean they are underfunded, that support for families is often rhetorical rather than practical and that the state is not trusted to deliver good-quality and reliable services.

During the 1990s, the value of child benefit fell well below inflation. Universalistic provision was largely replaced by means testing and targeting, and low-cost facilities for pre-school children and other workplace benefits, which had previously been the counterpart of high female employment rates, were severely cut back. Policy priorities fluctuated between targeting families as units, and especially large families, pro-natalist measures to encourage family building, and protection for individuals most at risk. The need for social assistance, which was a weak instrument under Soviet rule, became widespread, but the system proved difficult to manage because of the large informal economy, often extending to informal payment for services, as for example in Latvia (Bite and Zagorskis, 2003, p 113).

Subgroups are not easy to identify within this cluster with regard to the funding and delivery mechanisms of family policy. The employment-insurance model has been widely adopted as the main funding instrument for social protection, but with a much reduced role for employers in delivery, generally in conjunction with state-financed family benefits and social assistance schemes. The Czech and Slovak governments were among the first to introduce a comprehensive reform of social assistance and to adjust benefits in line with inflation, although they also cut back family support in the mid-1990s, targeting benefits on low-income families (Elster et al, 1998, pp 230-2).

Despite the shared experience of socialism, some of the distinctive features of family welfare systems have not been eliminated. Although most CEE countries retained elements of their previously relatively generous paid parental leave arrangements for working mothers, in Poland paid leave became means tested. By contrast, not only are women in Slovenia entitled to 12 months leave on full pay, but they can also transfer payment for unused leave to services such as childcare or, in the case of students aged under 18, to grandparents. Parental allowance is granted for those not entitled to insurance-based compensation, and childcare provision is well supported by government subsidies. Women in Lithuania and Slovenia who are not entitled to maternity insurance benefit receive family benefit (Dobravolskas and Buivydas, 2003, p 34; Stropnik et al, 2003, pp 40-1, 45, 93).

The examples of Hungary and Poland show how changing political ideologies have shaped the reform process. In the pre-war period, Hungary had established a conservative, statist, corporatist welfare system, with a heavy state bureaucracy, based on the Bismarckian social insurance system, where the church and private charity ensured the welfare of the working classes. Socialism brought an expansion of entitlements and near universal coverage, at least for those who took up state employment, to the extent that social assistance was denied to families with children unless both parents were in work (Ferge, 1992, p 207). Ten years after the end of Soviet rule, under a conservative, Christian nationalist government, Hungarian family policy distinctly favoured middle-class families through generous tax allowances (Ferge, 2001a, p 125). The fall in the real value of benefits for families during the 1990s further limited the redistributive effects of policy.

Religion has remained a powerful force in Poland underpinning restrictive legislation. The focus of policy is the conventional two-parent married family, as in southern European countries and Germany. Governments have pursued policies designed to uphold traditional family forms and moral values, while also providing openly pro-natalist financial incentives to encourage family building. The priority given to pension reform in the late 1990s meant, however, that spending on family welfare was cut back and limited to families most at risk.

The eight CEE countries that joined the Union in 2004 had in common the progress they had made in implementing economic and democratic reforms, which clearly distinguished them from the other countries in the former Soviet Union (UNICEF, 2001, figure 1.10), marking their readiness for EU membership. The extent to which these fifth-wave member states will influence the European social model, or be influenced by it, remains an open question. Their track record during the 1990s suggests that they are unlikely to constitute an undifferentiated and stable block. Nor are they expected to reverse the overall trend away from direct state support for families through universal benefits towards more targeted means-tested provision in combination with privatised (market and family) care solutions.

Family policy learning and diffusion

Diversity in welfare arrangements has long been a factor restraining attempts to promote the harmonisation and convergence of social protection systems across Europe, but it has not prevented the development of agreed targets and indicators for benchmarking and assessing the relative performance of different countries. The OMC, which is being applied in the area of social policy to address labour market issues and the problems associated with unemployment, pensions and social exclusion, does not force governments to adopt policies through a process of obligated transfer. Rather, the expectation is that, by observing and comparing practices elsewhere, countries will learn from one another and find ways of improving their performance, with the possibility of raising standards across the Union. The annual reports required by the OMC may, however, be blunt instruments for checking on policy implementation when national interests are at stake, to the extent that they may provide an indication of good intentions rather than effective actions. Governments can, and do, nonetheless, use pressure from the Union as a pretext for introducing contentious and unpopular legislation. EU law can act as a prompt for action at national level or to move an issue onto the policy agenda. Candidate countries are obliged to meet EU criteria for membership, and to adopt the social *acquis*. Their progress in doing so is monitored by the Union during the period prior to accession.

No formal process has been initiated under the OMC to set targets for family policy. During the 1990s, however, the European Observatory on National Family Policies and the Mutual Information System on Social Protection (MISSOC), among others, collected information about national policies that are useful for comparative purposes (see Chapters Five and Six). At the turn of the 21st century, no specific European targets had been set for family benefits, although European directives and recommendations had laid down a framework for national policies on leave and childcare. As part of the European employment strategy (COM(2003) 6 final, 14.01.2003, p 22), national governments agreed that, by 2010, childcare places should be provided for at least 90% of children between the age of three and mandatory school age, and for at least 33% of children under the age of three. They did not specify how provision should be funded and delivered. No formal attempt was being made to 'name and shame' countries that had not reached the baseline standards, although the publication of 'league' tables and comparative reports on the social situation was having the effect of highlighting good and bad practices, and identifying countries that are trail blazers or laggards (European Commission, 2003).

When the aim is to improve employability or reduce social exclusion, it is not too difficult to set targets for raising the living standards of families or the number and quality of childcare places. It seems less likely that agreement could be reached over objectives, targets and instruments for achieving a specific family size, for curbing the number of divorces or regulating the distribution of household labour. Attempts to engineer family size by providing incentives for large families or to limit the number of children among particular social categories, age or minority ethnic groups are extremely controversial within societies, as are issues concerning household living arrangements. Countries that have offered incentives to encourage more equal sharing within households, as provided for in the Council Directive on parental leave (96/34/EC, *Official Journal* L 145/4 19.6.1996), by making the full allocation of parental leave conditional on fathers taking part of it, have struggled to meet their own targets, as exemplified by the limited take up of the Swedish 'daddy months'.

The materials presented in this book have shown that most EU member states do not have an explicit and coherent family policy. Although consensus may not have been achieved at EU level for a European family model or a European family policy, member states can, nonetheless, usefully look to one another for solutions to some of the common problems they are facing as a result of socio-economic change, with the Union providing a stimulus for policy reform. This concluding section examines the extent to which policy learning may be effective and feed into the development of family policy across the Union.

Preconditions for effective family policy learning

The transferability of policies between countries is largely dependent on the match between prevailing circumstances in the lesson-exporting and lesson-importing countries, and the interplay between policy environments and processes. A number of conditions need to be met before policies can be transported between countries (Rose, 2001, 2002). Firstly, the exporting and importing countries need to have common objectives and a shared definition of the issues to be tackled. Secondly, the policy process in provider and receiver countries needs to be both appropriate and compatible in terms of political ideology and values, welfare design principles, structure and agency for formulation, implementation and delivery. Thirdly, policy learning and transfer have to be seen as desirable, feasible and practical, implying consideration of national constraints and opportunities, covering legitimacy and social acceptability of state intervention, and sanctions for non-conformity. Account also needs to be taken of resistance to change. Fourthly, policy transfer must be affordable and accountable in terms of perceived economic and social benefits, the costs of transportation and adaptation, and the ability to demonstrate value for money, not only for families as users but also for other stakeholders, particularly in the labour market.

All EU member states and accession countries, by virtue of signing up to European treaties and legislation, affirm that they are committed to developing a social model aimed at promoting economic and social cohesion, without undermining social justice and economic efficiency (European Commission, 2000b). To meet the requirements of their treaty obligations, to comply with the social *acquis*, and in response to the challenges of socio-economic change, governments are expected to develop policies in line with Community objectives. Although they have not been written into European legislation, in the area of family policy, the Union's shared objectives can be identified as the creation of an economic and social environment where children and older people are not considered as a burden for individuals or society, where family life is positively valued, and where men and women have equal opportunities in their public and private lives and a work–life balance conducive to family solidarity.

The analysis in Chapters Five to Seven suggests that the EU member states where public policy most strongly supports these objectives, and where they most closely match public perceptions and aspirations, are the Nordic states and France. At the other end of the scale are many of the southern European and CEE countries, where supportive public policy falls far short of achieving Community objectives and does not live up to public expectations.

The extent to which shared objectives can be translated into practice using the same or similar policies depends not only on their appropriateness for the importing country but also on the compatibility of the socio-economic, political and cultural environments in the exporting and importing countries. The closer countries are in terms of their political and welfare structures, psychological proximity, ideological compatibility, and socio-economic and cultural characteristics, the more likely they are to be able to pool, and learn from, their policy experience. This does not mean that countries that are further apart may not also be able to learn from experience elsewhere, but they may need to make greater adaptations to the policies they are importing, or to consider radical changes to their structures of governance and instruments for policy delivery[2].

Even in the case of obligated policy transfer, in accordance with the principle of subsidiarity, governments are left to adapt policies to suit national circumstances. It is rare that a policy can be imported without being adjusted in some way, requiring consideration of feasibility and practicality. When the Union issues a framework policy or guidelines, as in the case of the agreement between the social partners on parental leave (96/34/EC) and the employment guidelines produced since 1998, member state governments are responsible for determining their own funding arrangements, regulatory mechanisms and methods of delivery. Policy learning may involve one or more of these stages, and exemplars may be sought in more than one country

---

[2] Most of the examples cited in this section are taken from 'policy learning case studies' conducted by partners in the 11 countries participating in the Framework Programme 5 project referred to in previous chapters (see Acknowledgements).

in accordance with national constraints and opportunities. Policies that are readily legitimated in one jurisdiction may not, however, command public acceptance in another context, as demonstrated, for example, by reactions to government intervention to regulate working hours and conditions and introduce family-friendly working practices. Legislation in the exporting country may impose strict regulatory conditions with high penalties for infringement, whereas, in the importing country, firms may be issued with general guidelines based on the business case, and left to devise their own implementation strategies.

Policies may be delivered at national or local level through public services in the exporting country, as with childcare provision in France and Sweden, and through partnerships with business and the voluntary sector in the importing country, as in Germany. Differences in the structure of public finances and welfare delivery, and the public–private mix are important factors limiting policy transfer from northern Europe to the southern European and CEE countries. For instance, a policy measure borrowed from Sweden, where funding is from general taxation and provision is universal, might be financed in the importing country by employment-related insurance contributions and confined to contributors in the scheme, as in Italy or Spain.

Predictably, the Scandinavians tend to compare notes between themselves, rather than looking elsewhere in Europe. Countries such as Germany or the UK that share some of the socio-economic and political characteristics of the Nordic and French family policy environments may also look in this direction for their preferred models, in response to changing family structure, and for examples of good practice. The Dutch model offers novel policies on working time and a liberal approach to living arrangements and relationships. In Italy and Spain, innovative policies developed in specific regions or towns serve as examples for other areas through a process of internal policy diffusion. The UK is most likely to turn for its policy models to the United States or other countries in the Anglo-Saxon world, with which governments feel they have greater ideological, socio-cultural and linguistic affinity. Ireland draws many of its examples from the UK, largely for similar reasons. Despite very different approaches to policy, the apparent lack of ideological compatibility and major differences in welfare design principles, structures and agency for formulation, implementation and delivery, the UK may have served as the conduit for activation policies pursued in France.

Southern European and CEE countries are influenced by policy developments elsewhere in the Union, not least due to obligated policy transfer. A certain degree of commonality is conferred by the need to reach consensus with European partners and to comply with European law, which, in the case of Italy, dates back to the 1950s as a founder member of the European Economic Community (EEC). If political and economic affinity are the main conditions determining the success of policy learning, CEE countries might be expected to turn to southern Europe to look for lessons that could be drawn from their experience of becoming EU members after a fundamental regime change, entailing far-reaching economic restructuring and adaptation of welfare institutions. In the area of social policy, they tend, however, to look in other directions, including their own pre-communist past. None of them has opted for a single western model. Relatively little policy learning seems to have occurred between countries within the former Soviet block (Elster et al, 1998, p 245). In areas such as old-age security, the Czech Republic, Hungary and Poland might have been expected to draw on their common legacy prior to and during the Soviet era. While the Czech policy choice can be seen as a return to its pre-communist welfare traditions and a move towards western Bismarckian and Beveridgean paradigms, Hungary and Poland were less restrained by their institutional legacy, and were encouraged by the World Bank to draw lessons from the Latin American pension reform models (Müller, 2001, pp 59-63).

The psychological affinity between the Baltic states would seem to be a major factor encouraging Latvia, Lithuania and, especially, Estonia to look to their Scandinavian neighbours for social policy lessons (Manning and Shaw, 1999). Family welfare in Estonia is not, however, resolutely universalistic as in the Nordic states; nor is it based on social democratic ideals. Aspirations are, therefore, often tempered by socio-cultural factors and, more especially, economic realities and the pressures exerted by political lobbies intent on promoting or preventing reform. As in the longer-standing EU member states, ideological compatibility may shift according to the government in power. This is illustrated by Hungary, with its three changes in government since the end of the Soviet era, each bringing a different approach to family policy in line with prevailing party ideology.

A major obstacle to policy transfer is affordability. A reason frequently cited to explain why southern European and CEE countries have problems implementing European law or transporting policies from their central and north European neighbours is the difference in per capita income and the funds available for social spending. For the CEE countries that became EU members in 2004, the cost of delivering western-style welfare was prohibitively expensive. They found themselves in a similar situation to southern European member states when they joined the European Community during their transition to democracy after a period of authoritarian rule. By the late 1990s, per capita spending on social protection was still well below the EU15 average in Greece, Portugal, Spain and Ireland (European Commission, 2002d, pp 13-14).

Affordability raises questions about the extent to which tax payers (individuals and businesses) are willing to contribute more for social protection, and about the most acceptable balance between public (national, regional or local government) and private (family and private sector) funding and delivery of welfare. In CEE countries, in particular, funding of universal family benefits and services from general taxation and employment insurance tends to be opposed on grounds of unfairness, due to the large informal sector and widespread tax evasion. The related question of cost-effectiveness and value for money of public policy moved onto the European agenda with the adoption of the Stability and Growth Pact and the commitment to fiscal austerity during the 1990s. The principle of ensuring value for money was a priority in the OMC reports on the funding of pensions, requiring governments to give a public account of their actions and progress at international level, a process that many of them had little experience of conducting.

When they are not obliged to follow EU prescriptions and are not exposed to international scrutiny, or compelled to exchange experience, policy actors, whether they be political, economic or civil society, may show little interest in policy innovations in other countries. They may not consciously draw lessons from elsewhere. Nor do they necessarily keep a record of any examples of good practice that they choose to emulate. Governments often believe they do not have much to learn from experience elsewhere, precisely because welfare systems and policy environments are so different. They, therefore, prefer to look to their own past and build on their own legacy.

The potential for family policy development

Although some convergence of policy objectives and measures may occur due to obligated policy transfer, no strong consensus can be found, either between or within countries, over the place of public policy with a family impact in European societies. The interest shown in family matters at EU level has generally been confined to issues concerned with working conditions and arrangements that impinge on family life, rather than family policies *per se*. The reluctance of policy actors to develop a supranational family policy can be explained not only by the need to observe the principle of subsidiarity, which is especially relevant for questions concerning family life, but also by the fact that family policy is an area displaying such great cultural and ideological diversity. Comparative analysis of national law and practice with respect to family life reveals the complexity of the family policy-making process to the extent that it raises questions about the value of the concept of family policy as an analytical tool and the mechanisms available to promote policy diffusion. Even if comparisons of family policies are confined to legal frameworks and benefits systems, as shown in Chapter Five, the target population remains difficult to define. When measures are designed to tackle the issue of 'guaranteeing sufficient resources', they usually cease to be the concern of family policy, further limiting its remit. The decision taken in 2001 to abandon the European Community Household Panel (ECHP) surveys after six waves, in favour of a survey of Statistics on Income and Living Conditions (EU-SILC) provides yet another indication of the Union's reluctance to devote resources to family policy as a specific policy domain. The ECHP was the closest Eurostat had come to capturing the dynamics of family life within the Union. The launch of the SILC survey marks the growing interest in income dynamics and social exclusion as a policy priority (European Commission, 2002b).

Another constraint on policy development results from differences in the levels of policy implementation and standards of monitoring both within and across countries, demonstrating that agreement at EU or national level over the adoption of a common policy is not necessarily matched in practice at the individual workplace or in the local community. In some instances, poor implementation can be attributed to fragmentation of responsibility, as with childcare provision, or excessive bureaucracy, which may explain low take up of benefits and services in some southern European and CEE countries.

Public policy is not a one-way process, as has been demonstrated throughout this book. Socio-economic change calls for policy responses, and policy matters insofar as it impacts on families, even if the precise effect is difficult to isolate and interpret, and the policy measures involved may not be directly targeting families. Political parties need to remain sensitive to the views of the electorate regarding the role government can legitimately play in family life, and they are aware of the vote-winning potential of family-friendly policies. At the one end of the spectrum in the countries where government intervention is welcomed, expected and accepted, as in France and the Nordic states, although for different reasons, the state assumes the role of legislator, provider, arbiter and enabler, working in partnership with economic and civil society actors, who represent the interests of families. At the other end of the spectrum, the state is seen at best as well meaning and supportive, but ineffectual, and at worst as partisan, corrupt, and not to be entrusted with family matters. Between these two extremes, governments may support families in their rhetoric, while remaining reluctant to take on responsibility for delivery of services, not only because of the need to respect privacy, but also because they are committed to the concept of less, rather than more, state involvement in family matters in an effort to cut costs.

Irrespective of the level of legitimacy and public acceptability of government intervention in family life, one of the problems in delivering family policy is that it often gives rise to ideological tensions between policy actors within societies over priorities, objectives and policy mechanisms, to the extent that the policy process may be severely hampered. The problem is exacerbated in countries that experience frequent changes of government, confirming that ideology does matter: conflicting ideologies would seem to result in inconsistent, if not incoherent, family policy.

A further impediment to effective policy development is that the time lag between the point when a topic requiring a policy response is identified and the point when the effects of a policy become visible may be very long, whereas the time horizons of political actors are usually short. Socio-economic change and its repercussions for policy extend over a much longer time scale than the life of a government. The issues raised by population decline and ageing, and changing family structure for intergenerational relations have, however, made policy actors acutely aware of the need to take account of the longer-term implications of socio-economic change. Even countries where the immediate situation is not a cause for concern, for example Ireland, have implemented pre-emptive measures to ensure the longer-term viability of pensions and care arrangements for older people. In the context of regime change, pension reform has been high on the agenda of the CEE countries, despite relatively low life expectancy.

The drivers for state intervention in family life are many and varied but, like governments and political ideology, they change over time and space. Central government generally recognises how important it is to work in partnership with local government, which is closer to families, and with economic actors to broaden the base for policy delivery. The business case is presented to encourage employers to see that they have an interest in creating a more family-friendly workplace. As paymasters, contributors to social insurance and regulators of working conditions, employers are gradually being alerted to the need to accommodate the care responsibilities of their employees and to retain older people in the workforce as a means of sustaining the skills base and labour supply. The involvement of civil society actors, who are close to the ground, is also being actively encouraged as a supplement, if not an alternative, to public policy.

As argued in Chapter Four, an additional justification for EU-level incursions into family matters has long been the need to ensure the equal treatment of men and women at work and in social security systems. At the turn of the century, an additional stimulus was the need to enable and facilitate the labour force participation of women with children, both as an equality objective and to bolster the labour supply. A further but, nonetheless, central argument in favour of intervention at EU and national level in family life has been the reduction of poverty, especially among categories of the population unable to earn a living from their own work, or that of family members, in societies where social protection is essentially an employment-related right.

By the end of the 20th century, a situation had arisen that was almost unprecedented since the founding of welfare states. Faced by severe economic constraints, governments, including those in the Nordic states, were turning to private (market, civil society and family) solutions as an alternative, or supplement, to public spending and provision. The growing emphasis on the role of the private sector and on work as the solution to many of the problems created by socio-economic change highlights major ideological differences in welfare design and delivery, according to whether benefits and services are conceptualised as a citizenship right based on the principle of social solidarity and funded from taxation, or whether they have to be earned by participation in the labour force. A work-based welfare system tends to act as a polarising force, separating work-rich from work-poor people, but it can also be a balancing force, if work is made to pay, and if non-stigmatising routes are provided for those unable to work.

Even in countries where the legitimacy of government intervention in family matters is questioned, markets and civil society are not considered by public opinion to be acceptable substitutes for the state as a family policy actor. When governments are shown to be inadequate or inappropriate providers, the preference is usually for families to assume responsibility. Rather than reversing the trend towards decommodification and defamilialisation, pressures to increase the labour supply, in conjunction with welfare-to-work programmes and offloading to the private sector, have had the effect of increasing the burden on family members, while also creating large numbers of low-paid, short-hours jobs that are mainly taken up by women. While they bolster employment figures and move countries closer to the Union's targets, such jobs often contribute little to public funds.

Payments to parents to stay at home to raise children, or to family members who leave work to care for older or disabled relatives, although they too are usually relatively low, are bringing carers into the labour force and giving recognition to the care function, thereby blurring the distinction between paid and unpaid family care work. The concept of 'social care' (Daly and Lewis, 2000, p 296) has been used to portray the growing importance of the market as an intervening factor in the state–family relationship, thereby diluting another of the possible functions of family policy. Whether the distribution of benefits specifically targeting families is a sufficient justification for preserving a designated family policy domain becomes a moot point. The analysis carried out in this book suggests that, for families, what really matters is for governments to ensure that support in cash and kind is available for individuals and families as units when they most need it. Europeans seem to want such support to be offered as a complement rather than a substitute for family provision. They are, therefore, looking for services that are affordable, accessible, adaptable, reliable and of good quality, which few governments at the turn of the century seemed in a position to deliver within the narrow confines of a family policy remit.

References

Abela, A.M. (2003) 'Family values and social policy in Europe', *Cross-National Research Papers*, vol 6, no 5, pp 16-28.

Abramovici, G. (2003) 'Social protection: cash family benefits in Europe', *Statistics in Focus: Population and Social Condition*, no 19.

Afsa, C. (1996) 'L'activité féminine à l'épreuve de l'allocation parentale d'éducation', *Recherches et prévisions*, no 46, pp 1-8.

Alcock, P. (1996) 'Welfare and self-interest', commentary in F. Field, *Stakeholder welfare*, Choice in Welfare, no 32, London: IEA Health and Welfare Unit, pp 47-59.

Algava, E. (2002) 'Les familles monoparentales en 1999', *Population-F*, vol 57, nos 4-5, pp 733-58.

Algava, E. and Avenel, M. (2001) 'Les bénéficiaires de l'allocation de parent isolé (API)', *Études et résultats*, DREES, no 112.

Aliaga, C. and Winqvist, K. (2003) 'How women and men spend their time: results from 13 European countries', *Statistics in Focus: Population and Social Condition*, no 12.

Allan, G. (ed) (1999) *The sociology of the family: a reader*, Oxford/Malden, MA: Blackwell.

Allsopp, V. (1995) *Understanding economics*, London/New York, NY: Routledge.

Amaro, F. (1994) 'Portugal: improvement of the quality of family life', in W. Dumon (ed) *Changing family policies in the member states of the European Union*, Brussels: Commission of the European Communities, DG V, pp 255-70.

Anxo, D., Stancanelli, E. and Storrie, D. (2000) 'Transitions between different working-time arrangements: a comparison of Sweden and the Netherlands', in J. O'Reilly, I. Cebrián and M. Lallement (eds) *Working-time changes: social integration through transitional labour markets*, Cheltenham/Northampton, MA: Edward Elgar, pp 93-131.

Appleton, L. and Byrne. P. (2003) 'Mapping relations between family policy actors', *Social Policy and Society*, vol 2, no 3, pp 211-19.

Arber, S. and Attias-Donfut, C. (eds) (2000) *The myth of generational conflict: the family and state in ageing societies*, London/New York, NY: Routledge.

Attias-Donfut, C. and Arber, S. (2000) 'Equity and solidarity across the generations', in S. Arber and C. Attias-Donfut (eds) *The myth of generational conflict: the family and state in ageing societies*, London/New York, NY: Routledge, pp 1-21.

Badia i Ibáñez, M. (2003) 'Difficulties ahead for Spanish families', *Cross-National Research Papers*, vol 6, no 6, pp 60-6.

Barre, C. (2003) '1,6 million d'enfants vivent dans une famille recomposée', *Insée première*, no 901.

Becker, G.S. (1981) *A treatise on the family*, Cambridge, MA/London: Harvard University Press.

Bégeot, F. and Fernández Cordón, J-A. (1997) 'Demographic convergence beyond national differences', in J. Commaille and F. de Singly (eds) *The European family: the family question in the European Community*, Dordrecht: Kluwer Academic Publishers, pp 23-44.

Bekkengen, L. (2002) *Man får välja: om föräldraskap och föräldraledighet i arbetsliv och familjeliv*, Malmö: Liber.

Berglund, S., Hellén, T. and Aarebrot, F.H. (1998) *The handbook of political change in Eastern Europe*, Cheltenham/Northampton, MA: Edward Elgar.

Berthoud, R. (2000) 'Introduction: the dynamics of social change', in R. Berthoud and J. Gershuny (eds) *Seven years in the lives of British families: evidence on the dynamics of social change from the British Household Panel Survey*, Bristol: The Policy Press, pp 1-20.

Berthoud, R. and Gershuny, J. (eds) (2000) *Seven years in the lives of British families: evidence on the dynamics of social change from the British Household Panel Survey*, Bristol: The Policy Press.

Bielenski, H., Bosch, G. and Wagner, A. (2002) *Working time preferences in sixteen European countries*, Luxembourg: Office for Official Publications of the European Communities.

Bite, I. and Zagorskis, V. (2003) 'Study on the social protection systems in the 13 applicant countries: Latvia', unpublished report to the European Commission.

Bogenschneider, K. (ed) (2002) *Family policy matters: how policymaking affects families and what professionals can do*, Mahwah, NJ/London: Lawrence Erlbaum.

Bradshaw, J., Ditch, J., Holmes, H. and Whiteford, P. (1993) 'A comparative study of child support in fifteen countries', *Journal of European Social Policy*, vol 3, no 4, pp 255-71.

Bradshaw, J., Kennedy, S., Kilkey, M., Hutton, S., Corden, A., Eardley, T.,

Holmes, H. and Neale, J. (1996) *Policy and the employment of lone parents in 20 countries*, Brussels/York: European Commission/Social Policy Research Unit, University of York.

Brannen, J., Lewis, S., Nilsen, A. and Smithson, J. (eds) (2002) *Young Europeans, work and family: futures in transition*, London/New York, NY: Routledge.

Brannen, J., Mészáros, G., Moss, P. and Poland, G. (1994) *Employment and family life: a review of research in the UK (1980-1994)*, Research Series, no 41, Sheffield: Employment Department.

Bréchon, P. (2002) 'Des valeurs politiques entre pérennité et changement', *Futuribles*, no 277, pp 95-128.

Bréchon, P. and Tchernia, J-F. (2002) 'Les enquêtes sur les valeurs des Européens', *Futuribles*, no 277, pp 5-14.

Burgess, E.W. and Locke, H.J. (1945) *The family: from institution to companionship*, New York, NY: American Book Company.

Calot, G. (1980) 'Niveau de vie et nombre d'enfants: un bilan de la législation familiale et fiscale française de 1978', *Population*, vol 35, no 1, pp 9-56.

Carling, A., Duncan, S. and Edwards, R. (2002) *Analysing families: morality and rationality in policy and practice*, London/New York, NY: Routledge.

Castel, R. (1995) *Les métamorphoses de la question sociale: une chronique du salariat*, Paris: Fayard.

Cebrián, I., O'Reilly, J. and Lallement, M. (2000) 'Introduction', in J. O'Reilly, I. Cebrián and M. Lallement (eds) *Working-time changes: social integration through transitional labour markets*, Cheltenham/Northampton, MA: Edward Elgar, pp 1-21.

Chambaz, C. (2000) 'Les familles monoparentales en Europe: des réalités multiples', *Études et résultats*, no 66.

Cheal, D. (1999) 'The one and the many: modernity and postmodernity', in G. Allan (ed) *The sociology of the family: a reader*, Oxford: Blackwell, pp 56-85; first published as chapter 5, in D. Cheal, *Family and the state of theory*, 1991, Hemel Hempstead: Harvester Wheatsheaf.

Chester, R. (1994) 'Flying without instruments or flight plans: family policy in the United Kingdom', in W. Dumon (ed) *Changing family policies in the member states of the European Union*, Brussels: Commission of the European Communities, DG V, pp 271-301.

Coleman, D. (2000) 'Population and family', in A.H. Halsey with J. Webb (eds) *Twentieth-century British social trends*, London/New York, NY: Macmillan/St Martin's Press (3rd edn), pp 27-93.

Coleman, D. (ed) (1996) *Europe's population in the 1990s*, Oxford: Oxford University Press.

Coleman, D. and Chandola, T. (1999) 'Britain's place in Europe's population', in S. McRae (ed) *Changing Britain: families and households in the 1990s*, Oxford: Oxford University Press, pp 37-67.

Commaille, J., Strobel, P. and Villac, M. (2002) *La politique de la famille*, Paris: Éditions La Découverte.

Cooper, D. (1971) *The death of the family*, Harmondsworth: Penguin.

Council of Europe (1997) *Recent demographic developments in Europe 1997*, Strasbourg: Council of Europe Publishing.

Council of Europe (2002) *Recent demographic developments in Europe, 2002*, Strasbourg: Council of Europe Publishing.

Cristofari, M-F. and Labarthe, G. (2001) 'Des ménages de plus en plus petits', *Insée première*, no 789.

Daly, M. (2001) 'Globalization and the Bismarckian welfare states', in R. Sykes, B. Palier and P.M. Prior (eds) *Globalization and European welfare states*, Basingstoke/New York, NY: Palgrave, pp 79-102.

Daly, M. and Lewis, J. (2000) 'The concept of social care and the analysis of contemporary welfare states', *British Journal of Sociology*, vol 51, no 2, pp 281-98.

Davies, H., Nutley, S. and Smith, P. (2000) 'Introducing evidence-based policy and practice in public services', in H.T.O. Davies, S.M. Nutley and P.C. Smith (eds) *What works? Evidence-based policy and practice in public services*, Bristol: The Policy Press, pp 1-11.

de Hoog, K., Presvelou, C. and Cuyvers, P. (1993) *Family arrangements and policy in the Netherlands*, The Hague: Netherlands Family Council.

Dekeuwer-Defossez, F. (1999) *Rénover le droit de la famille: propositions pour un droit adapté aux réalités et aux aspirations de notre temps*, Rapport au Garde des Sceaux, Ministre de la Justice, Paris: La Documentation française.

Del Re, A. (2000) 'The paradoxes of Italian law and practice', in L. Hantrais (ed) *Gendered policies in Europe: reconciling employment and family life*, London/New York, NY: Macmillan/St Martin's Press, pp 108-23.

Department of Trade and Industry (2001) *Work–life balance: the business case*, London: Department of Trade and Industry.

de Singly, F. and Commaille, J. (1997) 'Rules of the comparative method in the family sphere. The meaning of a comparison', in J. Commaille and F. de Singly (eds) *The European family: the family question in the European Community*, Dordrecht: Kluwer Academic Publishers, pp 3-20.

Desrosières, A. (1996) 'Statistical traditions: an obstacle to international comparisons', in L. Hantrais and S. Mangen (eds) *Cross-national research methods in the social sciences*, London/New York, NY: Cassell, pp 17-27.

Dingledey, I. (2001) 'European tax systems and their impact on family employment patterns', *Journal of Social Policy*, vol 30, no 4, pp 653-72.

Ditch, J., Barnes, H. and Bradshaw, J. (1996a) *A synthesis of national family policies 1995*, Brussels: European Commission.

Ditch, J., Barnes, H. and Bradshaw, J. (eds) (1996b) *Developments in national family policies in 1995*, Brussels: European Commission.

Ditch, J., Barnes, H. and Bradshaw, J. (eds) (1998a) *Developments in national family policies in 1996*, Brussels: European Commission.

Ditch, J., Barnes, H., Bradshaw, J. and Kilkey, M. (1998b) *A synthesis of national family policies 1996*, Brussels: European Commission.

Dobravolskas, A. and Buivydas, R. (2003) 'Study on the social protection systems in the 13 applicant countries: Lithuania', unpublished report to the European Commission.

Donzelot, J. (1980) *The policing of families: welfare versus the state*, London: Hutchinson.

Drew, E., Emereck, R. and Mahon, E. (eds) (1998) *Women, work and the family in Europe*, London/New York, NY: Routledge.

Dumon, W. (1991) *National family policies in EC-countries in 1990*, Brussels: Commission of the European Communities and European Observatory on National Family Policies, V/2293/91-EN.

Dumon, W. (1994) 'National family policies in the member states: current trends and developments', in W. Dumon (ed) *Changing family policies in the member states of the European Union*, Brussels: Commission of the European Communities, DG V, pp 303-26.

Eekelaar, J. (1997) 'From "privacy" to the Leviathan state. The case of the child', in J. Commaille and F. de Singly (eds) *The European family: the family question in the European Community*, Dordrecht: Kluwer Academic Publishers, pp 205-16.

Ekert-Jaffé, O. (1986) 'Effets et limites des aides financières aux familles: une expérience et un modèle', *Population*, vol 41, no 2, pp 327-48.

Elias, P. (2003) 'Female employment and family formation in national institutional contexts (FENICs)', in L. Hantrais (ed) *Policy relevance of 'Family and Welfare' research*, Luxembourg: Official Publications of the European Communities, pp 21-6.

Elster, J., Offe, C. and Preuss, U.K. (1998) *Institutional design in post-*

communist societies: rebuilding the ship at sea, Cambridge: Cambridge University Press.

Ermisch, J. (1996) 'The economic environment for family formation', in D. Coleman (ed) *Europe's population in the 1990s*, Oxford: Oxford University Press, pp 144-62.

Ermisch, J.F. (2003) *An economic analysis of the family*, Princeton, NJ/Oxford: Princeton University Press.

Ermisch, J. and Francesconi, M. (2000) 'Patterns of household and family formation', in R. Berthoud and J. Gershuny (eds) *Seven years in the lives of British families: evidence on the dynamics of social change from the British Household Panel Survey*, Bristol: The Policy Press, pp 21-44.

Esping-Andersen, G. (1990) *The three worlds of welfare capitalism*, Cambridge: Polity Press.

Esping-Andersen, G. (1999) *Social foundations of postindustrial economies*, Oxford: Oxford University Press.

European Commission (1995) *The demographic situation in the European Union: 1994 report*, Luxembourg: Office for Official Publications of the European Communities.

European Commission (1996a) *The demographic situation in the European Union: 1995*, Luxembourg: Office for Official Publications of the European Communities.

European Commission (1996b) *Employment in Europe 1996*, Luxembourg: Office for Official Publications of the European Communities.

European Commission (1998) *Demographic report 1997*, Luxembourg: Office for Official Publications of the European Communities.

European Commission (1999a) *Affirming fundamental rights in the European Union: report of the Expert Group on Fundamental Rights*, Luxembourg: Office for Official Publications of the European Communities.

European Commission (1999b) *Employment in Europe 1999*, Luxembourg: Office for Official Publications of the European Communities.

European Commission (1999c) *Reconciliation of work and family life for men and women and the quality of care services*, Luxembourg: Office for Official Publications of the European Communities.

European Commission (2000a) *Living conditions in Europe: statistical pocketbook*, Luxembourg: Office for Official Publications of the European Communities.

European Commission (2000b) *Social policy agenda*, Luxembourg: Office for Official Publications of the European Communities.

European Commission (2000c) *The social situation in the European Union 2000*, Luxembourg: Office for Official Publications of the European Communities.

European Commission (2001) *The social situation in the European Union 2001*, Luxembourg: Office for Official Publications of the European Communities.

European Commission (2002a) *Employment in Europe 2002: recent trends and prospects*, Luxembourg: Office for Official Publications of the European Communities.

European Commission (2002b) *Joint report on social inclusion*, Luxembourg: Office for Official Publications of the European Communities.

European Commission (2002c) *The life of women and men in Europe: a statistical portrait. Data 1980–2000*, Luxembourg: Office for Official Publications of the European Communities.

European Commission (2002d) *Social protection in Europe 2001*, Luxembourg: Office for Official Publications of the European Communities.

European Commission (2002e) *The social situation in the European Union 2002*, Luxembourg: Office for Official Publications of the European Communities.

European Commission (2003) *The social situation in the European Union 2003*, Luxembourg: Office for Official Publications of the European Communities.

Eurostat (1988) *Labour force survey results 1986*, Luxembourg: Office for Official Publications of the European Communities.

Eurostat (1992) *Fertility: measurement and changes in the European Community*, Luxembourg: Office for Official Publications of the European Communities.

Eurostat (1994) *Definitions and methods of collecting demographic statistics in the European Community countries*, Luxembourg: Office for Official Publications of the European Communities.

Eurostat (1995a) *Demographic statistics 1995*, Luxembourg: Office for Official Publications of the European Communities.

Eurostat (1995b) 'Households and families in the European Economic Area', *Statistics in Focus: Population and Social Conditions*, no 5.

Eurostat (1996) *The European Union labour force survey: methods and definitions*, Luxembourg: Office for Official Publications of the European Communities.

Eurostat (1997a) *Education across the European Union: statistics and indicators 1996*, Luxembourg: Office for Official Publications of the European Communities.

Eurostat (1997b) *Labour force survey results 1996*, Luxembourg: Office for Official Publications of the European Communities.

Eurostat (1998) *A social portrait of Europe*, Luxembourg: Office for Official Publications of the European Communities.

Eurostat (1999) *Guidelines and table programme for the Community Programme of Population and Housing Censuses in 2001*, vol. 1, *Guidelines*, vol 2, *Table programme*, Eurostat Working Papers, 3/1999/E/No10, Luxembourg: Office for Official Publications of the European Communities.

Eurostat (2000) *European social statistics: migration*, Luxembourg: Office for Official Publications of the European Communities.

Eurostat (2001) *European social statistics: labour force survey results 2000*, Luxembourg: Office for Official Publications of the European Communities.

Eurostat (2002a) *European social statistics: demography*, Luxembourg: Office for Official Publications of the European Communities.

Eurostat (2002b) *European social statistics: labour force survey results 2001*, Luxembourg: Office for Official Publications of the European Communities.

Eurostat (2002c) *Key data on education in Europe – 2002*, Luxembourg: Office for Official Publications of the European Communities.

Eurostat (2002d) *Yearbook 2002. The statistical guide to Europe: data 1990-2000*, Luxembourg: Office for Official Publications of the European Communities.

Fagan, C. and Burchell, B. (2002) *Gender, jobs and working conditions in the European Union*, Luxembourg: Office for Official Publications of the European Communities.

Fagnani, J. and Letablier, M-T. (2003) 'La réduction du temps de travail a-t-elle amélioré la vie quotidienne des parents de jeunes enfants?', *Premières informations et premières synthèses*, DARES, no 01.2, Paris: Ministère des Affaires sociales, du Travail et de la Solidarité.

Ferge, Z. (1992) 'Social policy regimes and social structure: hypotheses about the prospects of social policy in Central and Eastern Europe', in Z. Ferge and J.E. Kolberg (eds) *Social policy in a changing Europe*, Boulder, CO: Campus/Westview, pp 201-22.

Ferge, Z. (1997) 'A central European perspective on the social quality of Europe', in W. Beck, L. van der Maesen and A. Walker (eds) *The social quality of Europe*, The Hague/London/Boston, MA: Kluwer Law International, pp 165-81.

Ferge, Z. (2001a) 'Disquieting quiet in Hungarian social policy', *International Social Security Review*, vol 54, nos 2-3, pp 107-26.

Ferge, Z. (2001b) 'Welfare and "ill-fare" systems in Central-Eastern Europe', in R. Sykes, B. Palier and P.M. Prior (eds) *Globalization and European welfare states*, Basingstoke/New York, NY: Palgrave, pp 127-52.

Fernández Cordón, J.A. (1994) 'Spain: adjusting to the new family structures', in W. Dumon (ed) *Changing family policies in the member states of the European Union*, Brussels: Commission of the European Communities, DG V, pp 105-22.

Festy, P. (2001) 'Pacs: l'impossible bilan', *Population et sociétés*, no 369.

Field, F. (1996) *Stakeholder welfare*, Choice in Welfare, no 32, London: IEA Health and Welfare Unit.

FitzGerald, M. (2000) 'Ireland before and after accession to the European Union', *Cross-National Research Papers*, vol 6, no 2, pp 61-7.

Flaquer, L. (2002) 'Family policy and the maintenance of the traditional family in Spain', in A. Carling, S. Duncan and R. Edwards (eds) *Analysing families: morality and rationality in policy and practice*, London/New York, NY: Routledge, pp 84-92.

Fox Harding, L. (1996) *Family, state and social policy*, London: Macmillan.

Franco, A. and Blöndal, L. (2002) 'Labour force survey: principal results 2001. Candidate countries', *Statistics in Focus: Population and Social Conditions*, no 20.

Franco, A. and Jouhette, S. (2002) 'Labour force survey: principal results 2001. EU and EFTA countries', *Statistics in Focus: Population and Social Conditions*, no 19.

Franco, A. and Winqvist, K. (2002) 'Women and men reconciling work and family life', *Statistics in Focus: Population and Social Conditions*, no 9.

Frey, M. (2001) 'Nok és férfiak a munkaeropiacon' ('Women and men on the labour market'), in I. Nagy, T. Pongrácz and I.Gy. Tóth (eds) *Szerepváltozások (Changing roles)*, Budapest: TÁRKI-Szociális és Családügyi Minisztérium, pp 9-29.

García-Ramon, M.D. and Monk, J. (eds) (1996) *Women of the European Union: the politics of work and daily life*, London/New York, NY: Routledge.

Gauthier, A.H. (1996a) 'The measured and unmeasured effects of welfare benefits on families: implications for Europe's demographic trends', in D. Coleman (ed) *Europe's population in the 1990s*, Oxford: Oxford University Press, pp 297-331.

Gauthier, A.H. (1996b) *The state and the family: a comparative analysis of family policies in industrialized countries*, Oxford: Clarendon Press.

Giddens, A. (1998) *The third way: the renewal of social democracy*, Cambridge: Polity Press.

Ginsburg, N. (2001) 'Globalization and the liberal welfare states', in R. Sykes, B. Palier and P.M. Prior (eds) *Globalization and European welfare states*, Basingstoke/New York, NY: Palgrave, pp 173-91.

Glover, J. (2002) 'The "balance model": theorising women's employment behaviour', in A. Carling, S. Duncan and R. Edwards (eds) *Analysing families: morality and rationality in policy and practice*, London/New York, NY: Routledge, pp 251-67.

Golinowska, S., Pietka, K., Sowada, C. and Zukowski, M. (2003) 'Study on the social protection systems in the 13 applicant countries: Poland', unpublished report to the European Commission.

Gornick, J.C., Meyers, M.K. and Ross, K.E. (1997) 'Supporting the employment of mothers: policy variation across fourteen welfare states', *Journal of European Social Policy*, vol 7, no 1, pp 45-70.

Guillén, A. and Álvarez, S. (2001) 'Globalization and the southern welfare states', in R. Sykes, B. Palier and P.M. Prior (eds) *Globalization and European welfare states*, Basingstoke/New York, NY: Palgrave, pp 103-26.

Hakim, C. (2000) *Work–lifestyle choices in the 21st century: preference theory*, Oxford: Oxford University Press.

Halsey, A.H. (2000) 'Twentieth-century Britain', in A.H. Halsey with J. Webb (eds) *Twentieth-century British social trends*, London/New York, NY: Macmillan/St Martin's Press (3rd edn), pp 1-23.

Hantrais, L. (2000a) *Social policy in the European Union*, London/New York, NY: Macmillan/St Martin's Press (2nd edn).

Hantrais, L. (ed) (2000b) *Gendered policies in Europe: reconciling employment and family life*, London/New York, NY: Macmillan/St Martin's Press.

Hantrais, L. (ed) (2003) *Cross-National Research Papers*, vol 6, no 7.

Hantrais, L. and Letablier, M-T. (1996) *Families and family policies in Europe*, London/New York, NY: Addison Wesley Longman.

Harding, S., Phillips, D. and Fogarty, M. (1986) *Contrasting values in western Europe: unity, diversity and change*, London: Macmillan.

Herpin, N. (2002) 'Postmatérialisme et structure des opinions sur la famille', *Futuribles*, no 277, pp 41-61.

Hobcraft, J. and Kiernan, K. (1999) *Childhood poverty, early motherhood and adult social exclusion*, CASEpaper, no 28, London: Centre for Analysis of Social Exclusion, London School of Economics.

Hoem, B. (1993) 'The compatibility of employment and childbearing in contemporary Sweden', *Acta Sociologica*, vol 36, no 2, pp 101-20.

Humphreys, P., Fleming, S. and O'Donnell, O. (2000) *Balancing work and family life: the role of flexible working arrangements*, Dublin: Department of Social, Community and Family Affairs.

Istat (2003) *Famiglia, abitazioni e sicurezza dei cittadini*, Rome: Istat.

Jeandidier, B. (1997) 'La spécificité des politiques familiales en Europe', *Recherches et prévisions*, no 48, pp 27-44.

Kamerman, S.B. and Kahn, A.J. (1982) 'Income transfers, work and the economic well-being of families with children: a comparative study', *International Social Security Review*, vol 35, no 3, pp 345-82.

Kamerman, S.B. and Kahn, A.J. (eds) (1978) *Family policy: government and families in fourteen countries*, New York, NY: Columbia University Press.

Karelson, K. and Pall, K. (2003) 'Estonian self-reliance', *Cross National Research Papers*, vol 6, no 6, pp 40-5.

Kaufmann, F-X., Kuijsten, A., Schulze, H-J. and Strohmeier, K.P. (eds) (1997) *Family life and family policies in Europe*, vol 1, *Structures and trends in the 1980s*, Oxford: Clarendon Press.

Kaufmann, F-X., Kuijsten, A., Schulze, H-J. and Strohmeier, K.P. (eds) (2002) *Family life and family policies in Europe*, vol 2, *Problems and issues in comparative perspective*, Oxford: Clarendon Press.

Kay, T. (2003) 'The work–life balance in social practice', *Social Policy and Society*, vol 2, no 3, pp 231-9.

Kazimierz, P. (ed) (2000) *Kodeks Rodzinny I Opiekuñczy z komentarzem (Family and Custody Code with commentary)*, Warsaw: Wydawnictwo Prawnicze.

Kende, A. (2000) 'The Roma (gypsies) in Hungary', *Cross-National Research Papers*, vol 6, no 2, pp 50-5.

Kiely, G. and Richardson, V. (1994) 'Ireland: family policy in a rapidly changing society', in W. Dumon (ed) *Changing family policies in the member states of the European Union*, Brussels: Commission of the European Communities, DG V, pp 151-72.

Kiernan, K. (1997) 'Becoming a young parent: a longitudinal study of associated factors', *British Journal of Sociology*, vol 48, no 3, pp 406-28.

Kosononen, P. (2001) 'Globalization and the Nordic welfare states', in R. Sykes, B. Palier and P.M. Prior (eds) *Globalization and European welfare states*, Basingstoke/New York, NY: Palgrave, pp 153-72.

Kumar, K. (1995) *From post-industrial to post-modern society: new theories of the contemporary world*, Oxford: Blackwell.

Kutsar, D. and Tiit, E-M. (2000) 'Comparing socio-demographic indicators in Estonia and the European Union', *Cross-National Research Papers*, vol 6, no 2, pp 27-34.

Lambert, Y. (2002) 'Religion: l'Europe à un tournant', *Futuribles*, no 277, pp 129-60.

Landgren-Möller, L.E. (1997) 'Att ha familj', *Välfärd och ojämlikhet i 20-årsperspektiv 1975-1995*, Rapport, no 91, Stockholm: Statistiska Centralbyrån, pp 269-85.

Lanquetin, M-T., Laufer, J. and Letablier, M-T. (2000) 'From equality to reconciliation in France?', in L. Hantrais (ed) *Gendered policies in Europe: reconciling employment and family life*, London/New York, NY: Macmillan/St Martin's Press, pp 68-88.

Legros, F. (2003) 'La fécondité des étrangères en France: une stabilisation entre 1990 et 1999', *Insée première*, no 898.

Lesthaeghe, R. (1995) 'The second demographic transition in western countries: an interpretation', in K.O. Mason and A-M. Jensen (eds) *Gender and family change in industrialized countries*, Oxford: Clarendon Press, pp 17-62.

Letablier, M-T., Pennec, S. and Büttner, O. (2003) *Opinions, attitudes et aspirations des familles vis-à-vis de la politique familiale en France*, Rapport de recherches, no 09, Noisy-le-Grand: Centre d'études de l'emploi.

Lewis, J. (1992) 'Gender and the development of welfare regimes', *Journal of European Social Policy*, vol 2, no 3, pp 159-73.

Lewis, J. (2002) 'Individualisation, assumptions about the existence of an adult worker model and the shift towards contractualism', in A. Carling, S. Duncan and R. Edwards (eds) *Analysing families: morality and rationality in policy and practice*, London/New York, NY: Routledge, pp 51-6.

Lewis, J. and Knijn, T. (2002) 'The politics of sex education policy in

England and Wales and the Netherlands since the 1980s', *Journal of Social Policy*, vol 31, no 4, pp 669-94.

Lister, R. (1997) *Citizenship: feminist perspectives*, London: Macmillan.

Longo, V. and Sacchetto, D. (2003) 'Traditional and modern policy responses to Italian family diversity', *Cross-National Research Papers*, vol 6, no 6, pp 67-73.

Maclean, M. (2002) 'The Green Paper *Supporting families*, 1998', in A. Carling, S. Duncan and R. Edwards (eds) *Analysing families: morality and rationality in policy and practice*, London/New York, NY: Routledge, pp 64-8.

Mangen, S.P. (2001) *Spanish society after Franco: regime transition and the welfare state*, Basingstoke/New York, NY: Palgrave.

Manning, N. and Shaw, I. (1999) 'The transferability of welfare models: a comparison of the Scandinavian and state socialist models in relation to Finland and Estonia', in C. Jones Finer (ed) *Transnational social policy*, Oxford/Malden, MA: Blackwell, pp 120-38.

Mateman, S. and Renooy, P.H. (2001) 'Undeclared labour in Europe: towards an integrated approach of combatting undeclared labour', Final report, Regioplan Publication, no 424, Amsterdam: Regioplan Research Advice and Information.

McGlone, F., Park, A. and Roberts, C. (1999) 'Kinship and friendship: attitudes and behaviour in Britain, 1986-1995', in S. McRae (ed) *Changing Britain: families and households in the 1990s*, Oxford: Oxford University Press, pp 141-55.

McLaughlin, E. and Glendinning, C. (1994) 'Paying for care in Europe: is there a feminist approach?', *Cross-National Research Papers*, vol 3, no 3, pp 52-69.

McRae, S. (1999) 'Introduction: family and household change in Britain', in S. McRae (ed) *Changing Britain: families and households in the 1990s*, Oxford: Oxford University Press, pp 1-33.

Méda, D. and Orain, R. (2002) 'Transformations du travail et du hors travail: le jugement des salariés sur la réduction du temps de travail', *Travail et emploi*, no 90, pp 23-38.

Meulders, D. and O'Dorchai, S. (2002) 'The rationale of motherhood choices: influence of employment conditions and of public policies', *Newsletter*, no 1.

Meulders-Klein, M-T. (1992) 'Vie privée, vie familiale et droits de l'homme', *Revue internationale de droit comparé*, vol 44, no 4, pp 767-94.

Mezei, S. (1997) 'Family policy in Communist Europe as an incitement to passive citizenship', in J. Commaille and F. de Singly (eds) *The European family: the family question in the European Community*, Dordrecht: Kluwer Academic Publishers, pp 217-27.

Millar, J. (2003) 'Social policy and family policy', in P. Alcock, A. Erskine and M. May (eds) *The student's companion to social policy* (2nd edn), Oxford: Blackwell, pp 153-9.

Millar, J. and Warman, A. (1996) *Family obligations in Europe*, London: Family Policy Studies Centre.

MISSCEO (Mutual Information System on Social Protection of the Council of Europe) (2002) *Comparative tables of social protection systems in 21 member states of the Council of Europe, Australia, Canada and New Zealand*, 11th edn, Strasbourg: Council of Europe.

MISSOC (Mutual Information System on Social Protection) (2001) 'Evolution of social protection in the European member states and the European Economic Area', *Missoc-info*, no 02, Luxembourg: Office for Official Publications of the European Communities.

MISSOC (2002) 'Family benefits and family policies in Europe', *Missoc-info*, no 01, Luxembourg: Office for Official Publications of the European Communities.

MISSOC (2003) *Social protection in the EU member states and the European Economic Area: situation on January 1st 2003 and evolution*, Luxembourg: Office for Official Publications of the European Communities. http://europa.eu.int/comm/employment_social/missoc/index _en.html

Mooney, A., Stratham, J. and Simon, A. (2002) *The pivot generation: informal care and work after fifty*, Bristol/York: The Policy Press/Joseph Rowntree Foundation.

Morgan, D.H.J. (1975) *Social theory and the family*, London/Boston MA: Routledge and Kegan Paul.

Morgan, P. (1995) *Farewell to the family? Public policy and family breakdown in Britain and the USA*, London: IEA Health and Welfare Unit.

Moussourou, L. (1994) 'Family policy in Greece: traditional and modern patterns', in W. Dumon (ed) *Changing family policies in the member states of the European Union*, Brussels: Commission of the European Communities, DG V, pp 87-104.

Müller, K. (2001) 'The political economy of pension reform in eastern Europe', *International Social Security Review*, vol 54, nos 2-3, pp 57-79.

Munoz-Pérez, F. and Prioux, F. (1999) 'Les enfants nés hors marriage et leurs parents: reconnaissances et légimitations depuis 1965', *Population*, vol 54, no 3, pp 481-508.

Murdock, G.P. (1949) *Social structure*, New York, NY: Macmillan.

Myrdal, A. (1945) *Nation and family: the Swedish experiment in democratic family and population policy*, London: Kegan Paul, Trench, Trubner and Co (first published 1941).

Neményi, M. and Tóth, O. (2003) 'Differential modernization in Hungary: families and family values after transition', *Cross-National Research Papers*, vol 6, no 6, pp 60-6.

Neyens, M. (1994) 'A leading sector in Luxembourg social policy: family policy, from its genesis to its diversity: its future challenges', in W. Dumon (ed) *Changing family policies in the member states of the European Union*, Brussels: Commission of the European Communities, DG V, pp 199-224.

NSO (National Statistics Office) (2003) *Demographic review 2002*, Valetta: National Statistics Office.

O'Dorchai, S. (2003) 'The rationale of motherhood choices: influence of employment conditions and of public policies (MoCho)', in L. Hantrais (ed) *Policy relevance of 'Family and Welfare' research*, Luxembourg: Official Publications of the European Communities, pp 27-30.

OECD (Organisation for Economic Co-operation and Development) (2001) *Education at a glance: OECD indicators*, Paris: OECD.

ONS (Office for National Statistics) (1998) *Social trends*, no 28, London: The Stationery Office.

ONS (2001a) *Birth statistics: review of the Registrar General on births and patterns of family building in England and Wales, 2001*, Series FM1, no 30, London: The Stationery Office.

ONS (2001b) *Living in Britain: results from the 2001 General Household Survey*, London: The Stationery Office.

ONS (2001c) *Social trends*, no 31, London: The Stationery Office.

ONS (2002a) 'Social focus in brief: ethnicity', National statistics online, London: ONS. http://www.statistics.gov.uk/cci/nugget.asp?id=272

ONS (2002b) *Social trends*, no 32, London: The Stationery Office.

ONS (2003a) 'Census 2001: children', National statistics online, London: ONS. http://www.statistics.gov.uk/cci/ nugget.asp?id=348

ONS (2003b) *Labour Market Tends*, vol 111, no 11.

ONS (2003c) *Social trends*, no 33, London: The Stationery Office.

Paoli, P. and Merllié, D. (2001) *Third European survey on working conditions 2000*, Luxembourg: Office for Official Publications of the European Communities.

Parsons, T. and Bales, R.F. (1956) *Family: socialization and interaction process*, London: Routledge and Kegan Paul.

Pascall, G. and Manning, N. (2000) 'Gender and social policy: comparing welfare states in Central and Eastern Europe and the former Soviet Union', *Journal of European Social Policy*, vol 10, no 3, pp 240-66.

Pashardes, P. (2003) 'Study on the social protection systems in the 13 applicant countries: Cyprus', unpublished report to the European Commission.

Penn, R. and Lambert, P. (2002) 'Attitudes towards ideal family size of different ethnic/nationality groups in Great Britain, France and Germany', *Population Trends*, no 108, pp 49-57.

Pfau-Effinger, B. and Geissler, B. (2002) 'Cultural change and family policies in East and West Germany', in A. Carling, S. Duncan and R. Edwards (eds) *Analysing families: morality and rationality in policy and practice*, London/New York, NY: Routledge, pp 77-83.

Potoczna, M. and Prorok-Mamińska, L. (2003) 'Polish paradoxes', *Cross-National Research Papers*, vol 6, no 6, pp 52-9.

Pringle, K. and Hearn, J. (2003) 'Thematic network on the social problem and societal problematization of men and masculinities (MEN)', in L. Hantrais (ed) *Policy relevance of 'Family and Welfare' research*, Luxembourg: Office for Official Publications of the European Communities, pp 43-6.

Prodi, R. and Kinnock, N. (2000) 'The Commission and non-governmental organisations: building a stronger partnership', Commission discussion paper, Brussels, 18 January.

Roll, J. (1991) *What is a family? Benefit models and social realities*, London: Family Policy Studies Centre.

Rose, R. (2001) *Ten steps in learning lessons from abroad*, Future Governance Discussion Paper, no 1, Strathclyde: Centre for the Study of Public Policy.

Rose, R. (2002) *When all other conditions are not equal: the context for drawing lessons*, Studies in Public Policy, no 366, Strathclyde: Centre for the Study of Public Policy.

Rostgaard, T. and Fridberg, T. (1998) *Caring for children and older people – a comparison of European policies and practices*, Social Security in Europe, no 6, Copenhagen: Danish National Institute of Social Research.

Rubery, J., Figueiredo, H., Grimshaw, D. and Smith, M. (2001) 'Adaptability: households, gender and working time', unpublished report for Applica, as part of a project for Directorate General Employment and Social Affairs, European Commission.

Rubery, J. and Smith, M. (1999) *The future of the European labour supply*, Luxembourg: Office for Official Publications of the European Communities.

Rubery, J., Smith, M. and Fagan, C. (1999) *Women's employment in Europe: trends and perspectives*, London/New York, NY: Routledge.

Rys, V. (2001) 'Social protection in central and eastern Europe ten years after', *International Social Security Review*, vol 54, nos 2-3, pp 3-6.

Sardon, J-P. (2002) 'Recent demographic trends in the developed countries', *Population-E*, vol 57, no 1, pp 111–56.

SCB (Statistiska Centralbyrån) (2000) *Barn och deras familjer 1999. Om familjesammansättning, separation mellan föräldrar, boende, inkomster, barnomsorg och föräldrars sysselsättning*, Demografiska rapporter, no 2, Stockholm: Statistiska Centralbyrån.

SCB (2001) *Befolkningsstatistik*, part 4, *Födda och döda, civilståndsändringar m.m.*, Stockholm: Statistiska Centralbyrån.

Schmid, G. (2000) 'Foreword', in J. O'Reilly, I. Cebrián and M. Lallement (eds) *Working-time changes: social integration through transitional labour markets*, Cheltenham/Northampton, MA: Edward Elgar, pp xix-xxi.

Schultheis, F. (1990) 'Familles d'Europe sans frontières: un enjeu social par dessus le marché', *Actes du colloque: Familles d'Europe sans frontières, 4-5 December 1989*, Paris: Institut de l'Enfance et de la Famille, pp 73-80.

Scott, A., Pearce, D. and Goldblatt, P. (2001) 'The sizes and characteristics of the minority ethnic populations of Great Britain – latest estimates', *Population Trends*, no 105, pp 6-15.

Seccombe, W. (1993) *Weathering the storm: working-class families from the industrial revolution to the fertility decline*, London/New York, NY: Verso.

Simões Casimiro, F. and Calado Lopes, M.G. (1995) 'Concepts and typologies of household and family in the 1981 and 1991 population censuses in the twelve Community countries', unpublished report for Eurostat, Lisbon: Instituto Superior de Estatistica e Gestào de Informaçào.

Singleton, A. (1999) 'Combining quantitative and qualitative research methods in the study of international migration', *International Journal of Social Research Methodology: Theory & Practice*, vol 2, no 3, pp 151-7.

Sleebos, J. (2003) *Low fertility rates in OECD countries: facts and policy responses*, OECD Social, Employment and Migration Working Papers, no 15, Paris: OECD.

Sporton, D. and White, P. (2002) 'Fertility', in J. Haskey (ed) *Population projections by ethnic group: a feasibility study*, Studies on Medical and Population Subjects, no 67, London: The Stationery Office, pp 81-91.

Statistical Office of Estonia (1999) *The 2000 population and housing census: reference book*, Tallinn: Statistical Office of Estonia.

Statistical Office of Estonia (2000) *Statistical yearbook of Estonia 2000*, Tallinn: Statistical Office of Estonia.

Statistics Finland (2003) *Foreigners and international migration 2002*, Population, no 8, Helsinki: Statistics Finland.

Strobel, P. (2002) 'Avant-propos', in D. Debordeaux and P. Strobel (eds) *Les solidarités familiales en questions: entraide et transmission*, Paris: Librairie Générale de Droit et de Jurisprudence, pp 11-18.

Stropnik, N., Stanovnik, T., Rebolj, M. and Prevolnik-Rupel, V. (2003) 'Study on the social protection systems in the 13 applicant countries: Slovenia', unpublished report to the European Commission.

Taki, D. and Tryfonas, S. (2003) 'Family self-sufficiency and distrust of the state in Greece', *Cross-National Research Papers*, vol 6, no 6, pp 74-8.

Théry, I. (1997) 'Le contrat d'union sociale en question', *Esprit*, no 236, pp 159-211.

Théry I. (1998) *Couple, filiation et parenté aujourd'hui: le droit face aux mutations de la vie privée*, Paris: Odile Jacob/La Documentation française.

Threlfall, M. (2000) 'Comparing unemployment in the UK and the European Union: a gender and working time analysis', *Policy & Politics*, vol 28, no 3, pp 309-29.

Titmuss, R.M. (1974) *Social policy: an introduction* (edited by B. Abel-Smith and K. Titmuss), London: George Allen and Unwin.

Trost, J. (1988) 'Conceptualising the family', *International Sociology*, vol 3, no 3, pp 301-8.

UNAF (Union nationale des associations familiales) (2001) 'Le coût de l'enfant: un indicateur pour la politique familiale', interview with J-L. Dubelloy, UNAF: Paris.

UNESA (United Nations Economic and Social Affairs) (2002) *World population prospects: the 2002 revision and world urbanization prospects*, New York, NY: United Nations. http://esa.un.org/unpp

UNICEF (United Nations Children's Fund) (2001) *A decade of transition: the MONEE project CEE/CIS/Baltics*, Regional Monitoring Report, no 8, Florence: UNICEF.

UN/ECE (United Nations Economic Commission for Europe) (1987) *Recommendations for the 1990 censuses of population and housing in the ECE region: regional variant of the world recommendations for the 1990 round of population and housing censuses*, Statistical Standards and Studies, no 40, New York, NY: United Nations.

UN/ECE (1998) *Recommendations for the 2000 censuses of population and housing in the ECE Region*, Statistical Standards and Studies, no 49, New York, NY: United Nations.

UNSD (United Nations Statistics Division) (1998) *Principles and recommendations for population and housing censuses*, Statistical Papers, Series M, no 67/Rev1, New York, NY: United Nations.

Vagac, L. and Haulikova, L. (2003) 'Study on the social protection systems in the 13 applicant countries: Slovak Republic', unpublished report to the European Commission.

van Bastelaer, A. and Blöndal, L. (2003) 'Labour reserve: people outside the labour force', *Statistics in Focus: Population and Social Conditions*, no 14.

van den Brekkel, J. and van de Kaa, D. (1994) 'The Netherlands: aspects of family policy in the setting of the second demographic transition', in W. Dumon (ed) *Changing family policies in the member states of the European Union*, Brussels: Commission of the European Communities, DG V, pp 225-54.

van Oorschot, W. and Math, A. (1996) 'La question du non-recours aux prestations sociales', *Recherches et prévisions*, no 43, pp 5-17.

Vukovich, G. (2002) 'Fobb népesedési folyamatok' ('Main demographic processes'), in T. Kolosi, I.Gy. Tóth and G. Vukovich (eds) *Társadalmi Riport (Social report)*, Budapest: Tárki, pp 138-51.

Walby, S. (1986) *Patriarchy at work: patriarchal and capitalist relations in employment*, Cambridge: Polity Press.

Walker, A. (1997) *Combating age barriers in employment: research summary*, Luxembourg: Office for Official Publications of the European Communities.

Walker, A. (1999) 'Attitudes to population ageing in Europe: a comparison of the 1992 and 1999 Eurobarometer surveys', unpublished report for the European Commission, Directorate General Employment and Social Affairs, European Commission.

Walker, A. and Naegele, G. (eds) (1999) *The politics of old age in Europe*, Buckingham/Philadelphia, PA: Open University Press.

Walker, R. (2000) 'Welfare policy: tendering for evidence', in H.T.O. Davies, S.M. Nutley and P.C. Smith (eds) *What works? Evidence-based policy and practice in public services*, Bristol: The Policy Press, pp 141-66.

Wallace, C. (2003) 'Households, work and flexibility (HWF)', in L. Hantrais (ed) *Policy relevance of 'Family and Welfare' research*, Luxembourg: Official Publications of the European Communities, pp 36-9.

Warzywoda-Kruszyńska, W. and Krzyszkowski, J. (2000) 'Socio-demographic change in Poland', *Cross-National Research Papers*, vol 6, no 2, pp 56-60.

Weir, P. (2001) 'Smoking gun? Is it fair to make people clock in and out for a fag break?', *Guardian*, 14 February.

WHO (World Health Organisation) (1992) *International statistical classification of diseases and related health problems*, 10th revision (ICD-10), vol 1, Geneva: WHO.

WHO (1999) *Reproductive health: interagency manual*, Geneva: WHO.

Index

A

Abela, Anthony M. 66, 198
abortion
  definition 14
  measurement 45, 55-6
  social acceptability 65, 68, 70, 142,
    147, 151-3, 159, 161, 168, 173-4,
    176
adoption 109-10, 114-16, 135-6, 139,
  173, 180
age at childbirth 14, 54-5
age at first childbirth 54, 176
age at first marriage 42, 51-2, 92
age at leaving parental home 18, 61, 63,
  182
age at marriage 42, 51-2, 63, 92, 107
Arber, Sara 7, 36, 37, 70, 128, 130
asylum 15-17, 26, 35
Attias-Donfut, Claudine 7, 36, 37, 70,
  128, 130
Austria (AT)
  benefits and services 122-4, 126, 144
  employment rate 88-9, 92
  extramarital births 56-7
  family formation and structure 51, 53,
    59, 63-4
  family–employment relationship 99
  family–policy relationship 129, 138,
    143, 161, 200, 202
  fertility 22, 55-6
  gender equality 86-7, 117
  labour market entry 75, 77
  long-term care insurance 155
  migration and ethnicity 16, 25-6
  population ageing 28, 30, 34, 195
  retirement and pensions 76, 118-19,
    125
  value systems 99, 153-5, 198
  working arrangements 89, 94-5

B

baby boom 11, 26, 31, 33-5, 50
Belgium (BE)
  benefits and services 123, 126
  employment rate 86, 88-90, 92-3
  extramarital births 57

family formation and structure 38, 52,
  54, 62-4
family–employment relationship 92,
  99, 184
family–policy relationship 71, 115,
  123, 129, 137-8, 144, 178, 200-2
fertility 22
gender equality 97
labour market entry 75, 86
migration and ethnicity 16, 25-6
population ageing 28, 30
pro-natalism 137
retirement and pensions 76, 86, 119
value systems 99, 154
working arrangements 89, 95
benchmarking 74, 164, 194, 197, 206
benefit family 116, 122
benefits
  means testing 123-4, 161-2, 166, 168-
    9, 171, 174, 203-6
  universal provision 82, 117, 123, 127,
    137, 139, 146, 157-62, 168, 170,
    174, 200, 202, 204-6, 209-10
  see also child benefit; family
    allowances
birth rate see crude annual birth rate
business case 103, 156, 161, 209, 213

C

candidate countries
  data gathering 85
  employment rate 87, 90
  family–policy relationship 120, 151
  gender equality 62, 86, 90, 97
  migration 25, 36, 153
  NGOs 148
  population growth 24
  population size 21
  reform process 9, 74, 105-6, 206
  value systems 66-7, 153
  working arrangements 93-4
care benefit 167, 183
care for older people 34-6, 78, 105, 128-
  9, 155-7, 180-3, 213-14
  see also long-term care insurance;
    social care
care services 144

V

W

Guildford College
Learning Resource Centre

Please return on or before the last date shown.
No further issues or renewals if any items are overdue.
"7 Day" loans are **NOT** renewable.

2 1 MAR 2006

2 5 FEB 2010

- 5 JAN 2011

2 7 JAN 2012

1 6 APR 2012

Class: 306.85 HAN

Title: FAMILY POLICY MATTERS

Author: HANTRAIS, Linda